CAMDEN'S
BRITANNIA

EPITOMIZED AND CONTINUED;

BEING

A COMPENDIOUS ACCOUNT

OF THE

ANTIENT AND PRESENT STATE

OF THE

COUNTIES OF ENGLAND.

By SAMUEL TYMMS.

VOL. VII.—MIDDLESEX, LONDON, AND
WESTMINSTER.

LONDON:
HENRY G. BOHN, YORK STREET, COVENT GARDEN.

PREFACE.

In presenting the concluding volume of this series of Compendious Local Histories, the Author feels that some apology is due for the length of time which the work has been passing through the press. But when he states that it has been pursued, only as an instructive amusement, in the intervals, few and short, which could be snatched from literary labours of another kind, demanding close and continued application; and when the labour of reading and carefully digesting many hundred volumes is considered; he feels confident that those who kindly approved of the previous volumes, will forgive any inconvenience to which they may have been subject, while they rejoice with him at the conclusion of the work; which has been, to adopt the words of Antony à Wood, " A painfull work, I'll assure you; wherein what toyle hath been taken, as no man thinketh, so no man believeth, but he that hath made the trial." But painful as it at times has been,

PREFACE.

its progress has been cheered by many acts of friendship and kindly assistance ; and the Author parts from it with regret, as from a habit endeared by time and constant indulgence. To name those who have contributed their aid and advice would be a pleasing duty ; but as it might appear to emanate from vanity more than gratitude, the Author hopes to be excused for acknowledging, in general terms, the valuable help that has been so frankly given.

Should these little volumes afford amusement or convey instruction to a few, the Author's labour has not been in vain ; and he will have received his reward in knowing that what has been to him a source of knowledge has also afforded some pleasure to others. He now respectfully and gratefully bids his kind friends and patrons adieu.

S. T.

Oct. 1, 1842.

MIDDLESEX.

SITUATION AND EXTENT.

Boundaries. North, Hertfordshire. East, Essex. South, Surrey. West, Buckinghamshire.

Greatest length, 23; *greatest breadth,* 17; *circumference* 115; *square,* 282 *miles; statute acres,* 180,480.

Province, Canterbury. *Diocese,* London.

ANTIENT STATE AND REMAINS.

Antediluvian Remains. Near Old Brentford, in digging clay for bricks, were discovered bones of elephants, hippopotami, deer, and oxen, with shells of oysters, nautili, and other marine exuviæ. At Chelsea Hospital, very large bones, elk horns 4 feet 6 inches long, found in 1838, in digging for a sewer. Highgate, when excavating the tunnel by the Archway, fossil teeth, fish, fruit, wood, &c. Primrose Hill and neighbourhood, nautili, &c. while excavating for the London and Birmingham Railway.

British Inhabitants, Trinobantes, the first tribe that submitted to the Romans. *Encampments,* Bush Hill, Edmonton, remains of a circular one of considerable dimensions. *Earthworks,* Harrow Weald, Gryme's Dyke. *Remains,* Sunbury, two urns.

Roman Province, Flavia Cæsariensis. *Stations,* Sulloni-

acæ, Brockley Hill. *Encampments*, Highbury; Hounslow Heath, Cæsar's Camp; Islington, Reedmont or Red-
mote Field, supposed to have been the camp of Paulinus
Suetonius in A.D. 61; Kingsbury, of Cæsar, within which
is the church; Laleham, two; Sheperton; Somers Town,
the Brill; Stanmore Magna. *Roads*, Ermine Street,
from Cripplegate, in London, northward into Hertfordshire; Via Trinovantica, from the coast in Hampshire
to the coast in Suffolk, came into the Acton Road and
crossed the Watling Street at Tyburn, thence along Oxford Street, and continued to Old Street, going north of
London; Watling Street, from London, through Hampstead, Hendon, and Edgeware; at Hackney, are the
remains of a stone causeway. *Remains*, Bentley, gold,
silver, and copper coins, rings and bracelet of gold.
Breakspear, near Uxbridge, sepulchres. Enfield, coins,
urns, and tiles. Hackney, coins. Hammersmith bridge,
a Roman sword. Hampstead, sepulchral urns, near the
wells, in 1774. Sheperton, in 1812, a canoe rudely cut
out of a solid block of oak, probably used when Cæsar
passed the Thames at Coway Stakes in pursuit of the
British prince Cassivelaunus; spurs, swords, &c. Stanmore Magna, coins, urns, and rings. Turnham Green,
urn of coins.

Saxon Octarchy, Essex.

Priories. Bentley; Haliwell, founded before 1189; Riselip,
cell to Bec Abbey, Normandy.

Nunneries. Bromley, founded in the time of William I.
by William Bishop of London; Clerkenwell, by Jordan
Briset, and Muriel his wife, about 1100, the site marked
by St. James's church; Isleworth, Syon monastery,
for 60 Bridgetine nuns and 25 brethren, by Henry V.

and Henry Lord FitzHugh, in 1415; Kilburn, by the Abbot and Convent of Westminster temp. Henry I.

Preceptories and Commanderies. Clerkenwell, Hospitallers, St. John of Jerusalem, founded about 1110, by Jordan Briset, who founded the Nunnery, the church dedicated by Heraclius, Patriarch of Jerusalem, in 1185; under the present church of St. John is the old crypt. Harefield, cell to Clerkenwell, the chapel remains.

College. Marylebone, St. Katharine's, in Regent's Park, removed from the site of the St. Katharine's Docks, where founded by Queen Matilda wife of Stephen, in 1148; dissolved in 1272; and refounded the following year by Queen Eleanor; removed 1826 to the Regent's Park; the only ecclesiastical gift in the Queens Consort of England.

Hospitals. Brentford End, Guild and Chapel of All Angels, by John Somerset, D.C.L., Physician to Henry VI.; Highgate, for lepers, founded by William Pole, yeoman to the Crown, in the time of Edward IV.; Hounslow, Trinitarians, temp. John; Kingsland, before 1437; Knightsbridge.

Churches. Acton, some circular pillars; Bromley St. Leonard's, traces of Norman architecture, part of the nunnery church; Friern Barnet, Norman; Harmondsworth, Norman south doorway; Harrow-on-the-Hill, remains of the Norman church of Abp. Lanfranc temp. Will. I.; Harlington, Norman doorway, and square embattled tower; Hayes, early pointed and some small portions of Norman; Hendon, handsome and large, with Norman remains and embattled tower; Laleham, Norman remains; Pinner, erected 1321; St. Pancras, 14th century; Strat-

ford-le-Bow, built 1311 ; Wilsdon, some Norman remains.

Fonts. Acton ; Drayton, the most curious in the county ;
Harrow ; Hayes, circular, sculptured ; Hendon, Norman ;
Heston ; Stepney ; Wilsdon, Norman.

Mansions. Canonbury House, Islington ; Chelsea, the
White Horse inn, built in the time of Hen. VIII. or Eliza-
beth ; Fulham, Queen's Head public house, now pulled
down, and rebuilt as the Golden Lion ; Islington, the
Queen's Head public house (also rebuilt) ; Kirby Castle,
Bethnal Green, built by John Kirby, in the time of Eliza-
beth ; Marylebone, on the east side of High Street, a house
called the Rose of Normandy ; Stepney, called King
John's palace, gateway of variegated brickwork ; Fulham
Palace, part as old as the time of Henry VII.

PRESENT STATE AND APPEARANCE.

Rivers. Brent ; Colne ; Crane, rises near Harrow ;
Exe or Echel ; Lea, flows from Hertfordshire, through
the Vale of the Lea, to the Thames at Blackwall ; Mose
or Moselle ; the New river was begun to be brought
from Amwell, near Ware, in Hertfordshire, to Islington, February 20, 1608, by the patriotic Sir Hugh
Myddelton, at his own expense, a distance of 39 miles,
and the water was let into the basin there, a distance of
38 miles, called the New River Head, September 29, 1613,
whence it is conveyed by sluices into cisterns, and thence
by innumerable pipes over the Metropolis ; Serpentine,
in Hyde Park ; and the THAMES (for which see under
London).

Inland Communications :—Navigation. Grand Junction Canal, from the Thames near Brentford, begun 1794, goes to Northamptonshire. Isle of Dogs Canal (now converted into docks). Kensington Canal opened August 1828, from Chelsea Lot meadows to Kensington, three-quarters of a mile, cost 40,000*l.* Paddington Canal, opened 1801. Regent's Canal, begun 1812 and opened 1820, from Paddington, near the first bridge on the Harrow road; passes under the Edgware road by a tunnel 372 yards long, thence to the Regent's Park, which it goes round; and thence to Camden Town, and White Conduit Fields, where it goes through a tunnel 970 yards in length; thence it crosses the Kingsland and Hackney roads, and passes onward by Stepney fields to the Thames at Limehouse. Its length is 8 miles 6 furlongs; it has a descent of about 84 feet from its commencement to its termination; there are 12 locks and 40 bridges. River Lea, from Hertford to the Thames. A cut from the Lea at Bromley to the Regent's Canal, made by Sir Charles Ducket.

Railways.— London and Birmingham Railway, from Euston Square, act obtained 1833, commenced 1834, engineer Stephenson, opened 17th Sept. 1838; on the line are eight tunnels, cost £4,983,849. Great Western Railway, from Paddington, through or near to Acton, Ealing, Hanwell, Brentford, Southall, and Uxbridge, to Bristol, a distance of 117 miles. Birmingham, Bristol, and Thames Junction Railway, designed to connect the river Thames with the two preceding railways; the line of about three miles is almost entirely within the parish of Hammersmith; it passes under the Paddington Canal, over which is a roadway. Eastern Counties, from London into Essex, through

Stratford, Ilford, Romford, and Brentwood, opened 1840, North-Eastern, from the Eastern Counties line, near Stratford, into Hertfordshire, through Tottenham, Edmonton, Enfield, &c. opened September 15, 1840.

Eminences and Views. Barrow Point Hill, pleasing views; Bentley Priory, rich and extensive prospects; Belmont, in Stanmore grounds; Brockley Hill, fine prospects; Canonbury Tower, Islington, affords one of the most delightful panoramic views near the Metropolis; Hampstead Heath, the views excel in extent and felicity of combination any to be witnessed in the immediate vicinity of the Metropolis; and Child's Hill House, situation eminently beautiful; Hanger Hill Tower, 251 feet high; Hanwell, the parsonage-house commands pleasing views; Harrow-on-the-Hill, pleasing and varied; Harrow Weald; Hendon has many beautiful prospects; High Grove, Riselip, agreeable prospects; Highgate; Highwood Hill, whence the eye ranges over a wide and richly cultivated expanse; Kensington, Camden Hill; King's Arbour, 132 feet high; Mill Hill; Muswell Hill, beautiful and varied; Noel House, charming views of the Surrey hills; Strawberry Hill, pleasing views over a well-wooded and watered country; Twickenham, scenery soft, rural, and pleasing; Wilsdon, scenery invitingly picturesque, and from a knoll near the green Windsor castle, Leith hill, &c. may be seen; Winchmore Hill.

Natural Curiosities. Acton, mineral waters; three wells. Bagnigge, cathartic and chalybeate springs; Chelsea, Apothecaries Garden, two remarkably fine cedar trees, and many curious exotic and medico-botanic-rarities; Clerkenwell, a number of medicinal springs, formerly in great repute; Enfield, at the Manor-house, a very large cedar of Libanus ; * Hampstead chalybeate wells, first recommended by Dr. Gibbons, the "Mirmillo" of Garth's " Dispensary," and saline wells, dis→ covered 1804, by Mr. Goodwin. Hampton Court, the great vine of the Black Hamburgh kind, which has been known to produce in one year 2,200 bunches of grapes, weighing on an average one pound each ; Highwood Hill, Hendon, mineral spring impregnated with cathartic salt ; Hoxton, medicinal waters ; Islington, medicinal waters, formerly very celebrated under the name of the New Tunbridge Wells, combining a peculiar modification of sulphate of iron with an aperient of salt ; Kilburn, mildly aperient well ; Notting Hill, Kensington, mineral well ; Pancras, medicinal waters ; Syon House, mulberry trees, the first planted in this kingdom ; Shadwell (or Saint Chad's well), medicinal waters ; Tottenham, on the Green, a cluster of fine elms by the road side, called the " Seven Sisters ;" several wells, one resembling the Cheltenham waters.

PUBLIC EDIFICES.

Acton, conduit, constructed 1612 : the Goldsmiths' almshouses, handsome, finished in 1811.
Bayswater, Queen's lying-in hospital, removed here 1791.
Brentford, handsome stone bridge over the Thames to Kew.

---

* The Cedar of Libanus was first planted at Fulham in 1683. There was one at Hendon Place, blown down Jan. 1, 1779, height 70 feet ; circumference at seven feet from the ground, 16 feet ; diameter of the horizontal extent of its branches 100 feet. Another of nearly equal dimensions was cut down at Hillingdon in 1789. A third of large size at Hammersmith in 1836.

Bromley St. Leonard's, the Draper's almshouses, rebuilt 1806.

Camden Town, veterinary college, instituted 1791.

CHELSEA HOSPITAL, for wounded and superannuated soldiers, first stone laid by Charles II. on March 12, 1682, finished 1690, architect, Sir Christopher Wren; three courts; length of principal building, 790 feet; whole space occupied, 50 acres; cost £150,000; statue of Charles II.; ordinary number of in-pensioners, about 470. College Infirmary; architect, Soane. Royal Military Asylum, for soldiers' children, 700 boys and 300 girls; first stone laid by the Duke of York, second son of George III. on June 19, 1801, completed 1805; architect, Sanders; it has a very convenient detached chapel. Bridge, over the Thames, one furlong long, 28 feet wide, built of wood, in 1772, cost £20,000. National Schools, first stone laid June 18, 1824; finished 1826; handsome range of buildings; cost £3,000. In the Apothecaries' Garden, is a statue of Sir Hans Sloane, by Rysbrach.

Clapton, London Orphan Asylum, founded in 1813; cost £30,000.

Clerkenwell:—Finsbury dispensary, opened 1781. Middlesex House of Correction, 1794, cost £70,000 on plan of Howard; outer wall erected 1824. White Conduit House, for music and other entertainments, rebuilt on a large scale 1829. Friends' School. Lady Owen's Almshouses and Free Grammar School, built and endowed in 1613 by Lady Alice Owen, in commemoration of, says tradition, her narrow escape from death by the arrow of an archer in her younger days. London Female Penitentiary, Pentonville, instituted Jan. 1, 1807, east wing erected 1811, and further enlarged 1812, will accommodate 100 females. Claremont Chapel, erected for the Independents, by Thomas Wilson, esq. of Highbury, opened 1819; cost £7,000; will accommodate 1500 persons. Sadler's Wells Theatre (vide ISLINGTON). Sessions House, Clerkenwell Green, erected in 1778 at the expense of about £13,000, is 110 feet from east to west, and 78 from north to south; the hall is 34 feet square, with a dome; architect, Rogers. Charity School, Amwell Street, erected in 1829, capable of accommodating 1,000 children. New Prison, built 1774; nearly rebuilt 1818. Workhouse, enlarged in 1790 at an expense of £4,000. Spafields Chapel, Exmouth Street, originally a house of entertainment; converted into a chapel by Selina Countess of Huntingdon in 1779; built in the form of a rotunda.

Fulham, bridge of wood, from plan of the surgeon Cheselden; length 789 feet, width 24; cost £23,075.

Hackney, bridge over the Lea, of iron, erected at a cost of £4,500 in 1821; National Schools, large, erected in 1811; cost £4,500; Dissenters' College, established 1730, present edifice erected in 1823, cost £10,000.

Hammersmith, Suspension Bridge, foundation laid May 7, 1825; opened October 6, 1827; engineer, William Tierney Clark, Esq., F.R.S.; cost £45,000; the clear extent of water-way between the suspension towers 400 feet; length of road-way 688 feet, being 135 feet more than the Menai Bridge.

Hampton Court, bridge of wood, eleven arches, opened December 13, 1753.

Hanwell, lunatic asylum, for the county.

Harrow, School, founded by John Lyon, yeoman, and the rules made by him, 1590; had 353 students, the greatest number, in 1804.

Hendon, at Mill Hill, Protestant Dissenters' grammar school, founded 1807, cost building £25,000.

Heston, magazine of gunpowder.

Highgate Archway, foundation laid Oct. 30, 1812; opened Aug. 21, 1813; 36 feet high, 18 wide, erected in consequence of the falling in of an intended tunnel under the hill, which had proceeded 130 yards, April 12, 1812.

Holloway, Whittington's College, founded in 1421 by will of Sir Richard Whittington, thrice Lord Mayor of London; erected 1824 by Mercers' Company; cost £20,000; here twenty-nine alms-women reside.

Homerton, Widows' Retreat, founded 1812, for eight widows of Independent Ministers, handsome range of buildings in the pointed style, erected at the sole expense of Samuel Robinson, esq. and endowed by him.

Hounslow Heath, cavalry barracks, erected 1793.

Hoxton, Aske's Hospital, or Haberdashers' Almshouses, founded by the Company of Haberdashers in 1692, in pursuance of will of Robert Aske, esq. who left £30,000 for their endowment; re-erected in a very handsome manner in 1826.

Islington.—Church Missionary Society's College, for the preparation of young men for foreign missions, erected 1827. Proprietary School, Barnsbury Street, erected 1830. A great many Almshouses. Bakers' Almshouses; Metropolitan Female Asylum, for reclaiming women, established 1829. Church of England School, in union with King's College, London. Lady Owen's Almshouses and School (vide Clerkenwell). Quakers' Workhouse and School. Sadler's Wells, so called from one Sadler, who discovered the spa in 1683; present theatre erected 1765; enlarged 1778, 1802, &c. Caledonian Asylum, Copenhagen Fields, for educating children of soldiers, sailors, and marines, natives of Scotland, first stone laid by Duke of Sussex May 17, 1827; cost £10,000. Highbury College, for the education of ministers of the Independent denomination, erected 1826 ; cost £22,000.

Kensington, National Schools. Water Tower, built in the time of Queen Anne, for supplying the palace with water.

Littleton, stone bridge of seven arches, built 1785; cost £13,000 ; architect, Payne.

MARYLEBONE : — Eastern National School, adjoining All Soul's Church, instituted in 1824, will accommodate 500 children. Western National School, Wyndham Place, erected by James Tillard, esq. who advanced a sum of 4,000*l.* in 1824, which he bequeathed at his death in 1828; it is spacious and handsome.—Colosseum, Regent's Park, constructed for the exhibition of a panoramic view of London, taken from the summit of the cross of St. Paul's Cathedral, in 1822, by Mr. Horner; the building raised under the direction of Mr. Decimus Burton ; a polygon of 16 faces, each 25 feet in length, making the circuit of the building 400 feet ; commenced 1824, and completed 1827 ; doric portico one of the finest and best proportioned in the metropolis; the picture, building, and mechanism, are deserving of high admiration ; here is preserved the *original ball* of St. Paul's.—Diorama, Regent's Park, opened Oct. 6, 1823, cost 9,000*l.* ; architects, Morgan and Pugin, completed in four months; for the exhibition of pictures with the variety of light and shade, introduced from Paris by Messrs. Bouton and Daguerre ; machinery executed by Mr. Topham ; the spectators sit in a revolving theatre.—Clergy Orphan Schools, St. John's Wood, founded 1749, at Acton, erected 1812. Artillery Barracks and Riding School, St. John's Wood. Statue of Wm. Duke of Cumberland in Cavendish square, erected in 1770, by Chew,. at the expense of Lt.-Gen. Wm. Strode. Portman barracks, for 500 men. Parish Charity School, erected 1754, confined

to girls, of whom there are upwards of 100. Central
National School in High street, erected 1808, by Sir Thos.
Bernard, bart. for 500 children. Philological Society's
School, King Street, Bryanstone Square, founded 1792,
present school provided, 1827, for sons of clergymen,
officers, merchants, &c. Queen Charlotte's Lying-in
Hospital, instituted in 1752, at Bayswater, removed to
the New Road in 1810. Middlesex Hospital, facing
Berners-street, instituted 1745. Workhouse, spacious and
commodious, erected 1775; architect, John White, whose
services were given gratuitously. (See under LONDON.)

Mile End:—Newy Tozedik, or German Jews' Hospital, established 1806, enlarged 1818. Hospital of Portuguese
Jews, instituted 1748, rebuilt 1793. Trinity Almshouses,
founded in 1695 by the Trinity House for distressed
officers in the merchants' service, with handsome chapel.
Bancroft's Almshouses, founded by Francis Bancroft in
1727, belong to the Drapers' Company. Fullers' Almshouses. Vintners' Almshouses, rebuilt 1802. Skinners'
Almshouses, founded by Lewis Newbury, 1698. East
London Lying in Institution.

Pancras:—Foundling Hospital, instituted by royal charter
in 1739, through the exertions of Captain Thomas Coram,
who was buried in its vaults, 1751; first stone of the
present building laid 1742. Welsh Charity School, Gray's
Inn Lane, established 1718, by the Society of Antient
Britons, instituted on St. David's Day, March 1, 1714.
Small Pox Hospital, Battlebridge, the first in Europe,
established 1745; the present building, now chiefly devoted
to vaccination, erected 1794. Adjoining is a Fever Hospital. City Light Horse Barracks, Gray's Inn Lane.
King's Cross, Battlebridge. Theatre, Tottenham Street.
Bazaar, in Liverꝫol Street. Female Charity School,
Hampstead Road, for 65 girls. (See under LONDON.)

Poplar and Blackwall :—the West India Warehouses and Docks, first stone laid by Mr. Pitt and others July 12, 1800, finished 1802; import dock, thirty acres; export, dock, twenty-four acres; entrance basin, six acres; whole premises, 204 acres; cost £1,200,000. East India Company's Docks, exports, nine acres and a quarter; imports, eighteen acres and one-eighth; entrance basin, two acres and three quarters. Dock and Warehouses of Wigram and Green, the most considerable private dock in Europe, nineteen acres. Trinity Buoy Wharf. East India Company's Almshouses, for widows of officers and seamen in the East India Company's service, rebuilt 1802. Free School, instituted 1816, erected at the expense of the East India Company. Mercers' Almshouses.

Shadwell, barracks for the Lascars and Chinese. Protestant Dissenters' Charity School, founded 1712, with chapel attached. Cooke's Almshouses, founded 1713, by Captain J. Cooke.

Somers Town, Hospital for the French Clergy, instituted by Abbé Carron, opened 1810.

Staines, bridge of iron, of one arch, supported by wooden piles (two bridges having fallen there since 1797), completed 1807.

Sudbury, infirmary, built 1773.

Tottenham; Cross erected in 1600, by Dean Wood, repaired 1809, at a cost of £300; Schools. Almshouses, partly founded in 1600, by Balthasar Sanchez, a Spaniard, said to have been the first person in this kingdom who exercised the trade of a confectioner, or "comfit-maker."

Uxbridge, market-house, erected 1789, cost £3,000.

MODERN CHURCHES.

Bethnal Green ; St. Matthew, erected 1740, of brick ; St. John's, of Grecian architecture, architect, Sir John Soane ; built 1828; cost £18,000 ; St. Peter, first stone laid Aug. 3, 1840.

Brompton, erected 1829, in the pointed style.

CHELSEA, St. Luke's Church, in the pointed style, first stone laid Oct. 18, 1820; consecrated Oct. 18, 1824; architect James Savage, esq. ; cost more than 20,000*l.* ; the interior has much that is admirable, and the fittings-up are in excellent taste.

—— Sloane Street, also in the pointed style, erected 1830 ; cost £6,000.

—— St. Saviour, Elizabeth Street, Upper Chelsea, pointed style; architect, George Basevi ; consecrated May 27, 1840 ; will accommodate 1,200 persons.

CLERKENWELL, St. James, first stone laid Dec. 16, 1788, architect, James Carr, cost £12,000.

—— St. John's, built in 1723 by Mr. Simon Michell and Mr. Hutton ; bought by Queen Anne's Commissioners for £2,950 ; consecrated Dec. 23, 1723, and became the second of the 50 new churches.

—— St. Mark, Myddelton square, in the pointed style, consecrated Jan. 1, 1828 ; the site given by New River Company ; cost £16,000, defrayed by the Commissioners for Building New Churches ; the furniture provided by the parish vestry.

—— Pentonville Chapel, erected 1787 ; consecrated 1791, architect Mr. Aaron Henry Hurst ; stands north and south, and the altar is in the north.

Edmonton, Winchmore Hill, erected in 1828 ; cost £5,000.

Enfield, St. James, Enfield Highway, erected by subscription in 1831, pointed style ; architect, Lockner.

—— Forty Hill, pointed style, very pleasing.

Fulham, St. John's, Walham Green, erected 1829 ; cost £10,000.

front faces the south instead of the west, and the altar
is at the north end; Ionic portico from the temple on
the Ilyssus at Athens; the columns to the first story of
the tower, which is a beautiful work, are insulated, and
of the "Tivoli Corinthian order;" and the second story
is a peristyle of six columns of the same order as the
Tower of the Winds at Athens; the interior is generally
admired for its decorations ; will accommodate 2,000
people ; cost 21,829*l.* 10*s.*

Paddington, Bayswater, built in 1818.

St. Pancras, Euston Square, (acts 1816 and 1821,) architects
the Messrs. W. and H. W. Inwood; first stone laid May 1,
1819; consecrated May 7, 1822; cost 76,679*l. 7s. 8d.*;
erected from models of the Erectheum ; the lateral
porticoes are from the southern portico of the Pandro-
sium ; the steeple 165 feet high, taken from the Octagon
Tower of the Winds at Athens; the interior particularly
elegant ; the communion table adorned with six antique
scagliola columns, with bases and capitals of white statuary marble, from the temple of Minerva.

—— Regent Square, Sidmouth Street, Gray's Inn Lane
Road, Ionic portico, erected 1824; cost £16,000.

—— Camden Chapel, erected in 1828 ; good Ionic portico.

—— Somers Town, erected by Messrs. Inwood; estimate
£14,291, 12*s.*

Poplar, All Saints, first stone laid March 29, 1821, consecrated July 3, 1823; entire cost, with parsonage house,
&c. 33,077*l.*; architect, Mr. C. Hollis ; the portico is from
the temple on the Ilyssus at Athens; the height of the
spire from the ground is 161 feet ; the interior is neat
and plain.

Shadwell, St. Paul, rebuilt 1820; architect, Mr. John Walters ; cost £14,000, "simply neat and elegantly chaste;"
the steeple is particularly beautiful.

STEPNEY, Mile End, first stone laid June 17, 1818, consecrated Jan. 9, 1823; pointed style of time of Henry VII.;
architect, Mr. John Walters.

—— St. Peter's, Globe Road, erected by the Metropolis
Churches Fund, consecrated Aug. 1838.

—— All Saints, Mile End New Town, partly erected by
the Metropolis Churches Fund, consecrated Nov. 9, 1839.

—— Tredegar Square, Mile End, built on ground the gift
of Sir Charles Morgan, bart.; consecrated Nov. 27, 1839.

—— Spicer Street, Mile End New Town, consecrated Nov.
25, 1839.

Tottenham Green, Trinity Chapel; consecrated May 26,
1830; architect, Savage; contract £4,893, 11s. 6d.

Twickenham, Holy Trinity, pointed style, foundation laid
Aug. 31, 1840.

SEATS.

Albemarle House, Hounslow, Rev. Joseph Benson, D.D.
Beauchamp House, Tottenham, Wm. Robinson, esq. LL.D.
Beech Hill, Archibald Paris, esq.
Belsize House, Hampstead, John Wright, esq.
Bentley Priory, Marquess of Abercorn.
Boston House, Brentford, Colonel Clitherow.
Breakspears, Harefield, Joseph Ashby Partridge, esq.
Broomfield House, Southgate, Henry Philip Powys, esq.
Bushy Park, the Queen Dowager.
Caen Wood, Hampstead, Earl of Mansfield.
Chelsea Park, Lady Wright Wilson.
Chiswick House, Duke of Devonshire.
Clock House, Ashford, A. Downes, esq.
Duncroft House, Staines, John Carmichael, esq.
Fulham Palace, Bishop of London.
Gunnersbury House, Baroness Rothschild.
Hadley House, Samuel Page, esq.
Hampton Court, Royal Palace.
Hanwell Grove, George Baillie, esq.
Hanwell Park, Charles Turner, esq.
Hanworth Park, Sir Frederick Pollock.
—— Little Park, Lady Laura Tollemache.

Harefield Grove, William Flower, esq.
Harefield Place, C. Newdigate Newdigate, esq.
Harlesden House, William Curtis, esq.
Heston Hall, John Whiting, esq.
Highwood Hill, Hendon, William Wilberforce, esq.
Hillingdon End, Sir W. Saltonstall Wiseman, bart.
Holland House, Kensington, Lord Holland.
Isleworth House, Dowager Lady Cooper.
Kempton Park, Fursan Manners, esq.
Kensington Palace, H. R. H. the Duke of Sussex.
Littleton, Colonel Wood.
Mill Hill, Hendon, Sir James Flower, bart.
Myddelton House, Enfield, Henry Carrington Bowles, esq.
Osterley House, Earl of Jersey.
Page Green, Tottenham, James Rowe, esq.
Park House, Fulham, J. P. Powell, esq.
Peterborough House, Parsons Green, —— Sampayo, esq.
Ravenscourt, Hammersmith, George Scott, esq.
Rose Bank, Fulham, Marquess of Londonderry.
Rosslyn House, Hampstead,
St. Margaret's, Isleworth, Marquess of Ailsa.
Seaton House, Isleworth, Lord Frederick Gordon.
Shepperton (Manor House), James Scott, esq.
Southall, Lord Montfort.
Spring Grove, Smallbury Green, Henry Pownall, esq.
Stanmore Hall, Thomas Teed, esq.
Stanmore, The Grove, Charles Poole, esq.
Stanwell Park, Sir John Gibbons, bart.
Strawberry Hill, Earl of Waldegrave.
Swakeleys, Ickingham, the late Thomas T. Clarke, esq.
Syon House, Isleworth, Duke of Northumberland.
Teddington House, Hon. William Jervis.
Teddington Place, Charles Devon, esq.
Tottenham Park, Joseph Rawlings, esq.
Trent Park, John Cumming, esq.
Twyford Abbey,
Wembly Park, the late John Gray, esq.
Whitton Dean, Hounslow, Lady Wood.
—— Place, Mrs. Gostling.
Worton Hall, near Hounslow, W. H. Story, esq.
—— House, Rev. John Keily.
—— Lodge, E. C. Southbrook, esq.
Wrotham Park, George Byng, esq. M.P.

Peerage. Chelsea, viscounty (1800) to Cadogan Earl Cadogan.

Caen Wood, Mansfield of, earldom (1792) to Murray.

Enfield, barony (1695) to Nassau, Earl of Rochford.

Harlington (written Arlington), earldom (1674) and barony (1664) to Fitzroy Duke of Grafton.

Hanworth, Vere of, barony (1750) to Beauclerk, Duke of St. Alban's.

Hendon, Tenterden of, barony (1827) to Abbott.

Kensington, barony (1622) to Rich, Earl of Holland; extinct 1759; Irish barony to Edwardes.

Middlesex, earldom (1622) to Cranfield; extinct 1651; recreated 1675, to Sackville, Duke of Dorset.

Ossulston (hundred), barony (1682) to Bennett, Earl of Tankerville.

Uxbridge, earldom (1714) to Paget; extinct 1769; revived in the same family 1784, now held by the Marquess of Anglesey.

Baronetage. Cadogan House, Chelsea, Farquhar, 1796. Camden Hill, M'Gregor, 1831. Castle Strange, Hort, 1767. Culland's Grove, Southgate, Curtis, 1802. Edmonton, Lake, 1711. Gray's Inn, Nelthorpe, 1666. Hadley, Smith, 1802. Harefield Place, Baynes, 1801. Stanwell House, Stanhope, 1807. Stanwell Place, Gibbons, 1752. Tottenham, Dyer, 1678. Twickenham, Johnson, 1755. Uxbridge, The Mount, Hamilton, 1776.

Representatives returned to Parliament, for the County, 2; Finsbury, 2; London, 4; Marylebone, 2; Tower Hamlets, 2; Westminster, 2; total, 14—The Reform Act created the Boroughs of Finsbury, Marylebone, and Tower Hamlets.

Produce. Clay, for bricks. Wheat, for which Heston was so famous that it was reserved for royal use, and Queen Elizabeth had her manchets made of it; barley; peas; beans; oats; hay; osiers; asparagus, and garden vegetables, extensive nursery grounds at Chelsea, Fulham, Hammersmith, Isleworth, &c.; raspberries for distillers, and strawberries, at Isleworth; lavender, cultivated at Baker Street, Enfield, in great quantities; potatoes and vegetables at Edmonton; fish, in the Thames and Lea.

St. George in the East, near Ratcliffe Highway, designed by Nicholas Hawksmoor, and commenced in 1715, consecrated by Bp. Gibson July 19, 1729; cost 18,557*l.*; massive and grotesque; interior heavy and gloomy.

Haggerstone, St. Mary, pointed style; architect, John Walters; the tower in imitation of that of Boston church, co. Lincoln, consecrated 1827.

Hackney, St. John the Baptist, erected 1797, of brick.

—— West, Kingsland Road, handsome Grecian edifice, erected in 1823, at a cost of near £16,000; architect, Smirke.

—— South, Well Street, built in 1810; cost £8,000.

—— Stamford Hill.

Hammersmith, St. Peter's, first stone laid May 10, 1827; consecrated Oct. 15, 1829; architect, Lapidge; Grecian Ionic.

Hendon, Mill Hill, erected at expense of William Wilberforce, Esq.; pointed style.

Hounslow, erected 1828-9; cost £5,310; pointed style; architect, Henry Mawley, Esq.

Hoxton, St. John, consecrated June 1829, very good steeple, cost £13,000, defrayed by the Parliamentary Commissioners.

ISLINGTON, St. John, Upper Holloway; pointed style; architect, Barry; completed 1828; cost £11,890.

—— St. Paul's, Ball's Pond; pointed style, architect, Barry, erected 1827; cost £11,000.

—— Trinity, Cloudesley Square, architect, Barry, erected 1830; cost near £12,000.

—— St. Mark, Pentonville.

—— Holloway, Chapel of Ease, consecrated Aug. 1814; cost £32,000.

—— St. Peter's, near Colebrooke Row.

—— St. James's, Holloway, architect, Clifton.

—— St. Stephen's, New North-road, architect, Clifton.

Kensington, in the Addison Road, erected 1829, in the pointed style.

Knightsbridge, now in the course of erection.

MARYLEBONE, St. Peter's, Vere Street, Oxford Street, erected about 1724 of brick; repaired 1832.

—— St. Paul's Chapel, in Portland Street, handsome brick building with stone steeple, erected 1766, on site of the Marylebone basin; consecrated in 1831.

—— St. John's Wood Chapel, of the Ionic order, designed by the late Thomas Hardwick, esq. consecrated in 1814.

—— Marylebone parish church, fronting the Regent's Park; architect Thomas Hardwick, foundation laid July 5, 1813; consecrated Feb. 4, 1817; interior magnificently fitted up, but with too theatric an effect; cost 60,000l.; the north front rich and elegant.

—— All Souls, Langham Place, first stone laid Nov. 18, 1822; consecrated Nov. 25, 1824; architect John Nash; cost 15,994l. defrayed by Government; a peripteral portico and multangular spire, of injudicious introduction.

—— St. Mary's, Wyndham Place, designed by Sir Robert Smirke and consecrated Jan. 7, 1824; the tower is circular over a portico of six Ionic columns; the height from the base to the top of tower is 135 feet, elevation of the body of the church 42 feet 6 inches, length of exterior 128 feet, height of portico pillars 33 feet; cost 20,000l.

—— Marylebone Old Church, on site of one taken down in 1740; opened in April 1742; converted into a parish chapel by Act of Parliament on Feb. 4, 1817.

—— Christ Church, near Lisson Green, designed by the late Philip Hardwick, esq. consecrated 1825; Ionic portico and plain square tower at east end, which is the principal front; the interior is Corinthian after Italian models.

—— Trinity Church, Portland Road, designed by the late Sir John Soane, and consecrated in 1828; the principal

Manufactures. Bethnal Green, cotton goods; waterproof hose for brewers and firemen; bricks.

Brentford, spirits; articles in iron.

Bromley St. Leonard's, a distillery.

Chelsea, tobacco pipes; oil cloth; soap; beer.

Clerkenwell, clocks and watches; mechanical tools; soap; spirits.

Edmonton, coaches.

Enfield, Ponder's End, crape, established 1809, by John Baylis.

Enfield Lock, fire arms, an extensive government establishment on the banks of the Lea, with residences for several hundred workmen and their families.

Fulham, brown stone ware.

Hackney, optical glasses; colours for painting; dyeing and calendering; bricks and tiles.

Hammersmith, bricks; bleaching and calendering muslins and calicoes; crucibles at Shepherd's Bush; varnish at Brook Green.

Harefield, copper sheets, bolts, and bars.

Heston, oil of vitriol.

Hounslow, gunpowder mills, and mill for dressing flax.

Hoxton, machinery; pins; vinegar.

Isleworth, beer.

Islington, white lead; floor-cloth.

Kensington, candles; cotton flocks for paper hanging manufacturers at Little Chelsea, North side.

Norwood, vitriol.

Ratcliff, sailcloth; chains; cables and ropes; machinery; sugar.

Stepney, beer; spirits; floor-cloth; tobacco pipes.

Teddington, wax candles, the most complete in the kingdom.

Tottenham, crape; pottery; beer; caoutchouc, or india rubber garments.

Twickenham, gunpowder; oil.

Uxbridge, flour; beer; bricks; implements of husbandry; Windsor chairs.

POPULATION IN 1831.

Hundreds, 6, one of which, Ossulstone, divided into 4 divisions; *Cities*, 2; *Boroughs*, 3.

Inhabitants, including the Cities of London and Westminster, Males, 631,410; Females, 726,920; total 1,358,330.

Houses, Inhabited, 180,493; Building, 3,919; Uninhabited, 14,413.

Families, 314,039; Employed in Agriculture, 9,882; in Trade, 173,822; in neither, 130,335.

Baptisms in the year 1830, Males, 17,682; Females, 17,712; total, 35,394; *annual average*, 33,312.

Marriages in 1830, 13,259; *annual average*, 12,834.

Burials in 1830, Males, 15,321; Females, 14,541; total, 29,862; *annual average*, 28,919.

Places having not less than 1,000 Inhabitants.

	Houses.	Inhab.		Houses.	Inhab.
London, within the walls	8,002	55,778	Hillingdon, including Uxbridge	1,315	6,885
London, without	8,733	67,905	Isleworth, including Hounslow	1,014	5,590
Westminster	20,616	201,842	Chiswick	876	4,994
Marylebone	11,608	122,206	Hornsey, including		
St. Pancras	12,369	103,548	Highgate	814	4,856
Shoreditch	10,698	68,564	Bromley	888	4,846
Bethnal Green	10,877	62,018	Twickenham	854	4,571
Clerkenwell	6,015	47,634	Hampton	700	3,992
St. Luke's	5,766	46,642	Harrow	609	3,861
St. George, East	5,764	38,505	Wapping	518	3,564
Islington	5,797	37,316	Stoke Newington	562	3,480
Mile End Old Town	6,028	33,898	Heston, including Hounslow, part	586	3,407
Chelsea	4,635	32,371	Stratford le Bow	603	3,371
Hackney	5,220	31,047	Finchley	540	3,210
Whitechapel	4,119	30,733	Hendon	454	3,110
Kensington	2,948	20,902	Staines	448	2,486
Spitalfields	2,271	17,949	Acton	426	2,453
Poplar	2,682	16,849	New Brentford	375	2,085
Limehouse	2,607	15,695	South Mims	393	2,010
Paddington	1,933	14,540	Wilsdon	326	1,876
Hammersmith	1,712	10,222	Sunbury	341	1,863
Ratcliffe	1,515	9,741	Hayes	300	1,575
Shadwell	1,493	9,544	Old Artillery Ground	187	1,411
Enfield	1,552	8,812	Stanwell	267	1,386
Hampstead	1,180	8,588	Norwood	212	1,320
Edmonton	1,394	8,192	Harefield	263	1,285
Ealing, with Old Brentford	1,325	7,783	Harmondsworth	232	1,276
Mile End New Town	990	7,384	Pinner	156	1,270
Fulham	1,168	7,317	Hanwell	214	1,213
Tottenham	1,298	6,937	Ruislip	248	1,197
			Great Stanmore	183	1,144

HISTORY.

61. The celebrated battle between the Roman general Suetonius Paulinus, and the British Queen Boadicea, is considered by some authors to have been fought on the site of the present Battle Bridge, Clerkenwell.

785. At Chelsea (Calcuith) a synod held before Gregory, Bp. of Ostia, and Theophylact, Bp. of Todi, the first legates sent by the Pope into this kingdom, when, at the instigation of Offa, the powerful King of Mercia, who was present, Lichfield was made an Archiepiscopal See.

879. At Fulham, Danish army wintered.

1009. The Danes, after burning Oxford, marched to London and crossed the Thames at Staines.

1016. At Brentford, Canute and the Danes, after being driven from London, were defeated by Edmund Ironside.

1170. Thomas à Becket, journeying towards Woodstock to pay respect to Prince Henry, was denied access to the court and commanded to repair immediately to his own diocese. He passed some days at his manor of Harrow on his return.

1217. At Hounslow, a conference was held between four Peers and twenty Knights on the part of Louis the Dau-

A. D.

phin, with the same number of nobles and knights on the part of the young King Henry III.

1250. Archbishop Boniface held a visitation at Harrow.

1263. Simon de Montfort, with the refractory Barons, encamped in the park of Richard Earl of Cornwall, at Isleworth.

1264. At Isleworth, the palace of Richard King of the Romans and Earl of Cornwall, brother of Henry III. destroyed by the Londoners under Sir Hugh Spencer.

1267. The Earl of Gloucester, at the head of the rebellious Londoners, assembled his troops on Hounslow Heath, intending to give Henry battle, but retreated before the arrival of the King's forces.

1299. At Stepney, Parliament held in the house of Henry Walleis, Mayor of London, when Edward I. confirmed the Charter of Liberties.

1381. The rebels under Wat Tyler burnt the priory of St. John of Jerusalem at Clerkenwell, and the prior's seat at Highbury. The Temple in Fleet Street, London, was also burnt and the prior beheaded on Tower Hill.

1386. At Hornsey, Thomas of Woodstock, Duke of Gloucester, Earls of Arundel, Warwick, and Derby, with other nobles, assembled to compel Richard II. to dismiss his favourite Robert de Vere, Duke of Ireland.

1391. The Company of Clerks played three days successively before Richard II. his queen, and the whole court, at Clerkenwell.

1437. Henry VI. held a council at the Hospitalers' Commandery, Clerkenwell, Nov. 13, and appointed Duke Humphrey one of his Regents.

1445. A chapter of the garter was held in the Lion Inn, at Brentford.

A. D.

1450. At Mile End, during the insurrection under Jack Cade, the Essex insurgents encamped.

1461. At Highgate, Thomas Thorpe, Baron of the Exchequer, beheaded by the insurgents of Kent.—The Earl of March, after the battle of Mortimer's Cross, mustered his army in St. John's Fields, Clerkenwell, and was there chosen King by the people's acclamation, and thence conducted in great state to St. Paul's, and proclaimed as Edward IV.

1465. The unfortunate Henry VI. being brought prisoner towards London, was met at Islington and arrested by the Earl of Warwick.

1471. April 14, was fought on Enfield chase that great battle between the Houses of York and Lancaster, generally known as the Battle of Barnet, in which the Lancastrians were defeated, and their commander, the Earl of Warwick, " that center-shaking thunderclap of warre," with his brother the Marquis of Montacute and 10,000 men, slain by Edward IV.

1483. At Hornsey, May 4, Edward V. accompanied by the Dukes of Gloucester and Buckingham (who had obtained possession of his person), met by the Lord Mayor and citizens, and conducted to the Bishop's palace in the city.

1516. Margaret dowager Queen of Scots, and sister to Henry VIII. visited Sir Thomas Lovell at Enfield.

1537. At Hampton Court, Oct. 14, Queen Jane Seymour died, two days after giving birth to Edward VI.

1540. At Hampton Court, Aug. 8, Katharine Howard openly acknowledged Queen.

1541. Syon House, the prison of Queen Katharine Howard, from Nov. 14 to Feb. 10, 1542, three days before her execution.

1543. At Hampton Court, Henry VIII. married to Katha-

A. D.

rine Parr, who was openly declared Queen, July 12, at this place. Here Henry VIII. entertained Francis Gonzaga, Viceroy of Sicily.

1548. The corpse of Henry VIII. rested in the conventual buildings at Syon House on its way to Windsor.

1553. At Syon House, Lady Jane Grey reluctantly accepted the crown, and was conducted hence with much pomp to the Tower.

1554. Philip and Mary kept their Christmas with great solemnity at Hampton Court.

1555. Aug. 8, Robert Smith burnt for his religious opinions at Uxbridge.

1556. At Stratford Bow, June 7, thirteen persons burnt for their religion.

1557. Sept. 17, four victims of bigotry burnt at one fire at Islington.

1558. At Brentford, July 14, six persons suffered martyrdom at the stake for their religion.

1572. Queen Elizabeth kept her Christmas at Hampton Court.

1578. Elizabeth visited Osterley House, and was magnificently entertained by Sir Thomas Gresham.

1586. At Uxendon, near Harrow, Anthony Babington and his fellow-conspirators against Elizabeth apprehended.

1593. Elizabeth passed her Christmas at Hampton Court.

1596. The Queen came from Theobalds to Enfield House to dinner, and to shoot at the buck.

1601. Queen Elizabeth visited Harefield place.

1602. Lord Russell at Chiswick honoured by a visit from his royal mistress.

1603. At Stamford-hill, May 7, James I. on his first entry into London received by the Lord Mayor and citizens, and conducted with great pomp through a field called

A. D.

Wood's Close, on the site of Northampton Street, Clerkenwell, " by a way that was cut of purpose through the bank," to the Charter-house.

1604. At Hampton Court, Jan. 14, commenced the Conference between the Presbyterians and the Members of the Establishment, which lasted three days ; James I. acting as Moderator. In consequence of this meeting a new translation of the Bible, and some alterations in the Liturgy, were made.

1625. At Stepney 2978 persons died of the plague.

1626. Queen Henrietta Maria was compelled by her priests to do penance under the gallows at Tyburn ; for which insolence King Charles drove them and all her Majesty's French servants out of the Kingdom.

1635. In August, the Queen and her whole court entertained at Hanworth by Lord Cottington.

1642. At Brentford, Nov. 12, Parliamentarians defeated, and the eccentric John Lilburne and 400 men taken prisoners by Charles I. The Earl of Essex, with an army of 24,000 men, marched from London to Turnham Green, on hearing that the King had carried the Parliamentarian works at Brentford. The King retreated to Kingston, and the Earl quartered his troops at Fulham, and built a bridge of barges across the Thames to Putney.

1643. There were three forts erected in Tyburn Road, now called Oxford Street.

1645. At Uxbridge, January, fruitless treaty between the Royal and Parliamentarian Commissioners.

1646. At the Red Lion, Hillingdon, Charles I. stopped when escaping from Oxford to the Scots.

1647. Several skirmishes took place near Brentford, at which time the Parliamentarian army was mustered on

A. D.

Hounslow-heath, and the guards were quartered at Brentford.—At Isleworth, August 4, head quarters of General Fairfax, who here received the Parliamentarian Commissioners.—At Hampton Court, Charles I. kept in imprisonment from August 24 until November 11, when he escaped, accompanied by Sir John Berkeley, Mr. Ashburnham, and Mr. Legge. He left three letters behind him, for the Parliament, for the Commissioners, and for Colonel Whaley. In the latter he assigned as a reason for escaping that he was "loath to be made a close prisoner under pretence of securing his life," and not from any fear of the talked-of plot of assassination to which the Colonel had alluded in conversation with him. Colonel Whaley, in his account of the transaction, did not consider it an escape, as the King had " never been in custody as a prisoner;" and if he had known of his going away he had no power to prevent it. It is generally thought that Cromwell was accessory to the escape, and it is known that its success gave him much exultation.

1651. At Acton, September 21, Oliver Cromwell congratulated on his victory at Worcester, and conducted to London by the Lord President and Council of State, many members of both houses of Parliament, with the Lord Mayor and Aldermen; in all a train of more than 300 coaches.

1656. The plot to assassinate Cromwell, designed by Miles Syndercomb and others, was to have been carried into execution while the Protector was on his way to Hampton Court. A house at Hammersmith, at the corner of Gould Hawk Lané, was hired, wherefrom to shoot at him. Various ineffectual attempts were made. Syndercomb was tried and sentenced to be executed, but committed suicide in prison.

A. D.

1660. General Monk drew up his forces at Finchley, Feb. 3. —Charles II. went to Hampton Court June 8, and returned, supping with Lord Campden at his house at Kensington, June 14.

1661. At the insurrection of the fifth-monarchy men, Caen Wood at Hampstead was the place of their retreat till driven out by a detachment of the guards.

1665. At Stepney 6583 persons died of the plague; 154 persons were buried in one day, September 11.

1678. At Primrose Hill, October 17, the body of the murdered Sir Edmondbury Godfrey discovered.

1686. James II. drew up his "large but shadowy" army on Hounslow Heath.

1688. James visited his encampment on Hounslow Heath formed of men destined to act against him. The plaudits of the soldiers on the arrival of the news of the acquittal of the seven Bishops, convinced him that his army was not sound.

1694. At Kensington palace, Dec. 28, Mary II. died; 1702, March 8, William III.; 1708, Oct. 28, Prince George of Denmark; 1714, Aug. 1, Queen Anne; and 1760, Oct. 25, George II. died.

1749. George III. and the Princess Augusta stood sponsors to Lady Georgiana Augusta, dau. of Earl of Berkeley, at Cranford Church.

1780. Dreadful riots in the Metropolis; the prisoners in Clerkenwell bridewell set free, &c.; troops in consequence quartered at Finchley.

1794. At Ratcliffe Highway, July 23, 455 houses and 36 warehouses burnt down. More than £16,000 was collected by subscription for the sufferers.

1807. A false alarm of fire at Sadler's Wells Theatre caused the loss of 18 lives, besides numberless severe injuries.

A. D.

The offenders were prosecuted to conviction and punishment.

1814. At Stanmore, April 20, Louis XVIII. accompanied by the Duchess d'Angoulême, from their asylum at Hartwell, in Buckinghamshire, was met by the Prince Regent and his illustrious guests the Emperor of Russia and the King of Prussia, and conducted in triumph to London.

1816. At Spa-fields, on what is now Wilmington Square, Nov. 15 and Dec. 2, were held two celebrated meetings of dissatisfied politicians, among whom were Henry Hunt and Arthur Thistlewood, the latter of whom was subsequently executed for the Cato-street Conspiracy, and the former became M.P. for Preston.

1820. The Cato Street Conspiracy to murder the Ministers at a Cabinet dinner at Lord Harrowby's, in Grosvenor Square, was frustrated through the information of a spy accomplice, and nine of the conspirators were captured at their rendezvous in Cato Street, Edgware Road, and several of them subsequently arrested, among whom was Thistlewood, who had been previously tried for High Treason with Dr. Watson, &c. Thistlewood with four others were executed, five were transported for life, and one pardoned.

EMINENT NATIVES.

Acton, John, divine, Acton (flor. 1290).

Acton, Ralph, divine, Acton (flor. 1320).

Aston, Sir Arthur, loyalist, Fulham, (murdered at Drogheda, by Cromwell, 1649).

Atkyns, Sir Robert, historian of Gloucestershire, Hadley, 1647 (died 1711).

Bennet, Henry, first Earl of Arlington, royalist; confidential minister of Charles II., one of the "Cabal;" Harlington, 1618 (died 1685).

Benson, William, auditor of the imprest, satirized by Pope, Bromley, 1682.

Berkeley, Sir John, Lord Stratton, loyalist general, Hanworth, 1607.

Berkeley, Sir William, brother of above, governor and historian of Virginia; dramatic author; Hanworth (or London) 1608 (died at Twickenham 1677).

Birch, Thomas, industrious and diligent historian and biographer, brought up a Quaker, afterwards ordained in the church; Clerkenwell, 1705 (killed by a fall from his horse in the road between London and Hampstead 1765). ·

Bishop, Samuel, divine and poet; St. John Street, Clerkenwell, 1731.

Blount, Charles, miscellaneous writer, favourer of Deism; his religious books burnt by order of the Church, and his political by order of the Parliament; shot himself because the Church would not sanction his union with the sister of his deceased wife, 1693; Holloway 1654.

Blount, Sir Thomas Pope, brother of above, Member of Parliament, and critical author; Holloway 1649 (died 1697).

Boyle, Charles, Earl of Orrery, antagonist of Bentley in the famous Phalaris controversy; author of a comedy, &c.; his name of Orrery was given to an astronomical instrument invented by Mr. George Graham; Chelsea 1676 (died 1731).

BUTLER, JAMES, first Duke of Ormond; honest statesman; Lord Lieutenant of Ireland, promoter of the restoration of Charles II.; Newcastle House, Clerkenwell, 1610 (died 1688).

Cæsar, Sir Julius, Master of the Rolls, Tottenham, 1557 (died 1636).

Chaloner, Edward, divine, Chiswick (died 1665).

Collins, Anthony, controversialist and metaphysical writer of considerable ability; opponent of revealed religion; Heston, near Hounslow, 1676 (died 1729).

Dancer, Daniel, miser, near Harrow, 1716.

EDWARD VI. amiable and pious, Hampton Court, October 12, 1537 (died 1553, aged 16).

Everitt, Thomas Hills, when only 11 months old 3 feet 3 inches high, girth round the loins 3 feet 1 inch, Enfield, 1779.

Fabell, Peter, magician and conjuror, subject of the play and a tract called "The merry Devil of Edmonton," attributed to the poet Michael Drayton, Edmonton (flor. temp. Hen. VII.)

Finch, Daniel, Earl of Winchelsea and Nottingham, K G. statesman, Kensington, 1689 (died at Parson's Green 1769).

Fox, Henry, first Lord Holland, statesman, rival of Pitt, Earl of Chatham, and father of Charles James Fox, Chiswick, 1705 (died 1774).

Fox, Stephen, first Earl of Ilchester, and brother of the preceding statesman, Chiswick, 1704 (died 1776).

Frowick, Sir Thomas, Lord Chief Justice to Henry VII. Ealing, 1466.

Gaskin, Dr. George, learned and amiable divine; Islington, 1751 (died 1829).

Gouge, Thomas, the son, nonconformist divine and author, Stratford Bow, 1605.

Gouge, William, puritan divine and author, Stratford Bow, 1575.

HALLEY, EDMUND, LL.D. astronomer and mathematician, author at 18 years of age of a pamphlet supplying a defect in the Keplerian theory of planetary motion; Haggerston, 1656 (died 1741-2 at Greenwich).

Harrington, John, Baron of Exton, accomplished nobleman and poet, Stepney, 1592 (died 1613).

Hawes, William, physician, author, and founder of Royal Humane Society; Islington, 1736; buried there in 1808.

Hewling, William, partizan of the Duke of Monmouth, Islington, 1665.

Hodges, Nathaniel, physician, who remained in London visiting the infected during the whole time of the great plague 1665, of which he wrote a Latin history; Kensington; (died in the prison of Ludgate in London in 1684, under what circumstances is unknown).

Holland, Charles, actor, Chiswick, 1733.

Hough, John, Bp. of Worcester, president of Magdalen College, Oxford, whose spirited resistance at his college to a mandamus of James II. which was contrary to the statutes, commenced that clerical resistance to the monarch which assisted in bringing about the revolution of 1688; successively Bishop of Oxford, Lichfield, and Worcester; born in 1650; died 1743, at the great age of 93.

Hough, Stephen, lawyer; Stepney, about 1741.

Hounslow, Robert, provincial of Trinitarian Friars, author, Hounslow (died 1430).

Hope, Sir Wm. Johnstone, admiral; Finchley, 1766.

Howard, John, the genius of active philanthropy; apprenticed to a grocer; married an elderly widow at Stoke Newington in gratitude for her care in nursing him; imprisoned during the French War; devoted his life to visiting prisons at home and abroad, suggesting improvements in their building and arrangement; building cottages for the poor, establishing schools, visiting hospitals, lazarettos, &c.; born at Clapton in Hackney, 1726; died 1790 of a malignant fever in Russia, where he was buried. His Statue is in St. Paul's Cathedral.

Killigrew, Henry, youngest brother, divine and dramatist, Hanworth, 1613.

Killigrew, Thomas, 2d brother, wit and dramatist, favourite of Charles II. Hanworth, 1611 (died 1682).

Killigrew, Sir William, eldest brother, dramatist and loyalist, Hanworth, 1606 (died 1693).

King, Dr. William, principal of St. Mary's hall, Oxford, politician and scholar, ingenious writer, Stepney, 1685 (died 1763).

Lawrence, George, nonconformist divine and author; Stepney, 1615.

Lyon, John, yeoman, founder of Harrow school, Preston, (died 1592.)

Mawson, Matthias, Bishop of Ely, Chiswick, 1682.

MEAD, RICHARD, physician, author on Poisons, Contagion, &c.; Stepney, 1673 (died 1754).

Nares, Sir George, judge, Stanwell, 1716.

Nares, James, musician, Stanwell, 1715.

NICHOLS, JOHN, F.S.A., "the modern Dugdale"; printer, successor to the learned Bowyer, of whom he published a life; antiquary and topographer of unequalled industry; for nearly half a century editor of the Gentleman's Magazine; voluminous author; born at Islington, 1744; died there 1826.

Northall, Richard, Archbishop of Dublin, Northall, (died 1397.)

Page, William, divine, schoolmaster, and translator; Harrow, 1590 (died 1663).

PARR, SAMUEL, divine, scholar, Greek critic; schoolmaster, politician, and author; Harrow, 1746-7; died 1825.

Percival, Sir Philip, statesman, Kensington, 1603.

PRATT, CHARLES, first Earl Camden, Lord Chancellor, independent and constitutional lawyer; Kensington, 1714, (died 1794.)

Rich, Henry, Earl of Holland, executed 1649, Stratford Bow, 1590.

Rose, Samuel, learned barrister; Chiswick, 1767.

Sadleir, Sir Ralph, Sec. of State to Hen. VIII.; Royal Falconer to Queen Eliz.; diplomatist, statesman, and warrior; born at Hackney, 1507; died 1587, aged 80.

Sawyer, Elizabeth, subject of the play, "The Witch of Edmonton," by Rowley, Decker, and Ford; Edmonton, (executed 1621.)

Simpson, Edward, divine, author of "Chronicon Catholicum," &c.; Tottenham, 1578, (died 1651.)

Skinner, Stephen, etymologist and antiquary; born 1622, (died 1667.)

Smith, Charles, able writer on corn trade; Stepney, 1713.

Snape, Andrew, learned divine; Hampton Court (died 1742).

South, Robert, "witty churchman," and controversialist, Hackney, 1633, (died 1716.)

Stamford, Sir William, Judge, author of "Pleas of the Crown," Hadley, 1509.

Steevens, George, commentator on Shakspere, dramatic critic and biographer; Stepney, 1735; died at Hampstead 1800.

Suckling, Sir John, poet, wit, courtier, dramatist; "spoke Latin fluently at five, and wrote it with ease and elegance at nine;" royalist officer; Whitton in Twickenham 1609,* died 1641.

Sydney, Dorothy, Countess of Sunderland, the "Sacharissa" of Waller; Syon house, 1617.

Taylor, Brook, musician, philosopher, and mathematician, author on linear perspective; Edmonton, 1685; died 1731.

Towerson, Gabriel, learned divine (died 1697).

Twiford, Roger, divine, Twiford (flourished 1390).

Wase, Christopher, learned and ingenious scholar and royalist; Hackney (died 1690).

Watson, Sir William, physician, botanist, and electrician; St. John's Street, Clerkenwell, 1715 (died 1787).

Wickham, William, Bishop of Winchester; Enfield, 1324 (died 1404).

Wilde, George, Bishop of Londonderry, dramatic writer; born 1601.

Wilkes, Alice, Lady Owen, foundress of Islington almshouses; Islington (died 1613).

Wilkes, John, political character, author of the North Briton, for No. 45 of which he was illegally apprehended and committed to the Tower, and for which he obtained damages against the Crown; M. P. for Middlesex; Lord Mayor of London; ugly, witty, elegant, and licentious man; born in St. John's Street, Clerkenwell, 1727 (died 1797).

William Duke of Gloucester, son of Queen Anne: Hampton Court, 1689.

Wolstenholme, Sir John, founder of the church, Stanmore Magna (died 1639).

Woodcock, Robert, painter of sea-pieces; Chelsea, 1690.

Yelverton, Sir Henry, judge, author of "Reports;" Islington, 1566 (died 1630).

* Other authorities, Witham, 1613.

MISCELLANEOUS OBSERVATIONS.

ACTON was the rectory of Daniel Featly, controversialist, author of "Clavis Mystica," who received this living from Archbishop Abbot as a reward for maintaining a public dispute with two jesuits, and died 1644-5; his house and church here were despoiled by the Parliamentarian soldiers in 1642; Philip Nye, one of the "Assembly of Divines," of Hudibrastic celebrity, who died 1673; Bruno Ryves, author of "Mercurius Rusticus," who died 1677.

Here were buried William Aldridge, wheelwright, aged 114, 1698; Margaret Fieldhouse, aged 100, 1761; Mary Hill, aged 100, 1762; Elizabeth Barry, actress, and pupil of the celebrated Earl of Rochester, 1713.

Here resided the Lord Chief Justices SIR MATTHEW HALE and Sir John Vaughan; the Bishops Lloyd of Norwich, one of the prelates who deprecated James the Second's assumed power of suspending the laws against popery, and Willis of Winchester; Francis Rous, Provost of Eton, and Speaker of the Little Parliament, who died here 1659; Philip Skippon, Parliamentarian General; RICHARD BAXTER, nonconformist, who retired hither on the passing of the Act against Conventicles; Sir Charles Scarborough, physician to Charles II.; and Philip Thicknesse, traveller in France and Spain, eccentric man and author, who died 1792.

d

BAYSWATER Tea Gardens were the property of the celebrated Sir John Hill, who there cultivated his medical plants, and prepared his celebrated " Water Dock Essence " and " Balm of Honey." Garrick characterised him thus:

> " For physic and farces his rival there scarce is,
> His farces are physic, his physic a farce is."

He died in 1775 of the gout, for which he professed to have a specific.

At these gardens died in 1793 Mrs. Kennedy, the singer.

Near Tyburn Turnpike is a burying ground belonging to the parish of St. George, Hanover Square. In it were buried Sterne, divine, wit, and sentimentalist; and Sir Thomas Picton, killed at Waterloo.

At BETHNAL GREEN resided Sir Richard Gresham, father of the founder of the Royal Exchange, London ; Sir Hugh Platt, author of "The Garden of Eden;" Sir Balthasar Gerbier, miniature painter, fanciful projector, died 1667 ; Robert Ainsworth, lexicographer, who kept a school here, and died 1743; and William Caslon, letter founder, who died here 1766.

The legendary "Beggar," in the well-known ballad (written in the time of Elizabeth, and embalmed in Percy's " Reliques," vol. ii.) was Henry de Montfort, who is supposed in the ballad to have survived the battle of Evesham, in 1265, where his father, Simon Earl of Leicester, was slain. It has been dramatised by Sheridan Knowles.

Here were buried Anne Postel, aged 100, 1749 ; Samuel Gates, aged 100, 1749-50 ; Bridget Fossett, aged 102, 1757; Mary Nash, aged 107, 1790; John Rosee, aged 102, 1795; Thomas Stamford, aged 104, 1799; Sarah Robertson, aged 100, 1804, &c. In the Jews' burial-ground was buried in 1782, Sarah Joseph, aged 107 years and 10 months.

At BRENTFORD were buried William Noy, Attorney-general, who suggested the tax of ship money, 1634; William Anslow, surgeon, aged 102, 1717 ; John Horne, whose son, the celebrated John Horne Tooke, was curate here for eleven years, 1766; Luke Sparks, comedian, 1769 ; Henry Gifford, actor and proprietor of Goodman's Fields theatre when Garrick first performed, 1772, and Anne Marcella Gifford, his wife, tragedian, 1777.

At BROMLEY ST. LEONARD'S was buried its native, auditor Benson, 1754.

In CHELSEA *Old Church* are monuments of Lord Chancellor SIR THOMAS MORE, with an inscription by himself: Jane, wife of the ambitious John Dudley, Duke of Northumberland, who died 1555; Gregory Lord Dacre, 1594, and his wife Anne, foundress of almshouses in Tothill-fields, 1595, with their effigies; and Lady Jane Cheyne (monument by Bernini, cost £500), 1669.

In the *New Church* is a beautiful monument, by Chantrey, to Lieut.-Col. the Hon. Henry Cadogan, who nobly fell at the battle of Vittoria, 1813.

In the old church and its cemeteries were also interred Sir Arthur Gorges, who built Stanley-house, translator of Lucan, 1625; Baldwin Hamey, physician and philosopher, 1676 ; Thomas Shadwell, poet laureate, 1692 ; its rector, Adam Littleton, lexicographer, 1694; Edward Chamberlayne, author of "Angliæ Notitia," 1703, his son John, linguist, 1723, and his daughter Anne, who fought as a sailor on board a fire-ship, wife of John Spragge, 1691 ; its native, Robert Woodcock, painter, 1728; Abel Boyer, historian, 1729 ; the learned Mary Astell, 1731 ; Thomas Barnardiston, serjeant at law, author of "Reports," 1752; SIR HANS SLOANE, President of the Royal Society and College of Physicians, 1753; Philip Miller, author of "The Gardener's Dictionary," 1771, monument 1815; Henry Mossop, actor, 1775; William Kenrick, critic, 1779; Sir John Fielding, magistrate, 1780.

, In the *Cemetery* in the *King's Road* were buried Andrew Millar, bookseller (his monument an obelisk), 1768; John Martyn, botanist, 1768; John Baptist Cipriani, artist (inscription by his friend Bartolozzi), 1785; Rev. Dr. Philip Withers, editor of the "Table of Cebes," who resided in Sloane Square, and died in Newgate, where he was imprisoned for libel 1790.

Ranelagh, so called from having been the residence of the paymaster-general, Richard Earl of Ranelagh, was once a very fashionable place of amusement and of public entertainment. The rotunda, first opened April 5, 1742, was 185 feet in diameter. All the buildings were taken down in 1805.

The famous coffee-house, called *Don Saltero's*, noticed by Sir Richard Steele, in the Tatler, No. 34, obtained its name from one Salter, a barber, who opened it in 1695. Most of his curiosities were given to him by Sir Hans Sloane, to whom he had once been a servant, and by Admiral Munden, who had been much on the coast of Spain, and who gave the house its Spanish appellation.

The *World's End* public house was a noted house of entertainment in the time of Charles II. It is mentioned in Congreve's comedy of "Love for Love," in a dialogue between Mrs. Foresight and Mrs. Frail.

At the *Apothecaries' Garden*, which was commenced 1673, and is maintained by the Society of Apothecaries of London, resided many years Philip Miller, who is honoured by having a new genus of plants consecrated to his name—*Milleria*. Here is a statue, by Rysbrach, of Sir Hans Sloane.

At *Stanley House* died, in 1743, Admiral Sir Charles

Wager; originally a quaker. It afterwards became the property of the accomplished and unfortunate Countess of Strathmore in 1777, who married A. B. Bowes, esq. and endured almost unheard of barbarities and cruelties from him, dying in 1800.

Ashburnham House was built in 1747, by Dr. Benjamin Hoadly, physician, philosopher, and author of "The Suspicious Husband."

Lindsey House, the late Moravian establishment, was built temp. Charles II. by Robert Bertie, Earl of Lindsey, on the site of a house of Sir Theodore Mayerne, physician to King James I. and his successor, who died there in 1655, aged 82. The Moravians were founded in 1750 by Count Zinzendorf, who lived here, presiding over the community. In the burial-ground, behind the house, lie Christian Renatus de Zinzendorf, only son of the Count, 1752 ; Peter Bœhler, their Bishop, 1775 ; William Hammond, author of "The Marrow of the Gospel," 1783; and Benjamin La Trobe, expositor of their religion, 1786.

Beaufort House, on the site of Beaufort St., was built about 1520, by Sir Thos. More, Lord Chancellor to Henry VIII. who here frequently visited him, and here obtained the Chancellor's assistance in writing the King's memorable answer to Martin Luther. Sir Thomas patronized the painter Hans Holbein, who lived three years in this house, when visiting England in 1526 : he was here introduced to Henry VIII. From this house More was taken to the Tower, where he suffered. It then became the residence of William Paulet, the first Marquess of Winchester, Lord High Treasurer to Queen Elizabeth ; of William Cecil, Lord Burghley, and his son Robert Cecil, the first Earl of Salisbury, who rebuilt the house of More ; and it subsequently became the property and residence of Lionel Cranfield, Earl of Middlesex, Lord Treasurer ; of George Villiers, the elegant and courtly

Buckingham, who was stabbed by Felton at Portsmouth in 1628; of his son, the witty and profligate author of " The Rehearsal;" of Sir Bulstrode Whitelocke, author of "Memorials of English Affairs " during the Commonwealth; and of Sir Hans Sloane, who pulled it down in 1740. Few houses can boast of having been the residence of such a succession of distinguished characters. *Vide* under Chiswick.

At *Shaftesbury House, Little Chelsea*, now the workhouse of St. George's, Hanover Square, resided Anthony Ashley Cooper, third Earl of Shaftesbury, author of " the Characteristics."

At *Little Chelsea* resided, in 1661, the philosopher and chemist Robert Boyle, seventh son of the Earl of Cork.

The sign of the Goat and Boots public house, Little Chelsea, was painted by Morland to defray expenses incurred at the house.

In *Church Lane* Dr. Atterbury, afterwards Bishop of Rochester, resided. He here became acquainted with Dean Swift, in 1711, who lodged in a house opposite to him.

Dr. John Arbuthnot, physician and wit, also resided in Church Lane.

On the site of *Lombard Terrace* resided Henry Sampson Woodfall, printer, and publisher of the Letters of Junius, for which he suffered by fine and imprisonment. He died in 1805, and had an inscription in the old churchyard.

In *Lombard Street* resided Lewis the bookbinder, companion of Dr. Smollett on his journey from Edinburgh to London, and the original of Strap the barber in Roderick Random.

In *Lawrence Street* resided Anne Duchess of Monmouth and Buccleuch, about 1714, and the poet Gay was for some time her secretary or domestic steward. In the same house afterwards resided Dr. Smollett, physician, novelist, historian, &c. The house was pulled down in 1839.

At *Shrewsbury* or *Alston House*, pulled down in 1813, resided George Talbot, Earl of Shrewsbury, generous and honourable keeper of Mary Queen of Scots; and Elizabeth his Countess, builder of Chatsworth, Hardwick, and Old-coates, who died 1643.

The old *Manor House*, situate in Cheyne Walk, was occupied by Katharine Parr, queen of Henry VIII. and her husband Sir Thomas Seymour, Lord High Admiral; and here had care of her ward the Princess Elizabeth. Anne of Cleves, after her divorce, also resided in this house, in which she died 1557. Charles Howard, Earl of Nottingham, Lord High Admiral, here frequently was honoured with visits from Queen Elizabeth. Sir Hans Sloane made it his retirement and a repository for his library and museum in 1742, till his death in 1753. In the gardens is a mulberry tree planted by the hands of Queen Elizabeth.

By the water side resided Sir Richard Steele, and here wrote some of the Spectators.

In *Cheyne Walk* were the baths of Dr. Dominicetti, an Italian charlatan of great celebrity. The House was afterwards the residence of the philanthropist, the Rev. Weeden Butler; and his friend James Neild, author on Prisons, resided in the same row of houses, which faces the Thames.

The Bishops of Winchester had a palace in Cheyne Walk, from 1664 to 1825, when it was pulled down. Here died Bishops Richard Willis, 1736; Benjamin Hoadly 1761; John Thomas, 1781.

Queen's Elm owes its name to the circumstance of Queen Elizabeth and Lord Burghley having found shelter under an elm tree here from a heavy shower of rain. An elm stood here until about the year 1835.

In *Salamanca Place* resided A. H. Haworth, esq. who had an unrivalled museum of entomology and natural history. He died in 1833.

In *Paradise Row* resided the statesman John Robartes, created Earl of Radnor, and there he entertained Charles II. in 1660; John Vaughan, last Earl of Carberry; Charles Duke of St. Alban's, natural son of Charles II. by Nell Gwynne ; the beautiful Duchess of Mazarine, whom Charles II. wanted in marriage, and who died here in 1699; Mrs. Mary Astell, learned friend of the accomplished Lady Elizabeth Hastings; Dr. Richard Mead, physician, about 1714; Thomas Stackhouse, historian of the Bible, 1750; Suett, the actor, who died here in 1805.

King James's College, for polemical divines, was founded in 1610, through the efforts of Dr. Sutcliffe, Dean of Exeter; but existed scarcely twenty years. Camden was one of its historiographers, in conjunction with Sir John Hayward.

The *Royal Hospital* for military pensioners, built on the site of the College, is said to owe its institution to the exertions and entreaties of Nell Gwynn, mistress to Charles II. The design was given by Sir Christopher Wren. In the centre of the Court is a bronze statue of Charles II. larger than life, by Grinling Gibbons. The Pensioners have a library of history, voyages, travels, and military memoirs. Dr. Messenger Monsey, physician to the hospital, a singularly accomplished and eccentric man, died here 1788, aged 96. On the morning of the day on which he died, while at breakfast, he said to the servant, "I shall certainly lose the game;" and upon her asking him what game? replied, "the game of a *hundred*, which I have played for very earnestly many years; but I shall lose it now, for I expect to die in a few hours."

In the *College* cemetery, William Hiseland, pensioner, aged 112, 1732; Christiana Davies, or Mother Ross, served as a dragoon under William III. and Duke of Marlborough, 1739; William Cheselden, surgeon, 1752; William Young, lexicographer, the original of Fielding's "Parson Adams,"

1757 ; James O'Hara, Lord Tyrawley, field-marshal, and John Ranby, surgeon, 1773; its governor, Sir William Fawcett, general, 1804; Alexander Reid, surgeon, 1789; Hannah Snell, female soldier, 1792; and Dr. Charles Burney, historian of music, 1814.

Near to the Hospital, on the west side, stood the house of Edward Russell, Earl of Orford, victor at La Hogue ; after him occupied by Sir Robert Walpole, statesman, who here employed as his architect Sir John Vanbrugh, and Lady Walpole here received visits from Queen Caroline. Part of the house is now the hospital infirmary.

Besides most of the above-mentioned, among the *Inhabitants* of Chelsea were, Thomas Beauchamp, Earl of Warwick, warrior at Cressy and Poictiers; Lord High Chamberlain, Robert Ratcliffe, first Earl of Sussex of his family, who died here 1542 ; the Parliamentarian, John Pym, for several years ; Edward Montagu, Earl of Manchester ; Sir Francis Wyndham, protector of Charles II. ; the prelates, Sharpe and Dawes of York ; Fletcher, of London, father of the dramatist; Fowler, of Gloucester, who died here 1714 ; Dr. Daniel Featly, controversial divine, provost of the college, where he died 1645 ; Philip Francis, translator of Horace, chaplain of the college ; Thomas Pelham, Lord Pelham ; Elizabeth Blackwell, herbalist ; James Glenie, mathematician and engineer, who died here 1817 ; and Richard Yates, D.D., F.S.A. chaplain of the College, 1834.

At CHISWICK were buried Sir Thomas Chaloner, statesman and naturalist, first discoverer of alum mines in this kingdom, 1615 ; Leonard Mawe, Bishop of Bath and Wells, 1629; Arthur Duck, civilian, biographer of Abp. Chichele, 1649 ; Barbara Villiers, Duchess of Cleveland, mistress of Charles II. 1709 ; Sir John Chardin, traveller, 1712 ; Mary, Countess of Fauconberg, third daughter of Oliver

Cromwell, 1713; Dorothy Linton, aged 105, 1728; William Kent, painter and architect, 1748; James Ralph, historian and poet, satirized by Pope, 1762; WILLIAM HOGARTH, painter (epitaph by Garrick), 1764; Charles Holland, a native, actor (epitaph by Garrick), 1769; Sir Thomas Robinson, first Lord Grantham, statesman, 1770; Christopher Strickland, esq. aged 102, 1782; Dr. Thomas Morell, editor of Ainsworth and Hederick, 1784; Dr. William Rose, critic, translator of Sallust (epitaph by Murphy), and Thomas, second Lord Grantham, statesman, 1786; Dr. Ralph Griffiths, original editor of the "Monthly Review," 1803; George Earl Macartney (below mentioned) 1806; Alexander Brodie, Esq. inventor of Register Stoves for Shipping, 1811; Philip James de Loutherbourg, painter, 1812; Sir James Earle, Surgeon to George III. and Chief Surgeon of St. Bartholomew's, 1817; William Sharp, Esq. historical engraver, 1824; Ugo Foscolo, dramatic author, 1827; and James Fittler, A.R.A., marine engraver to George III. 1835.

At *Corney House*, resided William, the brave Lord Russell of Thornhaugh; and his son Francis, first Earl of Bedford; and more recently, George, Earl Macartney, statesman. It was pulled down 1834.

At *Chiswick House*, after his disgrace, resided Robert Car, Earl of Somerset, favourite of James I. and his infamous Countess, previously Countess of Essex, who died here 1632.

At *College House* resided Busby and Freind, and other masters of Westminster School, it having been a country retirement provided for them, and occasionally for their scholars, on visitations of the plague or other epidemic sickness. In latter times it has been the printing office of Mr. Whittingham, celebrated for the beauty of his works. He died here 1839.

At *Turnham Green* resided George Elliot, Lord Heathfield, defender of Gibraltar, who died 1790.

At *Strand-on-the-Green* resided Joseph Miller, "honest Joe Miller," actor and jester, whose wit and humour contributed much to the success of Congreve's comedies, who died here 1738, and was buried in the Portugal Street burial ground; also J. Zoffany, painter, who died here 1810.

At *Chiswick* resided Sir Henry Sydney, Lord President of Ireland; Chief Justice Sir William Jones; ALLEN LORD BATHURST, who died 1775; RICHARD BOYLE, EARL OF BURLINGTON, who died 1753—

" Who plants like Bathurst, and who builds like Boyle ?"—POPE.

and Sir Stephen Fox, statesman, who was married here in 1703, to Christian Hope, whose two ennobled sons were born here, and who died here in 1716.

The present CHISWICK HOUSE was built by the classical Richard Earl of Burlington, and among its fine collection of paintings is the celebrated " Belisarius." In it died in 1806 the Right Hon. Charles James Fox, and in 1828 George Canning, both Prime Ministers of Great Britain; and here, in 1814, the Emperor of Russia and King of Prussia dined with the Duke of Devonshire.

In an avenue near the house, is the gate of Beaufort House, Chelsea, built by Inigo Jones in 1625, and given to the Earl of Burlington by Sir Hans Sloane 1737. On this removal, Pope wrote these lines:

Passenger.
O Gate, how com'st thou here?
Gate.
I was brought from Chelsea last year,
Batter'd with wind and weather.
Inigo Jones put me together;
Sir Hans Sloane
Let me alone;
Burlington brought me hither."

The beautiful iron gates recently erected at the entrance of the grounds, were removed from Heathfield House, Turnham Green, when that house was pulled down in 1838.

CLERKENWELL. The *Nunnery* is said to have possessed one of the six waterpots in which Jesus changed the water into wine !

In *St. James's old Church* was buried John Weever, the author of "Funeral Monuments," who lived in the Close, and died there in 1632; with a quaint poetical inscription, which may be seen in either Stowe or Strype.

In *St. James's Church* was buried Cave, the projector of the Gentleman's Magazine, who died in 1754, without any memorial. Could not the many who have been amused and instructed by that periodical, raise a tablet as a record of his worth and their gratitude ? The mite of the humble compiler of these pages would be cheerfully contributed.

In *St. John's Square* is a double-fronted house, with one bow-window, formerly the abode of Dr. Gilbert Burnet, Bp. of Salisbury, who accompanied William III. as his chaplain, when he came over as Prince of Orange, to take the throne. He died 1714-15, and was buried in Clerkenwell church. On the iron back of a stove is a bas-relief of Charles I. on horseback, trampling over a prostrate figure, with the initials C. R. and the date 1644.

In *St. John's Lane*, at the sign of the Baptist's Head, is a curiously carved stone mantle-piece, with the arms of Sir Thomas Forster, knt. one of the Judges of the Common Pleas, who resided here, and died in 1681. It is considered to have been a house of call of Drs. Johnson and Goldsmith, while contributors to the *Gentleman's Magazine*. On the wall of the tap-room is a picture of a Dutch fair, said to have been painted by Heemskirk ; but it is now nearly obliterated through neglect.

The *Gate* of the old Hospital of St. John of Jerusalem,
the superior of which was styled premier Baron of England,
is now used as the Old Jerusalem Tavern. Here was the
printing office of Edward Cave, whence issued the early
numbers of the Gentleman's Magazine, a periodical "of
which the scheme is known wherever the English language is spoken;" which has existed since the year 1731 ;
and which soon became, and has continued, the chosen
receptacle for the literary correspondence of the scholar and
the antiquary.   Among its early contributors were Dr.
Johnson, who supplied some of the Parliamentary debates,
and wrote several of the essays ; Dr. Hawkesworth; Dr.
Goldsmith ; and many of the most eminent literati of that
and subsequent periods.

In *Woodbridge Street* stood the Red Bull Theatre,
erected in the time of Elizabeth. In point of size it vied
with the Globe and Fortune, and excelled all the rest. It is
probable that the first English female performer belonged
to this theatre.

In *Jerusalem Passage* resided Thomas Britton, the eccentric "Musical Small-coal Man," the introducer of public
concerts, which were first held in a room over his coal warehouse, and to which access was made by a pair of steep steps
on the outside. This receptacle attracted all the fashion of
the age. The celebrated Dubourg here played the first solo
he ever executed in public, when a child, standing upon a
joint-stool.

What is now *Ray Street*, was formerly Hockley-in-the-
Hole, where was a celebrated bear garden. Mrs. Peachum,
in the inimitable Beggar's Opera, says to Filch, "You must
go to Hockley-in-the-Hole, and to Marybone, child, to learn
valour."

Hicks's Hall was so named from the Sessions House

having been built at the cost of Sir Baptist Hicks, 1612. It originally stood in St. John's Street, but now on Clerkenwell Green.

On the spot where now stands *Sutton Street*, were buried of the plague in 1349, 50,000 bodies. Soon afterwards a church, called Pardon Church, was erected for the saying of masses for the repose of their souls. The churchyard was subsequently used for such as desperately ended their lives or were executed for felonies.

Near to *Clerkenwell Green*, inserted in the wall of a little shop, is a pump with an inscription purporting that the water flows from the identical fountain, or "Clerks' Well," which gave rise to the name of the parish, and around which the Parish Clerks of London used annually to perform sacred plays. Among the former residents of the green was a notorious astrologer and fortune-teller, in the time of Charles II. named Jack Adams, or "*Jacko Cunningmanissimo.*"

Northampton House, was formerly a residence of the Comptons, Earls of Northampton; and previous to 1802, was a private lunatic asylum, in which the celebrated Brothers, "the prophet," was confined. Its gardens are now the site of Northampton Square.

Cobham Row marks the residence in the 15th cent. of Sir John Oldcastle, Lord Cobham, the first author as well as the first religious martyr among our nobility. He was hung in chains and then burnt in December 1417.

In *Great Bath Street*, Coldbath Fields, died, in 1772, the "highly illuminated" Emanuel Swedenborg, founder of a religious sect.

Bagnigge House is said to have been a residence of Nell Gwynn, and afterwards used as a public spa and place of entertainment.

Sadler's Wells Theatre, about 1780, was famous for its pantomimes, admirably supported "by that truly excellent master of dumb show, Signor Grimaldi," father and grandfather of the two celebrated Grimaldis. Here was first introduced, in 1804, the novelty of real water on the stage.

The *Three Hats*, near Islington turnpike, but in this parish, was formerly a well known place of resort. Mawworm, in Bickerstaffe's comedy of "The Hypocrite," says "Till I went after him (Dr. Cantwell) I was always a roving after fantastical delights. I used to go, every Sunday evening, to the Three Hats at Islington! it's a public house! Mayhap your ladyship may know it?"

In *Winchester Place*, Pentonville, resided for 15 years, "the rapacious and wicked old miser" Thomas Cooke, who died in White Lion Street in 1811, in his 87th year.

Near *John Street*, at a house called Hermes Hill, resided Dr. de Valangin, a pupil of the celebrated Boerhaave, and discoverer of the Balsam of Life. Here afterwards, in 1811, resided that remarkable man, William Huntington, S.S. (sinner saved), religious enthusiast.

At COWLEY were buried, in 1733, Barton Booth, tragedian, the original performer of Addison's Cato; on which occasion Lord Bolingbroke presented him, from the stage box, the sum of 50 guineas, an example which was immediately followed by that nobleman's political opponents ;• Hester, his widow, actress and dancer, 1773 ; and John Lightfoot, divine and botanist, 1788.

In CRANFORD were buried, in 1661, its rector THOMAS FULLER, D.D. royalist, ecclesiastical historian, and author of the "Worthies of England," and other works abounding with learning, intelligence, and playful wit; his memory was so excellent, that he could repeat 500 strange and unconnected words after twice hearing; and Sir Charles Scarborough, physician, 1693.

The philosophic JOHN WILKINS, one of the founders of the Royal Society, and afterwards Bishop of Chester, was rector here.

EALING was the vicarage of Thomas Gilbert, the first minister ejected after the Restoration, and of William Beveridge, afterwards Bp. of St. Asaph.

Here were buried old Sir John Maynard, King's Serjeant, 1690; John Oldmixon, historian 1742; Dr. William King, principal of St. Mary's hall, Oxford, scholar and politician, 1764; Elizabeth Platt, aged 100, 1772; Robert Orme, historian of the East Indies, 1801; Sir Frederick Morton Eden, author of "The State of the Poor," 1809; John Horne Tooke, philologist and politician, 1812.

Residents: At Gunnersbury, Sir Thomas Meautys, the Secretary of Lord Bacon; Princess Amelia, aunt to King George the Third.

At Pitshanger, Thomas Edwards, author of "Canons of Criticism."

At Ealing Grove, Joseph Gulston, print collector.

At Castle-hill, General Elliot, defender of Gibraltar, afterwards Lord Heathfield; Mrs. Fitzherbert; and Edward Duke of Kent.

At Fordhook, Henry Fielding, novelist, who died 1754.

At Little Ealing, Zachary Pearce, Bp. of Rochester, who died there 1774.

At Old Brentford, Mrs. Trimmer, a useful and pious writer for juvenile instruction, who died 1810.

At Elm grove, formerly called Hickes-on-the-Heath, Sir William Trumbull, Secretary of State, and friend of Pope; Dr. John Egerton, Bp. of Norwich; and the Right Hon.

SPENCER PERCEVAL, assassinated by Bellingham at the door of the House of Commons, 1812.

At Ealing, William Fleetwood, Recorder of London; Dr. John Owen, independent, who died here 1683; and Peter Francis le Courayer, French catholic divine, supporter of Church of England, who died 1776.

EDGWARE. The Lord of the manor used to provide a piper or minstrel for the diversion of the tenants while employed in his service. In 1552 the inhabitants were presented for not having a tumbrel and cucking-stool.

Edgware was the curacy of Francis Coventry, author of " Pompey the Little," and Thomas Martyn, professor of Botany.

EDMONTON. At Arnolds, Southgate, is a staircase painted by Lanscroon, a pupil of Verrio, 1723, representing the triumphal entry of Julius Cæsar into Rome, and his subsequent apotheosis.

At *Bury Hall* resided the regicide President Bradshaw, whose arms are over the chimney-piece in the dining room.

In *Bush Hill House* is the fine piece of carving, the stoning of St. Stephen, by Grinling Gibbons, the merit of which obtained for the artist an introduction to Charles II. by Evelyn, and the commendation of Sir Peter Lely.

At *Pymmes*, now demolished, resided the great Cecil Lord Burleigh, Lord High Treasurer; and afterwards his son, Sir Robert Cecil.

At the Rectory House resided the great Abp. Tillotson.

The Bell Inn, has acquired much celebrity from the poetic tale of " John Gilpin," by Cowper. A painting of the incident is exhibited outside the house.

In the workhouse died in October 1799, Mary Gillet, aged 100 years.

The Vicarage was possessed by Dr. Henry Owen, the author of " Critica Sacra," between the years 1776 and 1795, when he died, aged 80 years.　　　　　*e*

Peter Fabell, who was buried in the church in the time of Henry the Seventh, is the supposed original of "The Merry Devil of Edmonton," whose merry pranks were published in a scarce tract under that title, (reprinted in 1820,) and dramatised by Michael Drayton.

"The Witch of Edmonton," a tragedy, published in 1658, was founded on the history of Elizabeth Sawyer, or "Mother Sawyer," as she was called, who was executed as a witch in 1621.

In the *Church* were buried, Thomas Gill, physician, 1714; Charles Molloy, dramatist, 1767; James Barclay, poet, whose father, author of the Dictionary, was curate here in 1771; and James Vere, benefactor and author, 1779.

In the *Churchyard* was formerly a head-stone to one William Newberry, ostler, who is said to have lost his life in consequence of some improper medicines administered by an ignorant fellow-servant. The epitaph was as follows:

> " Hic jacet Newberry Will,
>   Vitam finivit cum Cochiæ Pill;
>   Quis administravit? Bellamy Sue;
>   Quantum quantitat? nescio—scisne tu?
>   Ne sutor ultra crepidam."

In the Burial-ground of the Society of Friends at Winchmore Hill, lie the remains of the celebrated physician, Dr. John Fothergill.

At the Independent Chapel, then used by the Presbyterians, the celebrated Dr. Price began his ministry in 1744.

ENFIELD was the residence of Edward VI. and Elizabeth in their childhood. Edward kept his court here immediately after his accession, and Elizabeth frequently visited it when Queen.

At *Elsynge Hall* resided the patron of Caxton, Tiptoft, Earl of Worcester, Lord High Treasurer, whose mother

Joyce died here in 1446, and is buried under a stately monument in the church; Sir Thomas Lovell, K.G. Treasurer of the Household, who died here 1524; and Philip Herbert, Earl of Pembroke, who condescended to accept a seat in Cromwell's House of Commons.

South Lodge, Enfield Chase, was left by will to William Pitt, afterwards Earl of Chatham, with a sum of £10,000. He observed that he should spend the money in alterations and improvements, and then grow tired of the place. He laid out the pleasure grounds at great expense, resided here a few years, and disposed of it.

East Lodge was a hunting-seat of Charles I., and the residence of Lord Chancellor Loughborough.

West Lodge, of Henry Coventry, Secretary of State to Charles II.

By *Enfield Wash* stands the cottage, now occupied by Green the baker, to which Elizabeth Canning, a servant girl of about 18 years old, swore that she was conveyed by two men in January 1753, and, having been robbed by Mary Squires a gipsy, after a confinement of a month, escaped out of the window. On this evidence Squires was sentenced to death; and Susanna Wells, the occupier of the cottage, to imprisonment; but through the exertions of Sir Crisp Gascoigne, Lord Mayor, Canning, after a trial of seven days, was convicted of perjury, and transported for seven years; whilst Squires and Wells were discharged. Canning was allowed to transport herself to America, where she formed an advantageous matrimonial alliance with a planter, and died there in 1773. This affair excited the greatest interest; and Lysons has enumerated 36 pamphlets and 14 prints published on the occasion; the respective parties being termed *Canningites* and *Egyptians.*

In the house now occupied by Mr. May as a boarding school, are to be found all that remains of the old palace.

Here resided Dr. Uvedale, the botanist, in honour of whom the plant *Uvedalia* is so named. He had a very curious garden here with the choicest exotics then in England; and here he planted a Cedar of Libanus, noticed under the head of "Natural Curiosities," which though mutilated is still an interesting object. The Dr. was Master of the Grammar School, and was buried in the church in 1722.

The old *Durants House*, or *Durance Harbour*, was a residence of the infamous Lord Chancellor Jeffries; and according to popular imagination the scene of "much bloody work." The old barns and moat remain, and surround a modern house.

Forty Hall was built by Inigo Jones. It contains many very valuable paintings.

The old *White Webbs House* was a house of the Gunpowder Plot Conspirators. Here they abided between the intervals of the last prorogation of Parliament.

Trent Place was the residence of Sir Richard Jebb, physician to George the Third, who conferred on him the honour of a baronetcy, and bestowed the title of Trent Place to his estate in commemoration of his successful attendance on the Duke of Gloucester when dangerously ill at *Trent.* The place called Camlet Moats, in the grounds, was the occasional lurking place of the notorious robber Turpin.

At the upper end of *Baker Street* resided Richard Gough, antiquary, author of the "Sepulchral Monuments," and editor of "Camden." He died there in 1809, and his widow in 1833.

Other eminent inhabitants were Edmund Calamy, nonconformist, who died here 1666; George Wharton, astrologer, died here 1681; Sir Richard Jebb, physician; and William Saunders, physician, died here 1817.

Enfield, during the last century, renowned for beautiful

women. Some lines on this subject were written by Mr. H. Baker in 1725, and are reprinted in Dr. Robinson's History of the parish.

In the *Church* are many old and interesting monuments.

In the *Churchyard* was buried Thomas Hills Everitt, aged 15 months, who, at the age of 11 months, weighed between 9 and 10 stone, was 3 feet 3 inches high, measured 3 feet 1 inch round the loins, and round the wrist 9 inches; had many teeth and a fine head of hair.

Here were buried William, Robert, and Margaret Deane, the first persons executed under the Coventry Act, 1667; John Truss, aged 112, 1723; and Susanna Wells, above mentioned, 1763.

At FELTHAM was buried William Wynne Ryland, engraver, executed for forgery, 1783.

FINCHLEY was the rectory of John de Feckenham, last abbot of Westminster; William Coton, Bp. of Exeter; John Bancroft, Bp. of Oxford; and John Barkham, real author of "Guillim's Heraldry."

Here were buried Sir Thomas Frowick, Chief Justice, 1506; Charles Lilly, perfumer, noticed in the Tatler, Nos. 92, 94, 101, 103, and 250, in the Spectator, Nos. 16 and 358, and Guardian, No. 64, 1746; Anne Maynard, aged 112, 1756; and "honest Tom Payne," one of the most eminent booksellers of this country, 1799.

Hogarth's "March to Finchley" represents the commencement of the march of the Guards towards Scotland in 1745. The scene is laid at Tottenham Court Turnpike, the King's Head, Adam and Eve, &c.

FRIARN BARNET was the residence of Chief Justice Sir John Popham.

FULHAM was the rectory of Richard Hill, Bp. of London, 1407; Henry King, Bp. of Chichester, 1641; Thomas

Howell, Bp. of Bristol ; and Dr. Michael Lort, antiquary. The vicarage of Adoniram Byfield (1649), celebrated by name by Butler ; and Dennison Cumberland (1757) afterwards Bp. of Kilmore.

In the *Church* are monuments of Sir William Butts, physician to Henry VIII., celebrated by Shakespeare, 1545 ; Sir Thomas Smith, statesman and scholar, 1609 ; John Viscount Mordaunt (by Bushnel and Bird, cost £400) 1675 ; a plain black stone to Humphrey Henchman, Bp. of London, 1675 ; Dorothy Lady Clarke, (by Grinling Gibbons, cost £300) 1695 ; her 2d husband, Dr. Barrow, physician to Charles II. 1682 ; and a tablet for BEILBY PORTEUS, Bp. of London, 1809.

In the *Churchyard* are tombs of the Bishops of London, HENRY COMPTON, 1713 ; John Robinson, 1723 ; EDMUND GIBSON (who has a cenotaph in the church), 1748 ; Thomas Sherlock, 1761 ; Thomas Hayter, 1762 ; Richard Terrick, 1777 ; ROBERT LOWTH, 1787 ; and John Randolph, 1813. In Fulham were also buried, Sir Sampson Norton, master of the ordnance to Henry VIII., 1517 ; John Tamworth, statesman, 1569 ; John Florio, translator of Montaigne, 1625 ; Sir Francis Child, Lord Mayor in 1699, 1713 ; Richard Fiddes, biographer of Wolsey, 1725 ; Christopher Wilson, Bp. of Bristol, 1792 ; William Cadogan, physician, 1797 ; and Granville Sharp, philanthropist and scholar, 1813.

Fulham palace contains some finely painted glass, and numerous portraits of its prelates. In it died Walter de Grey, Abp. of York, 1255 ; and the Bishops of London, Richard de Gravesend, 1303 ; John Aylmer, 1594 ; Compton, 1713, aged 81 ; Robinson ; and Lowth. A large chair in the shrubbery, in which the ferocious Bonner used to sit in judgment, is the subject of a pleasing little poem by

Mrs. Hannah More. In the palace garden, the Tamarisk was first planted; being introduced by Bp. Grindall, in 1560, from Switzerland. Many new plants from North America were introduced here by Bp. Compton. In 1683 the first Cedar of Libanus was planted here.

Sandford Manor House was a residence of Nell Gwynn. The walnut trees in front are said to have been planted by royal hands.

At *Sandy End* resided Addison the poet and essayist.

Mustow or *Munster House* was once a hunting seat of King Charles II.

At *Peterborough House* resided Charles Mordaunt, Earl of Peterborough, "Mordanto fills the trump of fame," sailor, soldier, orator, and statesman, who died in 1735; and his second wife the celebrated Mrs. Anastatia Robinson, an opera singer, who died in 1750.

At *Parson's Green* resided Admiral Sir Charles Wager, who died at Stanley House, Chelsea, 1743; Jeffrey Ekins, Dean of Carlisle, translator of Apollonius Rhodius, who died 1791; Sir Thomas Bodley, founder of the library at Oxford, between 1605 and 1609; Chief Justice Sir John Vaughan, to whose house here the great Lord Bacon retired when in disgrace, 1611; Chief Justice Sir Edward Saunders, 1682, in a house subsequently occupied by Mr. Samuel Richardson the novelist, on a visit to whom in 1757 Thomas Edwards, author of "Canons of Criticism," died here.

At *North End*, the novelist Richardson resided and wrote his "Clarissa Harlowe," and "Sir Charles Grandison." He removed hence to Parson's Green.—Jacob Tonson, the bookseller, had a house for some time in this hamlet. He was Secretary to the Kit Kat Club, and died in 1735, aged 80.—Foote, the comedian, had a house here for many years; and opposite to it was the house of Bartolozzi the engraver.

At *South Field Farm*, near Parson's Green, the first pine strawberry and Chinese strawberry, and also the first Auricula, were grown. Mr. Rench the proprietor instituted here the first annual exhibition of flowers ever known. His son, who died in 1783, introduced the moss-rose tree into this country from Holland.

Other inhabitants of Fulham were Chief Justice Sir Edward Saunders; George Hickman, Bp. of Londonderry, who died here 1713; the topographer Norden, who died 1624; and the naturalist Catesby.

GREENFORD MAGNA was the rectory of John de Feckenham, last Abbot of Westminster; and Edward Terry, Eastern Traveller, buried here 1660.

In GREENFORD PARVA, or PERIVALE, was buried Philip Fletcher, Dean of Kildare, poet, 1765.

In HACKNEY were buried Christopher Urswick, its rector, Dean of Windsor, statesman, 1521; Henry Percy, Earl of Northumberland, K. G. who arrested Cardinal Wolsey, 1537; Edward de Vere, Earl of Oxford, K.G. warrior and poet, 1604; Anthony, a poor old Negro, aged 105, 1630; David Doulben, its vicar, Bp. of Bangor, 1633; Owen Rowe, regicide, and Susanna Perwich, musician, 1661; Anne Pitts of Balmes, aged 105, 1664-5; William Spurstowe, its vicar, one of the authors of "Smectymnuus," 1666; John Worthington, its lecturer, editor of Mede's works, 1671; Timothy Hall, Bp. of Oxford, 1690; William Bates, nonconformist, author of "Harmony of the Attributes," 1699: Robert Fleming, nonconformist, author of "Christology," 1716; Peter Newcome, its vicar, author of Catechetical sermons, 1738; Richard Newcome, Bp. of St. Asaph, 1769; Joseph Egleton, aged 108, 1781; Francis Xavier de Oliveyra, Protestant proselyte and author, 1783;

Mary Wood, aged 104, 1796; and Ebenezer Radcliffe, dissenting minister, 1809.

Of this church was rector, Richard Sampson, Bp. of Lichfield and Coventry; Vicars, GILBERT SHELDON, Abp. of Canterbury, and Calybute Downing, Parliamentarian divine, who died here 1644; Lecturer, John Strype, antiquary, who died here 1737.

Of the old Dissenting meeting-house were pastors, Philip Nye, and Adoniram Byfield of Hudibrastic celebrity; Dr. William Bates, before mentioned; and Dr. Matthew Henry, biblical commentator.

Of the New, or Gravel-pit meeting, Dr. Richard Price, the calculator, who died here 1791; and Dr. Joseph Priestley, who, previously to his departure for America, preached his farewell sermon here, March 30, 1794.

Here, in 1637, Thomas Fairfax, afterwards the famous Parliamentarian General, was married to Anne daughter of Lord Vere.

Here were educated Catharine Phillips, generally known as "Orinda," and the brother dramatists Benjamin and John Hoadly.

Other inhabitants: Cecilia, the learned daughter of Sir Thomas More, wife of Giles Heron of Shacklewell, Esq.; Offspring Blackall, Bp. of Exeter; Thomas Wood, Bp. of Lichfield and Coventry, founder of Hackney alms-houses; Lord Brooke, Parliamentarian general, slain at Lichfield; Sir Julius Cæsar, Master of the Rolls; Colonel Okey, regicide; Sir Thomas Vyner, Lord Mayor, the first knight made after the Restoration, who died here 1665; Daniel De Foe, author of "Robinson Crusoe;" Dr. Bernard Mandeville, author of "The Fable of the Bees," who died here 1733; and John Ward, the usurer, celebrated by Pope, in the quaternion,

"To Ward, to Waters, Chartres, and the Devil."

Here died, in 1743, Mrs. Dowse, the Sexton, aged 100; Rev. Mr. Pratt, aged 102, 1771; Zachary Abingdon, aged 103, 1774; Mrs. Jane Davis, aged 113, 1777. In 1810 was living and receiving parochial relief, aged 103, Mary Thornbury.

At HADLEY were buried its native Sir William Stamford, Judge, 1558; Sir Roger Wilbraham, Master of Requests (monument by Nicholas Stone, cost £80), 1616; John Monro, physician, eminent in cases of insanity, 1792; Mrs. Hester Chapone, belles-lettres writer, 1801; Rev. David Garrow, father of the late Baron of the Exchequer (monument by Bacon), 1805.

John Booker, astrologer, was a writing master here.

An iron beacon still remains on the top of the church tower.

HAMMERSMITH was a chapelry of Fulham until 1834, when it was constituted a distinct parish. At *Fairlawn House* Dr. Charles Burney, the profound Grecian, kept a school and removed thence to Greenwich.

The *Nunnery*, near the Broadway, was established by Mrs. Bedingfeld about 1685. The buildings are very extensive, and contain some good pictures, and an antient wooden cross. The fine organ formerly belonged to Dr. Boyce. Cardinal Weld was private chaplain here from 1824 to 1829. In it is a school for educating daughters of Catholic nobility and gentry.

Of the *Independent Chapel*, the celebrated preacher, Dr. Thomas Raffles, was minister.

At *Lee's Nursery*, in 1787, was seen the first China rose.

At the *Chancellor's*, the residence of John Bowyer Nichols, esq. the proprietor of the Gentleman's Magazine, is a remarkably fine Gleditschia Triachanthos, one of the finest in England. In the grounds is an elegant pavilion of stone, erected by Lord Melcombe; and in it, and the house, are a number of curious antiquities, and many of the productions of Hogarth.

Brandenburgh House was built by the loyal Sir Nicholas Crispe. His nephew sold it to Prince Rupert, who gave it to his mistress the much admired Mrs. Margaret Hughes, one of the first who acted in female characters after they ceased to be performed by men. The celebrated Bubb Doddington, afterwards Lord Melcombe, resided and died here, 1762. The Margrave of Brandenburgh Anspach became its possessor, and his celebrated Margravine much improved it. It was lastly the residence of the ill-fated Queen Caroline, who here ended a life of disappointment and misery on the 7th of August 1821.

The enchanting singer Mrs. Billington resided in a villa near Brandenburgh House, called Sussex House, now the residence of Mrs. Copland.

On the *Lower Mall* is the Dove Coffee House, where the poet Thomson wrote the greater part of his " Winter."

On the *Upper Mall,* Catharine, dowager queen of Charles II. resided for several summers. The same house became the residence of Dr. Radcliffe, physician, and founder of the Radcliffe Library, Oxford.—Sir Leoline Jenkins, civilian, died at his house on the Mall in 1704.

On *Hammersmith Terrace* resided the dramatist, Arthur Murphy, who died at Knightsbridge in 1805, and was buried in Hammersmith Church.—At No. 13 resided Philip James de Loutherbourgh, painter, and here he died in 1812; and at No. 15, Sir Clifton Wintringham, bart. physician, who died in 1794.

On *Theresa Terrace,* resided a few years, James Elphinstone, author on philology, and friend of Dr. Johnson. He died here in 1809, and was buried at Kensington.

At *Ravenscourt Park* resided Alice Perers, " Lady of the Sun," the beautiful favourite of Edward III.

At *Palingswick Green,* is an antient Manor House, said to have been a hunting seat of Edward III. In it is the crest of Edward the Black Prince carved in oak, the preservation of which is especially provided for by the covenants of the original lease.

At *Kensal Green* is an antient cottage, formerly an inn, where the painter Morland spent much of his time towards the close of his life.

At Hammersmith died in 1723, Fortune Symons, aged 111; in 1776, Sarah Seekins, aged 104; in 1779, Martha Coxe, aged 105; in 1788, in the workhouse, Judith Thresher, aged 104; in Queen Street, in 1833, Mrs. Elizabeth Aberdien (the last descendant of the family of Cæsar Adelmar), aged 102; and in King Street, in 1836, Samuel Groves, aged 101.

In the *Church* is a bronze bust of Charles I. under which, in a marble urn, is the heart of the loyal donor, Sir Nicholas Crispe; who invented the present mode of making bricks, which were first used in building Brandenburgh house.

Here were buried Sir Samuel Morland, mechanic, inventor of the speaking-trumpet, 1696; William Lloyd, the deprived Bp. of Norwich, 1708; William Sheridan, Bp. of Kilmore, 1711; Sir William Meadows, diplomatist, 1718; George Bubb Doddington, Lord Melcombe, complimented by Young and Thomson, and celebrated for his wit, 1762; Thomas Worlidge, artist, 1766, who lived at Lee's Nursery; Hon. James Robert Talbot, Roman Catholic Bp. of Birtha, 1790; Arthur Murphy, dramatist, 1805; Sir Elijah Impey, Chief Justice at Calcutta, 1809; and the celebrated French royalist General Count de Puisaye, 1827, who died at Blithe House.

In HAMPSTEAD were buried Thomas Jevon and Christopher Bullock, comedians and dramatists, 1688 and 1722; George Sewell, poet and physician, 1726; James Pitt, political writer, the " Mother Osborne " of Pope, 1763; William Popple, dramatist, 1764; James Mac Ardell and

Charles Spooner, mezzotinto engravers, 1765 and 1767 ; Dr.
Anthony Askew, bibliographer and physician, 1774; James
Pettit Andrews, historian, 1797 ; Frances, wife of the great
Lord Erskine (monument by Bacon) 1809 ; and Dorothea,
the mother of Miss Joanna Baillie, dramatist of the Pas-
sions, who still reside at Hampstead.

Branch Hill Lodge was the seat of Lord Chancellor Macclesfield ; Rosslyn House, of Lord Chancellor Loughborough.

At the *Upper Flask Inn*, on Hampstead Hill, were held
the summer meetings of the Kit Cat Club; this house afterwards became the seat of George Steevens, whose fourth
edition of Shakespeare was revised here, and who died here
1800.

At the *Chicken House* in early life lodged Murray, afterwards LORD CHIEF JUSTICE MANSFIELD; and in it died
Samuel Gale, antiquary, 1754.

At *Frognall* lodged together the famous actors, Booth,
Wilkes, and Cibber.—Here Dr. Johnson took lodgings for
his wife in 1748, and thither himself occasionally resorted.
He here composed his " *Vanity of Human Wishes*, in
imitation of the 10th satire of Juvenal."—In this hamlet
died Lord Alvanley, Chief Justice of the Pleas, 1804.

On *Haverstock Hill* was the residence of Sir Charles Sed-
ley, wit and poet, who died there 1721 ; and the same house
was occupied in 1712 by Sir Richard Steele.

In Hampstead resided Sir Henry Vane, republican, who
was here seized and conveyed to the Tower, and in the same
house, JOSEPH BUTLER, Bp. of Durham, author of the
" Analogy;" John Wylde, Lord Chief Baron, who died
here 1697 ; Dean Sherlock, author on Death, who died here
1707 ; Thomas Rowe, biographer, (husband of the pious
Mrs. Elizabeth Rowe,) who died here 1715; Arthur Mayn-
waring, author of the Medley ; GAY and ARBUTHNOT,

who had lodgings here for the benefit of their health; MARK AKENSIDE, who practised as a physician here.

On the *Heath* the elections for the county were held previous to 1700-1, when they were removed to Brentford.

"Hampstead Heath" is the title of a comedy by Thomas Baker.

Belsize was the residence of Armigal Waad, voyager, and reputed discoverer of America, who died 1568, and was buried in the church; and his son, Sir Wm. Waad, Lieutenant of the Tower, who died 1623. Belsize house was a celebrated place of public entertainment for nearly 30 years previous to 1745, and afterwards the residence of Spencer Perceval, statesman, assassinated 1812.

At *Primrose Hill* was discovered the body of Sir Edmondbury Godfrey, whose murder has been justly termed "one of the most mysterious parts of the machinery of the Popish plot."

Sion Chapel was formerly a noted place, where a clergyman attended and married for nothing those who ordered their wedding dinner at the Wells tea-gardens.

On the hill above Ken Wood, resided the late eminent Lord Erskine, "whose splendid career at the English Bar is familiar to the whole nation."

At Hampstead died, in 1783, Miss West, the notorious female pickpocket and accomplice of Barrington; for many years celebrated by the appellation of the modern Jenny Diver. She bequeathed £3000 to her two children.

Here died, April 16, 1736, Andrew Pitt, eminent Quaker, "who inherited many virtues and wanted every vice."

HAMPTON was the vicarage of Samuel Croxall, author of the "Fair Circassian," and editor of Æsop's Fables.

Here was buried Richard Tickell, political writer, author of "Anticipation," 1793.

Near Hampton was the seat of Edward Lovibond, poet, author of "Tears of Old May Day," who died here 1775.

At Hampton Wick resided SIR RICHARD STEELE, at a house built by himself, and called the "hovel;" at Bushy Park the premier, Lord North; and the Duke of Clarence, afterwards William IV.; at Hampton House DAVID GARRICK, who erected here a temple in honour of Shakespeare, with a statue by Roubiliac, now in the British Museum.

HAMPTON COURT is the largest of all the palaces; and has been described by Grotius as " a residence for the Gods." It was built by Cardinal Wolsey, and presented by him to Henry VIII. Here Cardinal Wolsey lived in more than regal state; had 280 silk beds for visitors, and maintained nearly 1000 servants, including lords, knights, and squires. It subsequently became the occasional residence of our Sovereigns till the time of George III. Queen Jane Seymour died here October 14, after giving birth to Edward VI.; and here the ill-fated Katharine Howard, and Katharine Parr, were first received as Henry's queens. Queen Mary and Philip of Spain passed their honey-moon at Hampton Court; Elizabeth kept her Christmas here in 1572 and 1593; James had a festival here which lasted 14 days; his queen, Anne of Denmark, died here in 1618; and Charles the First spent his honey-moon here, and also some of his latter days as a prisoner. The oratory in which he is supposed to have offered up his devotions during his confinement, is "now too probably the receptacle of pickles and preserves." Oliver Cromwell occasionally resided here; and here his third daughter Mary was married, Nov. 18, 1657, to Lord Falconbridge; and his favourite daughter Elizabeth, Mrs. Claypole, died here Aug. 6, 1658. Cromwell was also attacked with his last illness here. On the Restoration it was given to George Monk, Duke of Albemarle; and Charles the Second's queen was brought hither on her arrival. James II. here received the Pope's Nuncio, and the canopy under which the reception took place is still to be seen.

Hampton Court was the scene of Pope's Rape of the Lock.

The Eastern front, 330 feet long, and the southern, 328 feet, were added by William III. and Sir Christopher Wren was the architect.

The remains of Wolsey's palace, which had 1500 rooms, consist of the first and second quadrangles.

Wolsey's Hall is 106 feet in length and 40 in breadth, and the roof is beautifully carved. Upon one of the panes of glass of the great window, Henry Howard, the poetical and gallant Earl of Surrey, wrote some lines with a diamond ring on the fair Geraldine, which excited the jealousy of Henry VIII. and perhaps assisted in bringing the Earl to the block in 1547. It is stated that the first play acted in this hall was that of Henry VIII. or the Fall of Wolsey, and that Shakespeare was one of the actors.

In Wolsey's withdrawing room are preserved some of the original tapestry hangings, of which an account has been recently for the first time published, by Mr. Jesse, in his " Summer's Day at Hampton Court."

In the middle Court is a curious astronomical clock, which was put up in 1540; and in King William the Third's bedroom is a clock that goes twelve months without winding up, made by the celebrated Daniel Quare.

One of the most curious pictures in the collection is a portrait of Queen Elizabeth, when twelve years old, by Holbein.

Among the numerous paintings, one room contains the beauties of King Charles's Court, by Lely and Verelst; another room those of Queen Mary II. and eight ladies of her court, by Kneller; and a third constructed for the purpose, holds the pictorial boast of Britain, Raffaele's seven cartoons. On these cartoons Oliver Cromwell obtained a loan of £50,000 from Holland.

Near the Stud House is a curiously shaped elm tree, called King Charles's Swing.

The Vine is 110 feet long, and has generally from 2000 to 3000 bunches of grapes upon it.

In the Orangery is an orange myrtle, said to have been brought to this country by William III., by whom the Wilderness and Maze were planted.

The public are freely admitted to see whatever is curious or interesting within the walls and gardens of the palace.

The Toy Inn is said to have been built by Oliver Cromwell as a dormitory for his round-head soldiers, not liking to admit them into the palace.

At Hampton Court Green, Sir Christopher Wren passed the latter part of his life.

HANWELL was the rectory of George Henry Glasse, Greek scholar, who died in 1809. Here were buried Jane Messenger, aged 101, 1741; Jonas Hanway, philanthropist, 1786; John Dimond, blind teacher, 1807.

In the register of Hanwell parish, Oct. 24, 1731, is mention of a child being called " by the midwife, at the font, a boy, and named by the godfather, Thomas, but proved to be a girl."

HANWORTH was the rectory of Adam de Brom, founder of Oriel College, Oxford. Here was a small but favourite palace of Henry VIII., in which his widow Katharine Parr and her third husband, Sir Thomas Seymour, Lord Admiral, with their ward Elizabeth, afterwards Queen, frequently resided. It subsequently was the seat of Francis Lord Cottington.

HAREFIELD *Place*, not now existing, was the residence of Lord Chief Justice Sir Edward Anderson;

f

Lord Keeper Egerton, Lord Ellesmere, and his wife
Alice Countess of Derby, who was complimented by Harrington in a poem on her marriage, by Spenser under the
name of Amaryllis, and by Milton, whose masque of " Ar-
cades " was first performed here before her in 1633. She
was buried in the church under a splendid monument in
1637. In this house also resided the loyal George Lord
Chandos, to whom the celebrated divine Dr. John Conant
(of whom it was said " *Conanti* nihil difficile ") was domestic chaplain. It afterwards became the property of the New-
digates, who have splendid monuments in the church, among
which are those of Sir Richard, Lord Chief Justice, 1678;
Mary, wife of his son Sir Richard, the second baronet (by
Grinling Gibbons) 1692; and Sir Roger, the last baronet,
founder of the Newdigate prize, Oxford, 1806. In the
church was also buried its former curate John Prickett,
Bishop of Gloucester, 1680.

HARLINGTON was the rectory of John Kyte, Bishop
of Carlisle; and Joseph Trapp, translator of Virgil, buried
here (epitaph by himself), 1747. Dawley house was the
favourite retirement of HENRY ST. JOHN, Viscount Bolingbroke.

HARROW was an antient occasional residence of the
Archbishops of Canterbury.

It was the Rectory of Cuthbert Tonstall, Bishop of Durham; and of William Bolton, the last Prior of St. Bartholomew's, Smithfield. The present vicar is the Rev. J. W.
Cunningham, author of that extremely pleasing tale, "The
Velvet Cushion."

Here were buried Sir Arthur Atye, public orator at Oxford, secretary to the Earl of Essex, 1604; Sir Samuel
Garth, poet and physician, 1719; Robert Sumner, head
master of its school (epitaph by Dr. Parr), 1771; and William Skenelsby, aged 118, 1775.

Here were educated William Baxter, author of "Glossa-

rium Antiquitatum;" Sɪʀ Wɪʟʟɪᴀᴍ Jᴏɴᴇs; the late Mr.
Pᴇʀᴄᴇᴠᴀʟ, and Mr. Sʜᴇʀɪᴅᴀɴ; with Dr. Bennett, Bishop
of Cloyne, Dr. Samuel Parr (whose father was an apothe-
cary here), Marquis Hastings, Earls Spencer and Aberdeen,
Lord Byron, the Right Honourable Sir Robert Peel, and
the Honourable William Spencer.

HAYES was an antient occasional residence of the Archbishops of Canterbury; the rectory of Robert Wright, Bishop of Lichfield and Coventry; and Patrick Young,
Greek scholar, translator of Clement; the vicarage of Henry
Gold, an accomplice of Elizabeth Barton, "the holy maid
of Kent," executed with her, 1534.

At HENDON were buried Sir William Rawlinson, commissioner of the great seal, 1703; Edward Fowler, Bishop
of Gloucester, 1714; Charles Johnson, dramatist, 1748;
James Parsons, physician, anatomist, and antiquary, 1770;
Edward Longmore, the "Herefordshire colossus," seven feet
six inches high, 1777; Sir Joseph Ayloffe, antiquary, 1781;
Nathaniel Hone, painter, 1784; and Sarah Gundry (beautiful epitaph), 1807.

In the village resided John Norden, topographer; at
Highwood-hill, Lord William Russell, previous to his arrest,
and Mrs. Porter, tragedian; and at Mill-hill, Peter Col-
linson, the naturalist, who was visited here by Linnæus,
. who planted some trees in his garden.

At *Hendon Place*, was a banqueting-house of Queen
Elizabeth. It was recently the residence of the late Lord
Tenterden, Chief Justice of the King's Bench.

The inhabitants of Hendon are exempt from all tolls at
fairs, markets, high-ways, and bridges, by charter, granted
by Edward the Confessor, 1066, confirmed by several suc-
ceeding sovereigns, and finally by William and Mary 1692.

The Manor belonged to Garrick the actor, who gave a
piece of land for the School.

HESTON. Osterley-house was built in 1577 by that

patriotic merchant Sir Thomas Gresham, who here entertained Elizabeth most sumptuously. It was afterwards the residence of Sir Edward Coke, when attorney-general; the parliamentarian general Sir William Waller, till his death in 1668; and the projector, Dr. Nicholas Barbon. Osterley-house was rebuilt by Francis Child, Esq. about 1760.

In HIGHGATE old chapel were buried, Sir Francis Pemberton, Chief Justice, 1699; Lewis Atterbury, divine, brother of the Bishop, 1731.

The great Lord Chancellor, Bacon, died at the Earl of Arundel's house, in this town, April 19, 1626, and the famous Dr. Henry Sacheverel at his own residence here June 5, 1724. Here also resided Sir Richard Baker, author of "Chronicles;" Sir Henry Blount, traveller in Turkey; and Sir John Pettus, mineralogist.

The burlesque nugatory oath imposed on strangers at the public-houses in this town is well known.

Here is a school, with a synagogue attached, for the children of Jews. There are generally about 100 pupils.

Here was confined for some time the ill-fated Lady Arabella Stuart, cousin of James I. in consequence of a stolen marriage into which she had entered with Mr. Seymour, afterwards Marquis of Hertford and Duke of Somerset.

At HILLINGDON was buried John Rich, patentee of Covent Garden theatre, inventor of the English harlequin . (who resided at Cowley-grove), 1761.

At LOWER HOLLOWAY, Mrs. Foster, grand-daughter of Milton the poet, kept a chandler's shop and died 1754, aged 66.

At Upper Holloway is the " Mother Redcap " public house, celebrated by Drunken Barnaby.

HORNSEY was the rectory of Thomas Westfield, afterwards Bishop of Bristol; Dr. Lewis Atterbury, brother of the Bishop of Rochester; and William Cole, the Cambridge antiquary.

In the church was buried Samuel Buckley, editor of Thuanus, 1741.

The learned Dr. John Lightfoot composed part of his Biblical criticisms in this village.

In HOUNSLOW chapel were buried Henry Elsynge, writer on parliaments, 1654; and Whitlocke Bulstrode, author on transmigration, 1724.

ISLEWORTH was the vicarage of John Hall, martyr, 1535; Nicholas Byfield, Calvinistic commentator; Dr. William Cave, author of "Historia Literaria;" and of W. Drake, a scholar and antiquary, who died 1801.

Here were buried, Anne Dash, foundress of alms-houses (monument by Halfpenny, cost £500), 1750; Richard Blyke, topographical collector for Herefordshire, 1775; and its native, George Keate, poet, (monument by Nollekens) 1797.

Here resided George Calvert, Lord Baltimore, original grantee of Maryland; Sir Ralph Winwood, author of "Memorials;" Sir William Noy, Attorney-general; its native, Dorothy Countess of Sunderland, the "Sacharissa" of Waller; Samuel Clarke, biographer, who died here 1682; Francis Willis, grammarian; Charles Talbot, Duke of Shrewsbury, who at the same time was Lord Chamberlain of the Household, Lord High Treasurer of England, and Lord Lieutenant of Ireland, died here 1718; the Duchess of Kendal, mistress of George I.; PULTENEY, Earl of Bath, the opponent of Walpole; and the late right honourable Richard Brinsley Sheridan.

SYON HOUSE was the residence of the Protector Seymour, Duke of Somerset; Dudley, Lord Guildford, and his accomplished and amiable wife, Lady Jane Grey; the children of Charles I. under the care of Algernon Percy, tenth Earl of Northumberland; and Queen Anne, when only Princess of Denmark. It was very much altered by Inigo Jones. In the vestibule are twelve columns and sixteen pilasters of verd antique, a greater quantity of this beautiful marble than in any other building in Europe; cost £27,000.

ISLINGTON. Vicars, Meredith Hanmer, chronicler of Ireland; and Dr. William Cave, author of "Historia Lite-raria," buried here 1713; Lecturer, Robert Browne, founder of the Brownists.

Here were interred Richard Cloudesley, benefactor to the parish, 1517; Sir George Wharton and Sir James Stewart, killed by each other in a duel, 1609; its native, Alice Lady Owen, foundress of almshouses, 1613; John Shirley, bio-grapher of Sir Walter Ralegh, 1679; William Baxter, author of "Glossarium Antiquitatum," 1723; Samuel Humphreys, poet, author of "Canons," 1737; John Black-bourn, Bishop of the Nonjurors, editor of Bacon, 1741; Robert Poole, institutor of the small-pox hospital in 1746, 1752; Hannah Carpenter, aged 103, 1752; Mary Hough-ton, aged 102, 1758; Launcelot Dowbiggen, architect of the church in 1754, 1759; John Lindsey, nonjuring divine, 1768; Elizabeth Button, aged 105, 1772; Susanna Wood-house, aged 101, 1778; John Hyacinth de Magelhaens, mineralogist, and proselyte from Catholicism, 1790; Judith Scott, aged 102, 1792; Elizabeth Robson, aged 103, 1793; J. Donaldson, artist and author, 1801; Alexander Aubert, who erected the observatory near Highbury-house (in which was the largest reflecting telescope ever made by Short), 1805; its native, William Hawes, physician, founder of the Humane Society, 1808.

In this town died John Bagford, typographical collector, 1716; Daniel De Foe, author of "Robinson Crusoe," 1731; Alexander Cruden, author of "Concordance," 1770; James Burgh, author of "Political Disquisitions," and Nicholas Robinson, physician, 1775; Joseph Collier, translator of the "Messiah" and "Noah," (whose wife, translator of the "Death of Abel," also resided here) 1776; Husband Mes-siter, physician, 1785; Isaac Ritson, translator of "Hymn to Venus," 1789; W. Pitcairn, physician, 1791; George Marriot, author of "Poems" and "Sermons," 1793; and Abraham Newland, chief cashier of the Bank of England, 1807.

Colonel Okey, the regicide, was a drayman in a brewhouse here.

Samuel Clarke, Orientalist, and Ezekiel Tongue, Protestant controversialist, were schoolmasters here.

At the Red Lion public-house in Islington road Thomas Paine composed his "Rights of Man."

Canonbury House, rebuilt by William Bolton, the last Prior of St. Bartholomew's, Smithfield, was the seat of "the rich" Sir John Spencer, Lord Mayor in 1593; and Lord Keeper Coventry. In it lodged Samuel Humphreys, poet, before-mentioned; Ephraim Chambers, Cyclopædist, who died here 1740; DR. OLIVER GOLDSMITH; and John Newbery, author of excellent books for children.

Its history has been recorded by the late John Nichols, the learned and estimable Editor of the Gentleman's Magazine, who was born (in 1745) in this village, and died at Highbury place in 1826, and was interred in the old churchyard.

At "Old Parr's Head" Henderson the player used to give recitations previous to his regular engagement.

Of the prebendaries were Edward Stillingfleet, Bishop of Worcester; and Archdeacon Nares.

Here was "Starvation farm," the farm of the execrable Baron d'Aiguilar, a Portuguese Jew.

The Pied Bull Inn, traditionally said to have been the residence of Sir Walter Ralegh.

In the fields the citizens used to amuse themselves with every sort of sport and pastime; and archery was particularly enjoined by royal ordinance. The sports here have been frequently alluded to in our early comedies, and several have taken their titles hence.

The Barley Mow public house, Long lane, was once the

temporary residence of the dissipated but great natural genius George Morland.

The Duke's Head was kept by Thomas Topham, "the strong man," or second Sampson.

At KENSINGTON were buried John Bullingham, Bishop of Gloucester, 1598; Henry Rich, Earl of Holland, whose title gave name to his seat here, beheaded 1649; its vicar, Thomas Hodges, Dean of Hereford, 1672; Charles Goodall, M.D. president and historian of the college of physicians, 1712; Charlotte, Countess of Warwick, widow of Addison, 1731; Bernard Lens, miniature painter, 1741; Richard Viscount Molesworth, field-marshal (saved the Duke of Marlborough's life at Ramillies), 1758; its vicar, Dr. John Jortin, biographer of Erasmus, 1770; Martin Madan, author of "Thelyphthora," 1790; George Colman, dramatist and essayist, 1794; Richard Warren, physician, 1797; Samuel Pegge, author of "Curialia," &c. son of the antiquary, 1800; James Elphinstone, philologist, 1809; Major-general SIR WILLIAM PONSONBY, slain at Waterloo, 1815; the Right Honourable GEORGE PONSONBY, statesman, leader of the Opposition, 1817; and the Rev. Thomas Rennells, vicar, 1824.

Here died Robert Nelson, author of "Fasts and Festivals," 1714; and Robert Price, judge, learned lawyer, 1732.

Here resided Lord Keeper Sir Orlando Bridgman; the Parliamentarian General Lambert; the brave William, first Earl Craven; Lord Chief Justice Pratt; the traveller Sir John Chardin.

At the entrance to Kensington, and nearly opposite the palace gates, is a large red house, which was the residence of the famous Duchess of Portsmouth, the French mistress of Charles the Second. Here he supped the night before he was seized with the illness of which he soon afterwards died.

The charity school was erected from designs by Sir John Vanbrugh.

The *Palace* was originally Nottingham House, built by the Lord Chancellor Heneage Finch, Earl of Nottingham. It was the favourite residence of all our Sovereigns from the Revolution of 1688 to 1760. It was nearly rebuilt by William III. by whom it was purchased, and his consort Mary died here of the small pox. He himself, and Queen Anne and her husband, George Prince of Denmark, and George II. also died here. The interesting collection of historical portraits has been recently removed to Hampton Court. The Duke of Sussex has an extensive library, particularly rich in biblical and theological works. The gardens are the subject of a poem by Tickell.

Holland House was erected by Sir William Cope, a gentleman of King James's Court, by whom it was bequeathed to his son-in-law Sir Henry Rich, afterwards Earl of Holland, courtier, and parliamentarian, who was beheaded as a loyalist 1649, and lies buried in Kensington Church. After his execution Fairfax occupied the house as his head quarters. —In 1716 it became the property and residence of ADDISON by his marriage with the Countess of Warwick ; and it was here that this accomplished and good man (on June 17, 1719) taught the young Earl of Warwick "in what peace a Christian can die." It was subsequently the residence of the celebrated statesman Henry Fox, Lord Holland, whose still more celebrated son, CHARLES JAMES FOX, spent much of his childhood and youth here, and displayed those talents which justified the predictions of the friends of his youth. The house contains a very extensive collection of works of art, and a choice collection of books. In the gardens, the Dahlia first made its appearance in this country, in the year 1803, from seeds sent from Spain by Lord Holland. On a column of granite is a bust of Buonaparte, then Commander in Chief of the army of Italy, by Canova.

Kensington House was occupied as a school by Mr. Elphinstone between 1776 and 1788, ludicrously characterised in Smollett's Roderick Random.

In *Kensington Square* resided the Duchess of Mazarine, 1692; Dr. Mawson, Bishop of Ely, who died here in 1770, aged 80; Sir Richard Blackmore, physician and poet; Dr. Herring, Bishop of Bangor, and in the same house Prince Talleyrand, when driven from France by Robespierre; Bishop Hough of Worcester; and the Rev. William Beloe.

In *Pitt Buildings*, then called Orbell's Buildings, resided Sir Isaac Newton, and here, in his 84th year, he had a fit of the gout, and shortly after died, in 1726.

Campden House was built about 1612, by Sir Baptist Hickes, afterwards Lord Campden. In it resided for five years Anne Princess of Denmark; and the accomplished Boyle Earl of Burlington.

At *Bayswater* died Cornelius Wood, the "Sylvio" of the Tatler, military officer, 1711; and Dean Swift had lodgings in 1712; the brave William first Earl of Craven.

At *Kensal Green* resided Morland the painter.

At *Earl's Court*, the celebrated surgeon John Hunter built himself a residence, and for many years spent his autumns there.

At *Brompton* the celebrated Arthur Murphy died 1805; Count Rumford resided.—Here was married, in 1653, Henry Cromwell, son of Oliver, who is said to have resided at Hale House, to Elizabeth, daughter of Sir Francis Russell.

Among the residents in this parish were William Penn, founder of Pennsylvania; James Ford, "the famous speaking doctor," ridiculed by Swift in the Tatler.

At KINGSBURY Dr. Goldsmith lodged whilst composing part of his "History of Animated Nature."

KNIGHTSBRIDGE was the residence of SETH WARD, Bishop of Salisbury, who died here 1689; WILLIAM PENN, founder of Pennsylvania; James Lane, Viscount Lanesborough, Pope's gouty dancer, who died at his house here, now St. George's hospital, 1724 ; and Bernard Lens, miniature painter, who died here 1741.

Kingston House, now occupied by the statesman and scholar, the Marquess of Wellesley, was the residence of Elizabeth Chudleigh, the eccentric and profligate Duchess of Kingston; and it was here she invited a large assemblage of people to her celebrated ball, and when they met she had made her escape to Calais.

MARYLEBONE. In the *Old Church* are monuments to James Gibbs the architect, ob. 1754, aged 71 ; Signor Giuseppe Baretti of the Royal Academy of Arts, 1789 ; Stephen Storace, ob. 1796, aged 34, whose life was "devoted to the study of musical science, and shortened by unremitted application and anxiety in the attainment of its object;" Caroline Watson, engraver to Her Majesty, who died June 9, 1814, aged 54, with poetical epitaph by Hayley.

Here were buried Humphrey Wanley, antiquary, 1726 ; John Abbadie, persecuted Protestant divine, 1727 ; James Figg, the prize-fighter, 1734, proprietor of the Boarded House, Marylebone fields ; Archibald Bower, author of " History of the Popes," 1766 ; Edmund Hoyle, whist player, 1769 ; John Michael Rysbrach, statuary, 1770 ; James Ferguson, philosopher, 1776 ; Charles Wesley, one of the founders of Methodism, 1788 ; William Cramer, musician, 1799 ; George Stubbs, painter, 1806 ; Alexander Dalrymple, traveller, 1808 ; Thomas Holcroft, linguist and novelist, 1809 ; Duke of Portland, Prime Minister, 1809.

In the *Parish Church* is a tablet to Richard Cosway, R.A., painter to the Prince of Wales, 1821, aged 80 years. In the spacious vaults underneath this church are deposited the remains of many of the nobility and distinguished gentry.

At *Harrow Road Cemetery*, among the interesting tenants of the tomb is John Hugh, eldest son of J. G. Lockhart, esq. and grandson of Sir Walter Scott, Bart. He was a favourite child of the novelist, who dedicated his " Tales of a Grandfather " to him under the title of Hugh Little John, esq. He died in his 11th year, 1831.

Of *Bentinck Chapel*, in Chapel Street, New Road, the Rev. Basil Woodd was minister for 45 years.

In *Little Titchfield Street* was Providence Chapel, under the ministry of Huntingdon, which was burnt down in 1810, when the minister observed " that Providence having allowed the chapel to be destroyed, Providence might rebuild it, for *he* would not."

In the *Cemetery* on the south side of Paddington Street, consecrated in 1733, it is computed that near 100,000 persons have been interred. An inscription here records the deaths of several infants, children of J. F. Smyth Stuart, "great grandson of King Charles II." Opposite to this cemetery is another not quite so large, consecrated in 1772, and containing a large number of tombs, some of them of a costly character.

In *St. John's Wood Chapel* are some beautiful specimens of modern sculpture, by Chantrey, Behnes, Wyatt, Austin, &c. In the vault lie the remains of the wife of Benjamin West, President R.A. Above 40,000 persons lie interred in the cemetery attached. On the west side is a flat stone, in memory of JOANNA SOUTHCOTT, who died Dec. 27, 1814, aged 65 years, at her house in Manchester Street, Manchester Square, with these verses thereon :

> " While through all thy wondrous days
> Heaven and earth enraptur'd gaz'd ;
> While vain sages think they know
> Secrets, Thou Alone cans't show ;
> Time alone will tell what hour
> Thou'lt appear in greater power.—SABINEUS."

Oxford Street, containing nearly 400 houses, is more than a mile in length, and of good width. It is a pleasing promenade; but if remembered as the way through which many unfortunate criminals have passed to pay the forfeit of their lives at Tyburn, must give rise to melancholy reflections.

At *Tyburn* was executed, Nov. 29, 1628, John Felton, who stabbed the Duke of Buckingham; Lord Ferrers, for murder, 1760; Dr. Dodd, for forgery, 1777; Hackman, for shooting Miss Ray, 1779; and the infamous Catherine Hayes, for the murder of her husband, who was literally burnt alive in consequence of the indignation of the populace preventing her being strangled by the executioner before the fire was kindled. Tyburn ceased to be a place of execution in 1783.

On the site of Beaumont and Devonshire Streets, was the *Marylebone Gardens*, a place of evening entertainment, the musical arrangements of which were for some time under the direction of Dr. Arne, and the music of Handel and other celebrated composers was often heard. They were suppressed in 1778 on account of the increase of buildings, and the use of fireworks.

From *Lord's Cricket Ground*, Garnerin made his second balloon ascent July 5, 1802.

Cato Street, where the conspiracy to assassinate in 1820 the Ministers of State was concocted by Thistlewood and others, passes from Queen Street to John Street; and is now called Horace Street.

In *Welbeck Street* was the residence of Lord George Gordon, who figured so conspicuously in the riots of 1780; Edmund Hoyle, the writer on Whist, &c.; and the miser John Elwes.

The house of the late Thomas Hope, author of Anastasius, in *Duchess Street*, was built by Adams. It has long been an object of interest to lovers of the Fine Arts on account of the valuable collection of sculpture, vases, pictures, and style of decoration.

In *Portland Road* died Sir Francis Bourgeois, in 1811, who bequeathed his pictures to Dulwich College.

Primrose Hill was formerly famous for primroses. Here was found the body of the murdered Sir Edmondbury Godfrey in Oct. 1678, for which, on the testimony of Oates, &c. four Roman Catholics, of whose guilt there are some doubts, were executed. Several fatal duels have also lent an historic interest to the spot. Here Colonel Montgomery was shot through the heart by Captain Macnamara, and the Captain just above the hip, 1803.

In *Marylebone Park* Queen Elizabeth entertained the Russian Ambassador with the diversion of hunting.

It is but a few years since the whole area of the *Regent's Park* was inclosed for grazing cows. An area of 357 acres was inclosed about 1818 as a park, and laid out in lawns, drives, plantations, &c. Since the year 1821 many ornamental detached villas, nine extensive terraces, &c. and public buildings, have been built; and the gardens of the Zoological and Botanical Societies are laid out.

In the *Hospital of St. Katharine*, in the Regent's Park, are preserved the curious old pulpit, carved stalls, and organ which belonged to the destroyed church near the Tower, and also the monument of the Duke of Exeter (died 1446).

NORTHALL was the vicarage of William Pierse, Bishop of Bath and Wells; Dr. John Cockburn, author of "Right Notions of God," buried here 1729; Samuel Lisle, Bishop of Norwich, buried here 1749; and Sir John Hotham, afterwards Bishop of Clogher.

Here was also interred Dr. Stephen Charles Triboude Demainbray, astronomer and electrician, 1782.

At PADDINGTON was married William Hogarth, "great painter of mankind," to Jane, daughter of his master Sir James Thornhill, 1729.

Here died George Colman, dramatist and essayist, 1794.

Here were buried, John Bushnel, statuary, 1701; Joseph

Francis Nollekens, painter, and Benjamin Parker, philosophical writer, 1747 ; Dr. Abraham Lemoine, author on
Miracles, 1757 ; Matthew Dubourg, musician, 1767 ; James
Lacy, patentee of Drury-lane theatre, 1774; Francis Vi-
vares, engraver, 1780 ; George Barret, landscape painter,
1784; Sir John Elliot, physician, 1787 ; William Arminger,
statuary, 1793 ; Thomas Banks, statuary, 1805 ; Lolli,
the musician, 1805 ; Marquess of Lansdowne, 1809; Lewis
Schiavonetti, engraver, 1810.

Mrs. Siddons, the tragedian, lived at Westbourn green.

In the Churchyard was buried, in 1802, aged 65, the
Rev. Dr. Alexander Geddes, learned Hebraist and translator
of the Historical Books of the Old Testament. On the
plain upright stone put up in 1804 by Lord Petre is this
extract from his works :—" *Christian* is my name, and
Catholic my surname ; I grant that you are a X" as well as I,
and embrace you as my fellow disciple of Jesus ; and if you
were not a disciple of Jesus, still I would embrace you as
my fellow man."

At PANCRAS were buried, Samuel Cooper, miniature
painter, 1672 ; Abraham Woodhead, Roman Catholic controversialist, 1678 ; Obadiah Walker, writer against Luther,
1699 ; John Ernest Grabe, editor of the Alexandrian Sep-
tuagint, 1711 ; Jeremy Collier, nonjuring Bishop, castiga-
tor of the stage, 1726; Edward Ward, author of the "London Spy," 1731 ; Edward Walpole, translator of Sannaza-
rius, 1740 ; James Leoni, architect, 1746 ; Simon Francis
Ravenet, engraver, and Peter Van Bleeck, portrait-painter,
1764 ; Abraham Langford, auctioneer and dramatist, 1774 ;
William Woollett, engraver, 1785 ; Stephen Paxton, musician, 1787 ; Timothy Cunningham, author of " Law Dictionary," 1789 ; Michael John Baptist Baron de Wenzel,
oculist, 1790 ; Mary Woolstonecraft Godwin, author of
" Rights of Women," 1797, with a square monumental pil-
lar with a willow-tree on each side ; Father O'Leary, the

amiable friar of the order of St. Francis, 1802 ; the Bishop
of St. Pol de Leon, 1806 ; John Walker, author of " Pro-
nouncing Dictionary," 1807 ; PASCAL DE PAOLI, Cor-
sican hero, 1807 ; Tiberius Cavallo, the Neapolitan philosopher 1809 ; the equivocal Chevalier d'Eon, political writer,
1810 ; J. P. Malcolm, historian of London, 1815 ; and the
Rev. William Tooke, translator of Lucian, 1820.

In *St. James's Cemetery*, Tottenham Court Road, were
buried Lord G. Gordon, 1797 ; M. Tomick, 7 feet 10 inches
high, 1794 ; Mr. Christie, auctioneer, 1803 ; Hoppner, the
painter ; G. Morland, the well-known painter ; and Dr.
Dickson, Bp. of Downe.

In *Camden-town* died Charles Dibdin, song and dramatic
writer, 1814.

In *Kentish-town* Chapel was interred Charles Grignion,
engraver, 1810.

In *Somers-town* Roman Catholic Chapel was buried the
Princess of Condé.

Among the portraits at CAEN WOOD is one of its illustrious inhabitant Lord Chief Justice Mansfield, who died
here 1793, by Sir Joshua Reynolds ; and a head of Betterton, the actor, by the poet Pope.

The reading desk and pulpit in the *New Church*,
Euston Square, are remarkable from having been constructed out of the remains of the celebrated Fairlop Oak,
which at one time shadowed an area of 300 feet in circuit,
was mainly destroyed by fire in 1805, and blown down in
1820.

The Chapel at the *Foundling Hospital* has an altar-piece
painted by West, and an organ presented by Handel. There
are several valuable pictures in the Hospital, particularly
Hogarth's " March to Finchley."

At PINNER were buried Sir Bartholomew Shower,
lawyer, author of " Cases " and " Reports," 1701 ; and
William Skenelsby, aged 118, 1775.

Here died in 1798 John Zephaniah Holwell, the governor of Bengal, who published a narrative of the sufferings of himself and his unhappy companions in the Black-hole at Calcutta.

At POPLAR resided SIR RICHARD STEELE, who had a laboratory here for his alchemical studies.

Here were buried Robert Ainsworth, lexicographer, 1743; James Ridley, author of "Tales of the Genii," 1765; his father, Dr. Gloster Ridley, divine and scholar (epitaph by Bishop Lowth), 1774; and George Steevens, commentator on Shakspere, (monument by Flaxman, epitaph by Hayley,) 1800.

At RISELIP were buried Mary, wife of Chief Justice Sir John Banckes, the heroic defender of Corfe Castle, Dorsetshire, 1661; and George Rogers, president of the college of physicians, complimented by Waller, 1697.

ST. GEORGE'S IN THE EAST. In the *Danish Church, Prince's Square,* are buried C. G. Cibber, the architect of the building, and his wife Jane Cibber, father and mother of Colley Cibber, the actor. In the church were buried Joseph Ames, poet and author on printing, 1759, who was a ship-chandler at Wapping; Joseph Reed, dramatist, resided at Sun-tavern-fields, as ropemaker.

Instances of longevity are numerous: 1764, Sarah Barton, aged 104; 1765, Geo. Hammond, aged 104; 1776, Anne Ball, aged 102; John Gynks, aged 104; 1780, James Miles, aged 102; 1783, Isabella Fennell, aged 103; and 1805, Mary Taylor, aged 103.

In the *Swedish Church,* Wellclose Square, lies buried the celebrated Baron Swedenborg, founder of a religious sect bearing his name, who died in 1772.

SHEPERTON was the rectory of William Grocyne, the

g

first Greek professor at Oxford ; and Dr. Lewis Atterbury, brother of the Bishop of Rochester.

Here it is supposed that Cæsar crossed the Thames in pursuit of Cassivelaunus, and that Coway stakes were placed there to prevent his passage. A rude canoe, cut out of a solid block of oak, was discovered here in 1812.

STANMORE MAGNA was the vicarage of Richard Boyle, afterwards Archbishop of Tuam.

Here were buried Charles Hart, the tragedian, 1683; Mary Smith, aged 102, 1780.—Here died Aaron Capadoce, a jew, aged 105.

At Stanmore hill resided James Forbes, author of " Oriental Memoirs."

Dr. Parr, on his removal from Harrow, kept a school here.

In STAINES is Duncroft House, where King John is said to have slept the night after he signed Magna Charta.

STANMORE PARVA, or WHITCHURCH, was the rectory of John Theophilus Desaguliers, experimental philosopher.

CANONS, the princely seat of James Brydges, Duke of Chandos, which cost £250,000, was on his decease pulled down, and the materials sold by auction in 1747 ; remarkably verifying the prophetic lines in Pope's epistle to Lord Burlington, in which the Duke is characterized under the name of " Timon." This satire, however elegant and poignant, is most discreditable to Pope, as the subject was his friend, who, though ostentatious, was benevolent and amiable, and whose taste in music, there ridiculed, is evinced in his selection of Handel, who composed the anthems, and Pepusch the morning and evening services for the church, which was re-edified at his expense, and in which he was buried 1744. The drama of Esther was composed by Handel for its consecration.

Here were also buried Sir John Lake, Secretary of State
to James I. 1630; Francis Coventry, author of "Pompey
the Little," 1754; Alexander Jacob, author of "Peerage,"
1785; Dennis O'Kelly, owner of the famous horse Eclipse
(whose bones lie in Canons park), 1788; and James, last
Duke of Chandos, 1789.

STANWELL was the vicarage of Dr. Bruno Ryves,
Dean of Windsor, author of "Mercurius Rusticus." In the
church is a monument (by Nicholas Stone, cost £215), for
Thomas Lord Knyvett, 1622. Mary, daughter of James I.
was entrusted to his care, and died at his seat here in 1607.

STEPNEY was the rectory of Stephen Segrave, Archbishop of Armagh; and Marmaduke Lumley, Bishop of
Lincoln, Lord High Treasurer. The vicarage of Richard
Fox, Bishop of Winchester, founder of Corpus Christi College, Oxford; John Colet, Dean of St. Paul's, founder of
St. Paul's school; Richard Pace, Dean of St. Paul's, statesman, who was buried here 1532; William Jerome, martyr,
1540; and William Greenhill, commentator on Ezekiel.

The Bishops of London had a seat here, in which died
Roger Niger, 1241; Ralph de Baldock, 1313; Ralph de
Stratford, 1355; and Robert de Braybrooke, 1404.

Edward Russell, Earl of Bedford, was here married to the
lovely and accomplished Lucy Harrington, 1594.

Here were buried Sir Henry Colet, father of the Dean,
Lord Mayor in 1495, who resided near the church;
John Kyte, Archbishop of Armagh, 1537; Sir Thomas
Spert, founder and first Master of the Trinity House,
1541; Roger Crab, "English hermit," 1680; William
Clarke, physician, author on nitre, 1684; Sir John
Berry, admiral, 1689; his widow Rebecca (pleasing
epitaph), 1696; Matthew Mead, puritan divine, father
of the physician, 1699; William Vickers, author of "Com-

panion to the Altar," 1719 ; Sir John Leake, admiral, 1720 ; Martin Bladen, translator of Cæsar, 1746 ; John Entick, school-master, voluminous writer, 1773; and Benjamin Kenton, who left £63,550, to charitable uses (monument by Westmacott), 1800. Two ludicrous epitaphs in the churchyard are noticed in the Spectator, No. 518.

Stepney was the residence of Sir Thomas Lake, Secretary of State to James I.; Henry first Marquis of Worcester, the gateway of whose house remains; and its native Richard Mead, who first practised as a physician in this place.

Here Nathaniel Bailey, the author of the "Etymological English Dictionary," which formed the basis of Dr. Johnson's Dictionary, kept a school. He was a good classical scholar, and died June 27, 1742.

In the Portuguese Jews burial ground were buried Emanuel Mendes Da Costa, author, 1791 ; Rabbi David Nietto, distinguished scholar and author, 1728; Raphael Meldola, Rabbi, oriental scholar, 1828; and in the same ground lies the wretched body of the miserable, inhuman, and unnatural Baron d'Aiguilar, who died 1802.

STOKE NEWINGTON. Inhabitants, THOMAS SUTTON, founder of the Charter-house; Sir John Popham, Chief Justice; Charles Fleetwood, Parliamentarian General; Daniel De Foe, author of "Robinson Crusoe;" DR. ISAAC WATTS, who died at Lady Abney's house here, 1748; Sir Thomas Abney, M.P. his great friend, who had a principal share in founding the Bank of England, and died in 1722, aged 83; Hannah Snell, female soldier, died Feb. 8, 1792, aged 69; Adam Anderson, commercial writer; Thomas Day, author of "Sandford and Merton;" John Howard, philanthropist; and James Brown, F.S.A. historian of Stoke Newington, his native place, who died Jan. 19, 1837.

Here died in 1603, Margaret Forster, widow, aged 103.

Here were buried, Edward Massie, Parliamentarian Governor of Gloucester, 1649 ; Thomas Manton, its ejected
vicar, voluminous writer, 1677 ; Bridget Fleetwood, wife of
the General, and eldest daughter of Oliver Cromwell, 1681 ;
Samuel Wright, dissenting divine, 1746; and James Brown,
who first projected the "London Directory," 1788.

Of the *Dissenters' Meeting-house* at Newington green
were ministers, Hugh Worthington ; Dr. Richard Price ;
Dr. Thomas Amory ; Dr. Joseph Towers ; and James
Lindsey.

At STRATFORD BOW, were married Dr. William
Whitaker, theologian, to Joan Fenner, 1591 ; William Pen-
kethman, comedian, to Elizabeth Hill, 1714; and "Orator"
John Henley to Mary Clifford, 1726.

Inhabitants, Edmund Lord Sheffield, one of the victors of
the Spanish Armada; John Le Neve, author of "Monu-
menta Anglicana;" and Samuel Jebb, physician.

Don Antonio Perez, Prior of Crato, who was crowned
King of Portugal at Lisbon, whence he was soon expelled
by Philip II. of Spain, resided here in 1591.

This place was of some note in the fourteenth century for
affording instruction in the French language.   Chaucer
thus contemptuously alludes to it :

> ———— " French she spake full fayre & fetisly
> After the scole of Stratford atte Bowe,
> For French of Paris was to hire unknowe."

In TEDDINGTON were buried Sir Orlando Bridgman,
Lord Keeper, and Thomas Traherne, its curate, author of
"Christian Ethics," 1674; Margaret Woffington, actress,
1760; Dr. Stephen Hales, its curate for 51 years, philosopher, 1761 ; Henry Flitcroft, architect, 1769 ; Paul Whitehead, poet, whose heart is at West Wycombe, co. Bucks.,

1775; and Richard Bentley, poet and dramatist, son of the critic, 1782.

Here resided Sackville, Earl of Dorset, Lord Treasurer; Dudley, Earl of Leicester, Elizabeth's favourite; William Penn, the Quaker; and Francis Manning, poet and dramatist.

Teddington was the curacy of Dr. Stephen Hales, philosopher for 51 years. He was here visited by Frederick Prince of Wales, father of Geo. III. and by many of the highest rank and taste; and died here in January 4, 1761, aged 84. He invented a ventilator for mines, prisons, hospitals, &c. which has proved most extensively useful.

TOTTENHAM was the vicarage of William Bates, nonconformist, author of "Harmony of the Attributes;" and Edward Sparke, author of "Scintilla Altaris."

Here were buried William Bedwell, its vicar and historian, 1632; Henry Hare, Lord Coleraine, another of its historians, 1708; Henry Hare, last Lord Coleraine of his family, antiquary, 1749; and Samuel Hardy, divine and astronomer, 1793.

Here also resided, in 1593, its native, Sir Julius Cæsar, civilian; Sir John Cooke, Secretary of State; and William Baxter, author of "Glossarium Antiquitatum," who was master of its free-school.

In the *Church* is a beautiful window of antient painted glass; and some old and good monuments.

Bruce Castle was the residence of Robert Bruce, father of Robert King of Scotland, who died in 1303; and subsequently of Sir William Compton, favourite of Henry VIII., and ancestor of the Earls of Northampton, who here entertained Henry VIII. and his sister Margaret Queen of Scots, in 1516. His grandson Henry Lord Compton in 1578 entertained Queen Elizabeth here. It has been of late occupied as a school.

Of the *Free Grammar School* was Master William Baxter, scholar, antiquary, and author, who died in 1723 in London.

Growing in the middle of the clump of elm trees, (before noticed, p. 7,) called the Seven Sisters, was formerly a walnut tree, which never grew greater or higher, but always threw out leaves. Tradition assigns it to having been planted on a spot where a Protestant martyr was executed.

Here died Hugh Broughton, learned divine and celebrated preacher, 1612, to whom the Chutch of Rome offered a Cardinal's hat if he would change his religion; Sir Abraham Reynardson, Lord Mayor in 1648, loyalist, 1661; Sir Michael Foster, Judge of the King's Bench, law writer, 1763.

In Robinson's History of Tottenham is a burlesque poem reprinted from the second volume of Percy's "Reliques," entitled "The Tvrnament of Tottenham: or the wooing, winning, and wedding of Tibbe, the Reeve's daughter there."

TWICKENHAM was the vicarage of Richard Meggott, Dean of Winchester, eloquent preacher; Samuel Pratt, Dean of Rochester; Daniel Waterland, author on the divinity of Christ; Richard Terrick, Bp. of London; and George Costard, astronomer and orientalist.

The house in which Pope resided for 29 years, in which his "Essay on Man," "Epistles," "Dunciad," and great part of his "Homer," were composed, and in which he died, is pulled down; as is also a large house erected on its site by the Baroness Howe; and Pope's celebrated cave,

"The Ægerian grot
Where nobly pensive St. John sat and thought,"

dilapidated. Pope was buried in the church, 1744, with a tasteless epitaph by Bishop Warburton; and a tablet, erected by him, commemorates the death of his father, 1713; his mother, 1733.

The *Eel Pie House* has been celebrated for more than two centuries.

Strawberry Hill, abounding with objects of high interest to the lover of antiquity, history, or vertu, is fully described in the works of its late acute and elegant possessor, Horace Walpole, Earl of Orford, who erected it on the site of a cottage in which Colley Cibber composed his comedy of "the Refusal," and in which Talbot, Bp. of Durham, and the French divine, Père Courayer, once resided. This "Castle of Otranto" is peculiarly rich in antient well-authenticated portraits; in the works of Holbein; in the finest miniatures and enamels of the Olivers, Petitot, and Zincke; and in such curiosities as the armour of Francis I. of France, the Cardinal's hat of Wolsey, and the wedding gloves of Hampden's wife. The house and its contents have been most strictly entailed.

At *Twickenham park*, resided in early life, "the father of experimental philosophy," Lord Chancellor Bacon; the lovely Lucy Harrington, Countess of Bedford; and the brave and loyal John Lord Berkeley of Stratton, who was buried here, 1678.

At *Marble Hill*, resided the Countess of Suffolk, mistress of George II. and correspondent of Pope; at Little Strawberry Hill, Mrs. Catharine Clive, comic actress, who was buried in the church in 1785.

At *Ragman's castle*, Mrs. Hannah Pritchard, actress, and George Hardinge, esq. the late eminent Welsh Judge.

At *Whitton*, Sir John Suckling, its native poet; Sir Godfrey Kneller, painter, who was buried here 1723; and Sir William Chambers, architect.

In *Twickenham* also resided Sir Humphrey Lind, Protestant controversialist; Sir John Finet, author of "Philoxenes;" Sir Benjamin Rudyard, statesman; the witty Richard Corbet, Bp. of Norwich; Edward Earl of Manchester, Parliamentarian General; the Speaker Lenthal; the philosopher Boyle; Secretary Craggs; the eccentric and versatile Duke of Wharton, whose house has been pulled down; Lady Macclesfield, the unnatural mother of Savage; John Gilbert, Abp. of York, who died here, 1761; the painters Hudson and Scott; the novelist Fielding; the physician Batty; Sir John Hawkins, historian of Music; Owen Cambridge, poet and essayist; Hickey, Goldsmith's "Special Attorney;" Paul Whitehead, poet, who died here 1775; Lady Mary Wortley Montagu; and Lord George Germaine.

Besides those already mentioned, here were buried Sir William Berkeley, governor and historian of Virginia, 1677; Lady Frances Whitmore (epitaph by Dryden) 1690; Nicholas Amhurst, author of "Terræ Filius," and the "Craftsman," 1742; the brave Admirals, Sir Chaloner Ogle, 1750; John Byron, 1786; and Sir John Pococke, 1792; and Edward Ironside, historian of Twickenham, 1803.

John Earl of Mar, General for the Stuarts at Sheriff's Muir, was married here in 1703 to Margaret Hay, daughter of the Earl of Errol.

At Twickenham the first weeping willow was planted early in the eighteenth century.

Louis-Philippe the present King of the French once resided at Twickenham.

At UXBRIDGE still remains the house in which the treaty between the Royalists and Parliamentarians occurred; now the Crown Inn.

Here died in 1788, John Lightfoot, botanist, and for some time curate of that place.

At **WEST TWYFORD** were buried Henry Bold, comic poet, 1683; and Fabian Phillips, antiquary, 1690.

At **WHITCHURCH** was Canons, the princely seat of the Duke of Chandos. (See under **STANMORE PARVA.**)

In **WILSDON** are seven prebends belonging to St. Paul's. In the church was buried Charles Otway, 1764.

List of Works consulted.

1. A description of the county of Middlesex.—8vo, 1775.
2. The history of the county of Middlesex. By Luke Pope.— 1 vol. 4to, 1795, *never continued*.
3. Beauties of England and Wales.
4. The history and antiquities of Canonbury House at Islington. By John Nichols, F.S.A.—4to, 1788.
5. The history and antiquities of Twickenham. By Edmund Ironside, Esq.—4to, 1797.
6. The Environs of London. By Rev. Daniel Lysons, A.M., F.R.S., F.S.A., L.S.—4to, 1810, vol. ii. iii. and v.
7. The history, topography, and antiquities of the parish of St. Mary, Islington. By John Nelson.—4to, 1811.
8. An historical and topographical account of Fulham, including the hamlet of Hammersmith. By T. Faulkner.—8vo, 1813.
9. The topography and natural history of Hampstead. By John James Park.—4to, 1818.
10. The history of the ancient town and borough of Uxbridge. By George Redford and Thomas Hurry Riches.—8vo, 1818.
11. The history and antiquities of the parish of Tottenham. By William Robinson, gent.—8vo, 1818. Second edit. 2 vols. 8vo, 1840.
12. Tour of the Grand Junction canal. By J. Hassell.—8vo, 1819.
13. The history and antiquities of the parish of Edmonton, &c. By William Robinson, gent. F.S.A.—8vo, 1819.
14. The history and antiquities of the parish of Stoke Newington. By William Robinson, gent. F.S.A.—8vo, 1820.
15. History and antiquities of Kensington. By Thomas Faulkner.—8vo, 1820.
16. Some account of Kentish Town, &c. By James Bennett.— 12mo, 1821.

17. The history and antiquities of Enfield. By W. Robinson, LL.D., F.S.A.—8vo, 1823, 2 vols.

18. History and description of the parish of Clerkenwell, embellished with numerous engravings by J. and H. S. Storer. The historical department by T. Cromwell.—8vo, 1828.

19. An historical, topographical, and statistical description of Chelsea, and its environs. By Thomas Faulkner.—2 vols. 8vo, 1829.

20. A topographical and historical account of the parish of St. Mary-le-Bone. By Thomas Smith.—8vo, 1833.

21. The history and antiquities of the parish of Hammersmith. By Thomas Faulkner.—8vo, 1839.

22. The history and antiquities of Syon Monastery, the parish of Isleworth, and the chapelry of Hounslow. By G. J. Aungier. —8vo, 1840.

LONDON AND WESTMINSTER.

SITUATION AND EXTENT.

The Cities of London and Westminster, forming the Metropolis of England, and the seat of the British Government, are situated on the northern bank of the river Thames, about 60 miles from its mouth. The site was originally fens and marshes at the foot of hills covered with forests. The opposite bank was a complete morass; and Finsbury was a fen communicating with the Essex marshes.—The Metropolis, in length, is nearly eight miles, its breadth three, and its circumference twenty-six.

Province, Canterbury. *Diocese*, London.—The City of Westminster was created a bishopric by Hen. VIII. with jurisdiction over all Middlesex, except Fulham, a peculiar of the see of London; but it was dissolved by Edw. VI.

ANTIENT STATE AND REMAINS.

BRITISH PERIOD :—Mr. Owen, the editor of the Welch Archæology, derives the name of London from *Llyn* a lake, and *din* a town,—the town by the lake. Others bring it from the Celtic *Lhongdun,* "a town of ships."

A British Trackway is considered to have gone from Old Street, St. Luke's, by the City Arms public house in the City Road, across the Holloway back road, near to the Adam and Eve, and by Hagbush Lane to the foot of Highgate Hill. There were houses and buildings in London when the Romans first came to our Island; and it was the capital of the Trinobantes, who were emigrants from Belgium.

ROMAN PERIOD :—London is not mentioned by Cæsar, but it became an important station of the Roman people, and is mentioned by their authors under the names of Londinium, Augusta, &c. In the time of Nero, Tacitus informs us that it was a famous city with extensive commerce and plenty of all things. In the time of Severus it was called by Herodian, a great and wealthy city. There were three temples : one to the Goddess Diana, on the site of the present Cathedral of St. Paul ; another to Apollo, on the site of Westminster Abbey ; and the third is presumed to have stood on the site of Bow Church.

The great *Roads* constructed by this people, were the Ermine Street, which went out of the city by Cripplegate; the Watling Street, which passed from Tyburn through St. James's Park to Westminster, and thence to Lambeth at Stangate, on its way to Dover; another road from Farnham along Oxford Street to High Street, Bloomsbury, and thence to Clerkenwell; and the Prætorian Way, which went from Dowgate along the present Watling Street, by Newgate, to the Oxford Road. There was also a vicinal way from Aldgate by Bethnal Green to Old Ford, in Essex.

The *Walls* of the city are supposed to have been built by Helena the mother of Constantine, about the year 306, or by her son Constantine. They began by the Tower, went along the Minories to Aldgate, by the back of Hounsditch to Bishopsgate, thence in a straight line by London Wall to Cripplegate, and by the other gates to the Thames by the River Fleet, a circuit of more than three miles. The walls were defended by towers and bastions. In thickness they were between eight and nine feet. Some remains are visible on Tower Hill, near to the Minories.

Remains of the works of this people have been very extensively discovered. Among others, at the following places:

Aldgate, when rebuilding the gate in 1606, coins.

All Hallows Barking, patera, 1796.

Bishopsgate Church, urns, pateræ, coin, arch, 1725.

Bow Lane, Cheapside, near the corner of Little St. Thomas Apostle, in Dec. 1839, was found the perfect skeleton of a man, in a coffin constructed of Roman pavement; the man must have stood 6 feet 7 inches high, and between the teeth was found clenched a coin too corroded to decipher; a great quantity of pavement was also found.

Bread Street, Cheapside, richly figured Samian vases, and specimens of painting from the walls of Roman dwellings, very interesting, and exhibiting great freshness of colours.

Broad Street, pavement.

Camomile Street, Bishopsgate, in 1711, a cemetery with tessellated pavement, and containing urns filled with burnt bones; a lachrymatory, rings, fibula, and a coin of Antoninus.

Cannon Street, the London Stone, generally supposed to have been a miliary. It is enclosed in the wall of the church of St. Swithin.

Christ's Hospital, sepulchral remains, 1826. In 1834 a beautiful gold ring set with a sapphire, ruby, and two turquoises. In 1837 part of a fluted column.

Church Lane, Whitechapel, sepulchral stone, 1776.

Coleman Street, near the public house called the Swan's Nest, a well 3 feet square, boarded on each side, full of vases regularly packed in the mud and sand.

College Street, Dowgate Hill, on site of Dyers' Hall, pavement, earthern jars, and a large quantity of animal bones.

Crosby Square, in 1835, extensive pavements and foundations.

Crutched Friars, pavement, 1787.

East Cheap, tesseræ, coins, amphoræ, and architectural fragments in 1831; fragments of a pavement, and adjoining St. Clement's Church, 12 feet below the present pavement, was found in 1834, a tessellated pavement, and fragments of domestic utensils, six small earthern lamps, rings, coins, &c.; one gilt ring, had an engraved turquoise, representing an augural priest feeding a cock.

Founders' Court, in 1834, tessellated pavement.

Gutter Lane, a great quantity of Samian pottery; glass bottle capable of holding 2 ounces; coins; and curved edged tiles, used for covering roofs of houses.

Holborn Bridge, two lares and a pavement.

Honey Lane, in 1834, while digging for the foundation of the new City School, glass bottles, coins, sacrificial knives, &c.

King William Street, numerous remains of habitations, and an abundance of pottery, &c. proving that spot to have been closely occupied by dwelling houses, were found while making some sewers in 1834.

Leadenhall Street, pavement, discovered in 1800, a square of 11 feet, in the centre Bacchus reclining on the back of a tiger, &c. preserved in the library of the East India House, where are remains of vases, tiles, bones, &c. discovered in 1822.

Lombard Street, in digging for the foundation of the church of St. Mary Woolnoth, in 1716, pottery, and tusks and bones of animals. Earthern lamp, pavement, aqueduct, 1730.

London Bridge, beautiful little statue of Harpocrates, of silver, 1825; figure of horse in lead, 1827; colossal head of Hadrian. In the bed of the Thames, in Jan. 1836, bronze figures of a priest or devotee of Cybele, a Mercury, an Apollo, an Atys, and the fragment of a Mercury or Jupiter; the work of the Augustan era, probably of Greek artists in the employ of the Romans. Several thousand coins, in very fine preservation, lying in the line of the trajectus, or bridge. Three gold medallions, two of which were under one of the piles of the old bridge.

London Wall, in 1834, needles, gold ring, engraved cornelian, pottery, brass tweezers, with earpick connected by a ring; instrument for fastening the hair like a packing needle at one end and flat and circular like a coin at the other, with helmeted head thereon.

Lothbury, pavement, 1805; another 1834.

Ludgate, in 1683, sepulchral monument to a Roman soldier,

preserved at the theatre at Oxford; in 1806, at back of London Coffee House, a stone to the memory of Claudia, wife of a Roman general.

Ludgate Hill, circular tower and staircase, trunk of a statue of Hercules, altars, head of a female, 1806.

Moorfields, rare coins, sepulchral inscriptions, and vases, 1839.

Moorgate, by the London Wall, in August 1837, 18 feet from the surface, a sepulchral stone with an inscription.

Prince's Street and Bank, in 1834, a pair of small brass scales, keys, spatulæ, fibulæ, styli, needles in brass and bone, coins; steel for sharpening knives, with handle ornamented with a lotus leaf and horse's head of bronze; knives with bone handles.

Pancras Lane, pavement.

Queen Street, Cheapside, in Oct. 1839, an elegant mosaic pavement.

St. Margaret's Church, in 1834, iron chisels, crowbars, hammers, &c.; leathern sandal with nails on the sole; pottery, coins.

St. Martin's in the Fields, brick arch 1722, and glass vases, stone coffins, and buffaloes heads.

St. Martin's le Grand, tile and coin, 1818.

St. Mary Hill, pavement, urns, bones, coins.

St. Mary-le-Bow, Cheapside, when building the church, walls, windows, and the pavement of a temple.

St. Paul's Cathedral site, urns, vases, ampullæ, &c.

Shadwell, cemetery, 1615.

Spitalfields, urns of ashes, coins, lachrymatories, pateræ, penates, 1576.

Tenter Ground, Goodman's Fields, urns, lachrymatories, sepulchral stone, 1787.

Thames Street, opposite to Vintners' Hall, wall of flint, chalk, and flat tiles, in alternate layers, Oct. 1839.

Threadneedle Street, on site of French Church, two fine
pavements, &c. 1841.

Tower, ingot of silver and coins.

Westminster, coins, and pottery.

SAXON PERIOD : —London was called by Bede, Londinia,
and a princely mart town; by King Alfred Lunden-
ceaster; and by other Saxon writers Lunden-berig, and
Lunden-wic. It became the capital of the kingdom of
Essex during the Octarchy ; and when all the petty
kingdoms came under the sway of Egbert, London became
the Metropolis of England. Westminster was called
Thorney Island, being insulated by a small stream, called
in modern times Longditch, the track of which has been
traced from the Thames at Manchester Buildings across
King Street by Gardeners Lane round to Tothill Street,
and thence to the river at the end of Abingdon Street, and
covered over with thorn bushes. It was named Westminster
from its Abbey, being situated to the west of London, or
to distinguish it from St. Paul's. In very old grants the
Abbey is described as being " in loco terribili ! "

Saxon Remains. Two stone coffins found in Cheapside,
Jan. 1837. In Thames Street, opposite Dowgate Lane,
was found, in April 1839, a very curious brooch, in the
possession of C. R. Smith, Esq. F.S.A. of gold and ena-
mel, representing a crowned head.

CATHEDRAL. Commenced in the seventh century, by King
Ethelbert, who had been converted by St. Augustine, the
Apostle of the English ; destroyed by fire in 1083 ; rebuilt in the time of William Rufus, by Bishop Maurice ;
and again burnt in Sept. 1666, in the great fire of London.
47,000 loads of rubbish were removed, and the first
stone of the present structure was laid June 21, 1675 ;
opened for divine service Dec. 2, 1697, on the occa-

sion of the thanksgiving for the peace of Ruyswick; begun and finished in a space of 35 years, by one architect, Sir Christopher Wren, one principal mason, Mr. Strong, and during one bishopric, that of Dr. Henry Compton; the total expense £736,752. 2s. 3d., of which £130,000 was raised by subscription. The dome, or cupola, is the most striking feature of the whole edifice. It is 112 feet in diameter, and 215 feet in height.* The following are the dimensions of the church:

	feet.
Length from east to west, within the walls . .	500
Length from north to south, within the doors of the porticos	286
The breadth of the west entrance . . .	100
Circuit of entire building	2292
Circumference of Cupola	430
Diameter of Ball	6
From the Ball to the top of the Cross . . .	30
Diameter of Columns of portico	4
Height to top of west pediment, under the figure of St. Paul	120
Height of Campaniles of west front . . .	287

ABBEYS. Our Lady of Grace, Tower Hill, founded by Edward III. 1349-50.

Westminster, generally believed to be founded by Sebert King of the East Saxons, previous to the year 616; destroyed by the Danes and rebuilt by King Edgar in 958; again rebuilt by Edward the Confessor in 1065,

---

* The Dome of St. Sophia at Constantinople, erected in the time of Justinian, is 115 feet diameter, and 201 in height; that of St. Maria delle Fiore, at Florence, 139 feet diameter, and 310 high; and that of St. Peter, at Rome, 139 feet diameter, and 330 high.

part of whose work remains on the south side; constituted
a place of inauguration for the kings of England by Pope
Nicholas II.; present church principally built by Henry
the Third; Our Lady's Chapel was begun in 1502, by
Henry the Seventh, and thence called after him; Henry
the Eighth converted it into a Cathedral and Bishop's See;
and Edward the Sixth dissolved the See and made it into
a College; Queen Mary again made it an Abbey; and
Elizabeth founded the present Dean and Chapter; Oliver
Cromwell converted it into barracks for soldiers; the
towers, 225 feet high, were erected by Sir Christopher
Wren, but have more in them to condemn than to admire.
The northern entrance is very beautiful, and is called
Solomon's Porch. The Abbey, in the interior, is 360
feet long, and from transept to transept 195 feet; the
nave is 72 feet broad; Henry the Seventh's Chapel is
99 feet in length, 26 in breadth, and 54 in height. Henry
the Seventh's Chapel was, early in the present century,
completely repaired with Bath stone, at a cost of £42,000;
executed by Mr. Gayfere, Master-mason of the Abbey.

PRIORIES. St. Bartholomew, founded by Raherus, the
king's justice, about 1102. (Vide under CHURCHES.)
Holy Trinity, Aldgate, founded by Matilda, queen of
Henry I. in 1108. It was the richest priory in England.

NUNNERIES. Holywell, between Holywell Lane and Norton
Falgate, founded temp. Richard I. by Sir Robert Fitz-
gelran; refounded by Sir Thomas Lovel in 1510.
Holy Trinity, Minories, founded by Edward Earl of Lan-
caster, brother of Edward I. 1293, and his wife Blanch
Queen of Navarre, for nuns of the order of St. Clare.
St. Helen's, Bishopsgate Street, founded 1212, by William
Basing.

FRIARIES. Augustine, near Broad Street, founded 1253 by Humphrey de Bohun, 9th Earl of Hereford ; remains used as a Dutch Church.

Black, between Ludgate and the Thames, where, among many other illustrious individuals, were interred, the heart of Queen Alianor, the foundress ; her son Alphonso ; Margaret Queen of Scots ; Hubert de Burgh, Earl of Kent ; John of Eltham, Duke of Cornwall, brother of Edward III.; and King James of Spain.

Crutched or Crossed, near Tower Hill, founded by Ralph Hosier and William Labernes, about 1298.

De Sacca, founded by Henry III. on site of the original synagogue of London at the corner of Old Jewry and Lothbury.

Dominican, by Hubert de Burgh in 1242, in Holborn ; re-founded at Ludgate by Archbishop Kilwarby, 1279.

Grey, or Franciscan, near Christ's Hospital, founded 1225, by John Ewin, mercer. Here were buried, Margaret, queen of Edward I.; Isabel, queen of Edward II. with the heart of her husband ; Joan, wife of Edward Bruce, King of Scots ; and many other persons of high rank and distinction.

White, or Carmelite, near the Temple, founded by Richard Gray, knight, in 1241.

PRECEPTORY. The order of Knights Templars was instituted about 1117 or 1118, and were bound to wage war against the pagans, and defend the pilgrims to the Temple at Jerusalem ; they established themselves in England temp. Stephen, and first settled near Holborn, on the site of the present Southampton Buildings, where upwards of a century ago some remains were discovered of their original temple, constructed in a circular form, like the more ancient part of the present church, erected by them on

their removal, in the time of Hen. II. to an extensive plot
of ground between Fleet Street and the Thames. The
Knights were suppressed and dispossessed in 1312 ; the
estates regranted to the Knights Hospitallers of St. John
of Jerusalem, by order of the Council of Vienna, in
1324. The Temple Church was dedicated in honour of
the blessed Mary by Heraclius, Patriarch of Jerusalem,
about 1185, who was at that time being entertained by
the Knights Templars. It was most probably the western
or round tower part. The body of the church was completed in 1240, and is a pure specimen of the period.
(Vide under *Churches.*)

COLLEGES. Allhallows Barking, founded by Richard III.
Corpus Christi, in St. Lawrence Pountney, by Sir John de
    Poultney 1346.
Holy Ghost, founded by Roger Holmes, 1400.
Jesus Commons, Dowgate.
Lancaster, founded by Henry IV. and the executors of
    John of Gaunt,
St. Martin's le Grand, founded by Ingelricus and Edward
    or Gerard, his brother, 1056.
Saint Michael, Paternoster Royal, founded by the celebrated
    Sir Richard Whittington (four times Lord Mayor of
    London), between 1396 and 1419, afterwards converted
    into almshouses for 13 poor men, and since taken down
    for removal to Highgate.

HOSPITALS. Saint Anthony's, in Threadneedle Street,
    founded by Henry II. as a cell to one at Vienna.
St. Augustine Papey, near Bevis Marks, founded 1430,
    by two or three priests.
Blessed Mary, Bishopsgate, founded by Sheriff Simon
    Fitzmary, 1246.

Domus Conversorum, founded by Henry III. on site of Rolls Chapel.

Elsynge in St. Alphage, founded 1331, by William Mercer, converted into a college 1340.

St. Giles, Whitecross Street, founded temp. Edw. I.

St. Giles in the Fields, for lepers, by Queen Matilda, 1102.

St. James, Westminster, for lepers, founded ante 1100.

St. Mary Bethlehem, Bishopsgate Street, by Simon Fitz Mary, 1246.

St. Mary Spital, without Bishopsgate, founded by Walter Brune and Roesia his wife, 1197.

St. Michael, Crooked Lane, by Sir William Walworth 1380.

Rounceval, Charing Cross, founded by William Marischal, . Earl of Pembroke, temp. Henry III. on site of Northumberland House.

Savoy, founded by Henry VII. for priests to stand at their gate to take in objects of charity and feed them; suppressed 7 Edw. VI. and re-founded by Mary.

St. Thomas of Acon, now Mercers' Hall, founded temp. Henry II. by Thomas Fitz Theobald de Heili and his wife Agnes, sister to the famous St. Thomas à Becket.

CHAPEL. St. Michael, built by Prior Norman, 1189; some remains exist under the house No. 71, Leadenhall Street.

•

HERMITAGES. All Hallows, London Wall.

St. James's on the Wall, near Lambe's Chapel, founded by Henry III. for Robert de St. Lawrence.

Tower, ante temp. Henry III.

Westminster, Charing Cross.

CASTLES. Baynard's, erected by one of William's Norman attendants of that name, and stood on the site of the Carron Iron Works, Thames Street, Blackfriars.

TOWER, begun, in 1076, by William the Norman, and completed by William Rufus, who surrounded it with walls and a ditch. Henry III. in 1240, added gates and other fortifications, and Edward IV. built the Lion's Tower. In the Keep or White Tower, is a Norman chapel, erected by Gundulph Bishop of Rochester. There is also another to St. Peter ad Vincula, erected temp. Edward I. Its extent is thirteen acres one rood, and the circuit round the ditch is about a quarter of a mile.

CROSSES. Charing, one of those erected in honour of Queen Eleanor.

Cheap, stood at the end of Wood Street, Cheapside.

Paul's, before the Cathedral on the north-east.

MANSIONS AND OLD HOUSES. Aldersgate Street, formerly Half Moon Tavern, and Thanet House, built by Inigo Jones.

Beech Lane, Barbican, Prince Rupert's.

Bishopsgate Street, Sir Paul Pindar's, now a public house, under the sign of "The Flying Horse."

Cock public house, in Tothill Street, where it is said the pay table during the building of Westminster Abbey was kept, temp. Henry III.

CROSBY HALL, Bishopsgate Street, built by Sir John Crosby, Sheriff of London, in 1470; the great hall (55 feet long, 27 broad, and 40 high), council chamber, and some vaults, remain; the roof or ceiling of the hall is "decidedly one of the finest specimens of timber work in existence." A committee was formed to secure its pre-

servation, and a public subscription entered into in 1832,
and, being now restored, it has been used for several public
purposes.

Ely House, the town mansion of the Bishops of Ely, chapel
of St. Etheldreda remains.

Golden Lane, Barbican, Queen's Nursery.

Grub Street, General Monk's.

Hounsditch, in Seven-step Alley, Gravel Lane, remains a
very handsome antient mansion.

Lincoln's Inn Gate and Hall, erected temp. Henry VII.

Northumberland House, Charing Cross, erected by Bernard
Janssen, temp. James I.

St. James's Palace Gate.

Staple's Inn.

Van Dun's almshouses, York Street, Westminster, erected
temp. Eliz.

Winchester House, Winchester Street, built by the Marquess of Winchester, temp. Hen. VIII. or Edw. VI.;
pulled down in 1839 (see in the Gentleman's Magazine,
for that year, a view of it taken just before its destruction).

PRESENT STATE AND APPEARANCE.

RIVER.

The THAMES, the great source of London's prosperity, is in length more than 200 miles. To Lechlade in Gloucestershire, a distance of 138 miles from London, it is navigable for vessels of 90 tons. In its progress it forms a boundary to the counties of Essex, Kent, Middlesex, Surrey, Bucks, and Berks. The tide flows as high as Richmond, a distance of 70 miles from the ocean, being a greater distance than the tide is carried by any other river in Europe. The jurisdiction of the Lord Mayor of London over it extends from Sheerness to Staines ; and he holds four Courts of Conservancy every year, in June and July.

RAILWAYS.

Great Western Railway, from Paddington to Bristol, a distance of 117¼ miles ; engineer, Brunel, jun.; date of Act 1835 ; partly opened at several times, and the whole way to Bristol, June 1841.

West London, or Thames Junction, from the Great Western and Birmingham Railways, near Holsden Green, to the Thames, 3 miles ; begun in 1836, but works suspended for want of funds.

London and Birmingham Railway, 112 miles from Euston Square, act obtained 1833, commenced 1834, engineer Stephenson, opened 17th Sept. 1838 ; on the line are eight tunnels ; cost £4,983,849 ; capital, £5,500,000.

Eastern Counties, from High Street, Shoreditch, by Colchester, to Norwich and Yarmouth, 126 miles; date of Act 1836; opened as far as Brentwood 1840; capital, £5,000,000; engineer, John Braithwaite.

Northern and Eastern Railway, from the Eastern Counties Line to Bishop's Stortford; Act obtained 1836; opened 1841, as far as Harlow; cost £26,000 per mile; engineers, Walker and R. Stephenson.

London and Blackwall, from Fenchurch Street 3½ miles to the Thames at Blackwall, where are extensive storehouses, and a spacious wharf; date of Act 1836; opened July 6, 1840, except half a mile at the London end; trains worked by stationary engines by means of ropes; the starting of the trains is regulated by an electric telegraph; the terminus at Blackwall is a large and well designed building; engineers, Stephenson and Bidder.

London and Greenwich Railway, 3¾ miles from London Bridge, on arches all the way (878 in number); date of first Act 1833; opened as far as Deptford in 1835; and the whole distance in 1838; probable cost, including stations at London, Greenwich, and Deptford, about £1,000,000; Landmann, engineer; the viaduct is now being widened for two lines of rails, so as to afford accommodation for the Brighton and South Eastern traffic.

London and Croydon, 8¼ miles, (and thence to Brighton 41¼ miles); date of Act 1835; opened to Croydon 1839; commences from the Greenwich Line; cost £661,000; engineer, Joseph Gibbs.

South Western Railway, from Nine Elms, near Vauxhall Bridge, to Southampton; date of Act 1834; opened May 12, 1838, as far as Woking Common, and the whole line, a distance of 76¼ miles, in 1840; capital, £2,140,000; cost £26,788 per mile; engineers, Giles and Locke.

PUBLIC EDIFICES AND INSTITUTIONS.

Active Life Assurance, Cornhill.

Adelaide Gallery (*vide* Royal Gallery of Practical Science).

Adelphi, The, buildings designed by Messrs. John, Robert, and James Adam, on the North bank of the Thames, near the Strand.

Adelphi Theatre, Strand; commenced in 1802; very rich façade, erected 1840, and completed within little more than a fortnight.

Admiralty, built by Ripley, temp. George II. on site of Wallingford House; the portico is heavy and tasteless; and a screen by Adams was afterwards erected to hide it; this screen was mutilated some years since to form new carriage entrances; on the top of the house is a semaphore telegraph.

Admiralty Court, Doctors' Commons.

Adult Orphan Asylum, Regent's Park, for the relief and education of daughters of clergymen, and of military and naval officers; founded in 1820.

Aged Christians' Society, 32, Sackville Street.

Agricultural (Royal) Society, Regent Street; incorporated 1840, for the improving of English agriculture.

Albany Chambers, Piccadilly, formerly the residence of the Duke of York, son of George III.; a fine range of buildings. The centre mansion was erected by Sir William Chambers, for Lord Melbourne.

Albion Club, 85, St. James's Street.

Alfred Club, 23, Albemarle Street.

Alien Office, Crown Street, Westminster.

Alliance British and Foreign Life and Fire Assurance Office, Bartholomew Lane.

Alliance Club, 79, Pall Mall.

i

Almack's Rooms, King Street, St. James's, where the most aristocratic assemblies are held.

Amicable Society, Life Insurance Office, Serjeants' Inn, incorporated by charter of Queen Anne in 1706; the oldest office of the kind in existence.

Antiquaries Society, Somerset House, originally founded about 1580; revived 1717; incorporated 1751.

Apothecaries' Hall, Union Street, Blackfriars, incorporated 1617.

Architects *(vide* Royal Institute of British Architects).

Architectural Society, 35, Lincoln's Inn Fields, instituted 1831.

Argus Life Assurance, Throgmorton Street, established 1833.

Armourers' and Braziers' Hall, Coleman Street; incorporated by Henry VI.

Army and Navy Club, St. James's Square.

Army Medical Officers' Benevolent Fund Society, 5, Berkeley Street, Piccadilly, founded in 1820.

Asiatic (Royal) Society, Grafton Street; incorporated 1824.

Astronomical (Royal) Society, Lincoln's Inn Fields; established 1820.

Athenæum Club House, Carlton Gardens, Pall Mall, established in 1824, for the association of literary and scientific gentlemen and their patrons; erected in 1829; architect, Decimus Burton; the frieze is a copy of the panathenaic procession, which formed the frieze of the Parthenon. The statue of Minerva, over the portico, is by Baily.

Atlas Assurance Company, Cheapside; established 1808.

Auction Mart, Bartholomew Lane, for the sale of estates, &c. erected by subscription, between 1808 and 1810; architect, John Walters. It contains a spacious saloon, coffee room, &c.; very elegant building.

Australian Agricultural Company, Coleman Street, established 1824.

Bakers' Hall, Harp Lane, Great Tower Street.

BANK, Threadneedle Street, incorporated by Act 1694 ; present building begun by George Sampson in 1732 ; extended by Sir Robert Taylor between 1766 and 1788 ; since which time so many alterations and erections have been made by Sir John Soane, that the whole pile of buildings may be considered to be from that architect's designs. They have been constructed with incombustible materials ; the principal entrance is on the south, in Threadneedle Street ; this façade is very profusely decorated ; but the north and west elevations are more simply grand. The Temple of Venus at Tivoli supplied the order and forms. This extensive pile covers an irregular area of about eight acres ; and comprises nine open courts, a spacious rotunda, an armoury, engraving and printing offices, library, apartments for officers and servants, and numerous large offices for the different public stocks. The south front measures 365 feet, west side 440 feet, north side 410 feet, east side 245 feet. The entrance to the Bullion Court was designed from the triumphal arch of Constantine at Rome, and the chief Cashier's office, from the temple of the Sun and Moon at Rome. In the Pay Hall is a marble statue of William III. by Cheere, and over this apartment, but in a separate building, is a clock, which shows the exact time in sixteen different offices, which is effected by brass rods weighing about 700 lbs. The late Dividend Warrant Office is a very richly decorated apartment ; built by Mr. Cockerell, the present architect of the Bank.

Bankruptcy Court, Guildhall, erected 1820 ; architect, Fowler.

Barber-Surgeons' Hall, Monkwell Street, erected by Inigo

Jones, and esteemed one of his best works. Here is a picture by Holbein of Henry VIII. giving the charter to the Company, in which is a portrait of Dr. Butts, who is mentioned by Shakspere. Part of the building was formed out of one of the barbicans of the old London Wall.

Belgrave Literary Institution, Pimlico, established 1833.

Bernard's Inn, Holborn, an appendage to Gray's Inn ; has a small hall.

Blackfriars' Bridge, of nine arches, erected with Portland stone; commenced in June 1760, and finished in 1770; Mr. Robert Mylne, a Scotch architect ; cost £152,840; length 995 feet, width 42, and height 62; the span of the centre arch is 100 feet; surface of waterway 793; and space of piers 207 feet ; breadth of carriage way 28 feet, footpath 7 feet, on each side ; repaired at an expense of £74,035 in 1840 ; when the road was lowered in the centre and raised at each end, and made equal to a new bridge.

Board of Control, Cannon Row, Westminster, for the direction of East Indian affairs ; architect, Wm. Atkinson ; brick, with stone Ionic portico.

Boodle's Club, 28, St. James's Street.

Botanic (Royal) Society, Pall Mall, established 1840. The Society are laying out gardens in the Regent's Park.

Brewers' Hall, Addle Street, Cheapside.

Bricklayers' Hall, Leadenhall Street; lately used as a Jews' synagogue.

Bridewell, Bridge Street, Blackfriars, founded (on site of a house inhabited by Cardinal Wolsey in 1522, and rebuilt by Henry VIII. for the accommodation of the Emperor Charles V.) in 1553, by Edward VI. ; destroyed by the fire in 1666 ; hospital rebuilt 1668 ; used as a house of correction for city apprentices, and for dissolute persons. Taking its name from the neighbouring well of St. Bride, it has given it to buildings for similar purposes elsewhere.

Britannia Life Assurance, Prince's Street, Bank, incorporated by Act, 1840.

British Artists' Society, Suffolk Street, Pall Mall East; established in consequence of the Royal Academy not having room for all the pictures sent in for exhibition; opened 1824.

British and Foreign Bible Society; instituted 1801. Offices, Earl Street, Blackfriars.

British Fire and Life Office, Strand; instituted 1799; rebuilt by Cockerell; of Grecian Doric.

British Institution, Pall Mall, founded June 4, 1805, principally through the exertions of Sir Thomas Bernard, for exhibiting the works of British Artists for sale; and of the most celebrated ancient and modern masters, for the study of pupils; the sculpture in front of the gallery, which was erected by Alderman Boydell for his Shakspere gallery, represents Shakspere, accompanied by Painting and Poetry, designed by Banks.

British Lying-in Hospital, Brownlow Street, Drury Lane; established 1749.

British Museum, Great Russell Street, Bloomsbury, originally Montagu House, built by Ralph first Duke of Montagu, about 1687; architect, Peter Puget; purchased and repaired by the Parliament, at a cost of £30,000, for the reception of the Sloaneian, Cottonian, and Harleian Collections, and opened for study and inspection, Jan. 15, 1759; enlarged 1804, architect, Saunders, for the reception of the Townleian Marbles. The whole Museum is in the course of being rebuilt after the designs of Sir Robert Smirke.

Brookes's Club, 61, St. James's Street.

BUCKINGHAM PALACE, St. James's Park, architect, Nash; begun 1826; first inhabited by Queen Victoria.

Burlington Arcade, a covered communication for foot passengers, from Piccadilly to Burlington Gardens, with a range of shops on each side, erected in 1815, by Lord George Cavendish, the owner of Burlington House; designed by Samuel Ware, Esq.

Butchers' Hall, Pudding Lane, rebuilt after being destroyed by fire in 1829.

Carlton Club House, Pall Mall, established 1834; architect, Sir Robert Smirke.

Carpenters' Hall, London Wall, with bust of Inigo Jones over the archway; now used as a carpet warehouse.

Central Criminal Courts, Old Bailey, for the speedy trial of prisoners charged with offences within ten miles of London; holds eight sessions in the year; tried in two Courts.

Charing Cross Hospital, for sick and accidents; established mainly through the exertions of Dr. Golding; first stone laid by the Duke of Sussex, Sept. 15, 1831; neat façade.

Charter House, formerly a Carthusian priory; converted, in 1611, into a hospital for eighty decayed gentlemen, who had been merchants or military men, by Thomas Sutton, Esq. who did not live to see it finished; there is also a school for forty-four boys, but the boys not on the foundation make it one of the largest public schools.

Christ's Hospital, or Blue Coat School, founded by Edward VI. on site of a house of Grey Friars, Newgate Street; a new infirmary was built in 1820; a noble hall of Haytor granite, commenced in April 1825, was opened May 29, 1829. It is in the Pointed style, on an arcade; architect, John Shaw; is 187 feet long, 51 wide, and 47 high, and is decorated by several fine pictures illustrative of the history of the place; grammar and mathematical schools, of brick, in the Elizabethan style, architect, Shaw;

opened 1832. From 1,000 to 1,400 are here educated annually; and the revenues of the hospital are estimated at £50,000.

Christian Knowledge Society's Offices, Lincoln's Inn Fields.

Church Building Society, St. Martin's Place, incorporated in 1818 to assist by grants of money the erection and extension of churches and chapels in the United Kingdom; nearly 400 have already been built through their help.

City of London Literary and Scientific Institution, Aldersgate Street, on site of house occupied by Milton; established June 1825.

City of London Royal British School, Poppin's Court, Fleet Street, for 600 children.

City of London School, on site of Honey Lane Market, founded by John Carpenter, Town Clerk, in the time of Henry VI.; first stone of present building, which is extensive, and in the Pointed style, was laid by Lord Brougham, Oct. 21, 1835; architect, J. B. Bunning.

Civil Engineers' Society, Great George Street, Westminster; incorporated 1828.

Clarence Club, 12, Waterloo Place.

Clement's Inn, Strand, appendage to the Inner Temple; has a hall with a portrait of Sir Matthew Hale, and in the garden is a sun-dial, supported by a kneeling negro, brought from Italy by Lord Clare.

Clerical and Medical Life Assurance Office, Great Russell Street, Bloomsbury; established in 1824.

Clifford's Inn, Fleet Street, appendage to the Inner Temple. It was formerly the mansion of the Lords Clifford. It has a hall in which is an oak case of great antiquity.

Clothworkers' Almshouses, Monkwell Street, for ten freemen of their company; chapel in pointed style; architect, Angel.

Clothworkers' Hall, Mincing Lane; the Court-room is handsome, and here are carvings of James I. and Charles I.

Coachmakers' Hall, Noble Street, Falcon Square.

Coal Exchange, Thames Street, erected in 1825; a convenient and neat structure.

Coldbath Fields Prison.—*Vide* Middlesex House of Correction, in the account of Middlesex.

College of Physicians. Their first College was in Knight Rider Street, in a house presented to them by Dr. Linacre, physician to Henry VII. and VIII., who died in 1524. They afterwards removed to Amen Corner, which was burnt in the fire of London in 1666. They then purchased an extensive plot of ground in Warwick Lane, Newgate Street, where a building, still existing, was erected between 1674 and 1689, from the designs, and under the superintendence of Sir Christopher Wren; and with statues of King Charles II. and Sir John Cutler, satirised by Pope. The college was removed to a new building in Pall Mall East, erected from designs by Sir Robert Smirke; hexastyle Ionic portico.

College of Surgeons, Lincoln's Inn Fields, incorporated in 1800; a spacious building containing a large museum, the basis of which was the collections of John Hunter; and to which the public are admitted by order of a member every Monday, Wednesday, and Friday.

Colosseum, Regent's Park. *Vide* under the head of MARYLEBONE, in Middlesex.

Commercial Hall, Mincing Lane, for public sale of Colonial produce, erected 1811; architect, Joseph Woods; in the front are emblematic basso-relievos by J. G. Bubb, of Husbandry, Science, Britannia, Commerce, and Navigation.

Coopers' Hall, Basinghall Street, of brick.

Cordwainers' Hall, Distaff Lane.

Corn Exchange, Mark Lane, (Old) a quadrangle, surrounded by a colonnade; (New) elegant building, adjoining the Old, with handsome fluted Doric portico at the entrance; the columns of the interior have capitals formed of wheat-sheafs; erected 1828; architect, Smith.

Covent Garden Market, the best in England for herbs, fruits, and flowers; the piazza designed by Inigo Jones; the present Market by C. Fowler; erected by the late Duke of Bedford in 1830.

Covent Garden Theatre; the first theatre on its present site built in 1730, and opened in 1733; ground rent to the Duke of Bedford £100 per annum; partly rebuilt in 1792, from a design by Holland, when the Duke granted a new lease at £940 per ann.; burnt down Sept. 20, 1808; present theatre commenced Dec. 31, 1808, and opened Sept 18, 1809, cost £150,000; the ground rent now above £2,000 per ann. The portico is Grecian Doric, from the temple of Minerva, in the Acropolis at Athens; the whole front of the theatre is decorated by basso-relievo representations of the drama, ancient and modern; in the ante-room is a large statue of Shakspere, by Rossi, in yellow marble; the form of the auditory is that of the horse-shoe; the width at the extremities is 51 feet 2 inches, and the depth, from the front lights to the front of the boxes, 52 feet 9 inches; the house will accommodate, in the boxes (exclusive of the private ones) 1,200 persons; the pit 750; second gallery 500; first gallery 350; in all, 2,800.

Council Chamber, Whitehall, architect, Sir John Soane; erected 1825.

County Fire Office, Regent Street, established 1806, chiefly by the exertions of Mr. Barber Beaumont; present edifice erected by Mr. Nash in 1819; "an indifferent copy" of the water front of Old Somerset House, designed by Inigo Jones.

COURTS OF LAW, on the western side of Westminster Hall, built by Sir John Soane, in 1827; they are seven in number, and have suitable rooms and passages; the *Queen's Bench Court* is 35 feet 6 inches long, 30 feet wide, and 26 feet 6 inches high; the *Bail Court*, 30 feet 6 inches long, 28 feet wide, and 23 feet 6 inches high; the *Court of Exchequer*, 52 feet long, 31 feet 7 inches wide, and 26 feet high; *Court of Equity*, 31 feet long, 23 feet 7 inches wide, and 24 feet high; *Court of Common Pleas*, 41 feet long, 33 feet wide, and 24 feet high; *Vice Chancellor's Court*, 36 feet long, 25 feet wide, and 29 feet high; *Lord Chancellor's Court*, 36 feet long, 33 feet wide, and 28 feet high. In these Courts the contrivances for light are admirable.

COURTS OF LAW, Guildhall, erected 1823; architect, W. Mountague.

Crockford's Club House, 50, St. James's Street.

Crown Life Assurance Office, Bridge Street, Blackfriars; established in 1824.

Curriers' Hall, London Wall, plain brick edifice, erected 1820.

Custom House, Lower Thames Street, spacious and commodious structure, erected from designs by David Laing, first stone laid Oct. 25, 1813; completed May 12, 1817; 480 feet long and 100 deep; cost £268,520; almost indestructible by fire; the long room, 190 feet long, 55 high, and 66 broad, fell in in 1825, but was subsequently rebuilt at the cost of the architect; the alto-relievos, in artificial stone, are by J. G. Bubb.

Cutlers' Hall, Cloak Lane, Great St. Thomas Apostle.

Cymmrodorian Society, established 1820.

Diorama, Regent's Park. *Vide* under MARYLEBONE, in the account of Middlesex.

Dissenting Ministers' Library, Red Cross Street, Cripplegate; founded by Mr. Daniel Williams, who died in 1716, for the use of Protestant Dissenting Ministers. Here is a collection of portraits of non-conformist divines.

Docks, East and West India. *Vide* POPLAR, in Middlesex.

Doctors' Commons, wherein is held the Admiralty Court; the Court of Arches, or highest Ecclesiastical Court in the kingdom; the Court of Delegates; and the Prerogative Court of Canterbury, for the probate and administration of wills.

Drapers' Hall, Throgmorton Street, on the site of the residence of Cromwell Earl of Essex, temp. Henry VIII.; purchased by the Drapers on his disgrace; a spacious quadrangle with broad piazza; architect, Jarman; the screen in the hall is very fine; south front by Adams.

Drury Lane Theatre; the first Theatre in Drury Lane was the Cockpit, opposite the Castle Tavern, built in 1617; rebuilt in 1629; new theatre upon nearly the site of the present edifice, opened in 1663; burnt down 1672; rebuilt by Sir Christopher Wren and opened in 1674; enlarged by Garrick and opened in 1762; pulled down in 1791, and rebuilt, the opening taking place on March 12, 1794; burnt to the ground Feb. 24, 1809; first stone of present edifice laid Oct. 29, 1811, and opened Oct. 10, 1812, architect Mr. B. Wyatt; it was partly built on the plan of the great theatre at Bordeaux, supposed to be the best theatre in Europe for the accurate conveyance of musical sounds; the rotunda and grand staircase have a peculiarly striking effect; the fronts of the dress boxes have a series of representations from the most popular of

Shakspere's dramas; the boxes (exclusive of private boxes, which hold 320) hold 1030; the pit 800; second gallery 550; upper gallery 350; total 3060; the stage, from the orchestra to the back wall, is 96 feet 3 inches, and the width from wall to wall 77 feet 5 inches.

Dutch Church, Austin Friars, formerly the nave of the friary church, and built temp. Edw. III. but has been recently covered with compo.

Dyers' Hall, College Street, Dowgate Hill, rebuilt 1839.

Eagle Life Office, Cornhill; established 1807.

East India House, Leadenhall Street, for conducting the affairs of the East India Company, commenced in 1799, on site of old building erected in 1726, from designs by Mr. R. Jupp; since altered and extended by Cockerell and Wilkins; the front is 190 feet in length; the tympanum of the Ionic portico is embellished with sculptures of emblematical figures by Bacon. The Museum, containing a vast collection of natural and artificial curiosities from the East, is open to the public every Saturday, from ten till four; and, with the whole of the interior, is well worth visiting.

Economic Life Assurance, Bridge Street, Blackfriars, established 1823.

Egyptian Hall, Piccadilly, erected by Mr. Bullock in 1812, and appropriated to the since-dispersed collection of the London Museum; architect, G. F. Robinson, whose design was taken from the great temple of Tentyra; now used as exhibition rooms.

Electrical Society, established 1837.

Emanuel Hospital, Tothill Fields, founded by Lady Anne Dacre, in 1601, for ten men and ten women, and twenty children; under the patronage of the Lord Mayor and Court of Aldermen.

Embroiderers' Hall, Gutter Lane, now used as a manufactory.

English Opera House, partly built by Dr. Arnold, but not licensed; rebuilt by his son at a cost of £80,000, and opened in 1816; destroyed by fire in 1830, and rebuilt the same year, near the former site; Beazley was the architect to the present and last theatres.

Entomological Society, Old Bond Street.

Erectheium Club, St. James's Square, opened 1840.

Excise Office, Broad Street, erected 1763, on site of Sir Thomas Gresham's college; spacious and noble.

Exeter Hall, Strand; erected for the holding of religious meetings of every character; opened March 1831; the hall is capable of containing 3,800 persons; architect, Gandy.

Farmers' Fire and Life Insurance, Norfolk Street, Strand, established 1840.

Farringdon Market, for eatables, a parallelogram of about one acre and a half; cost £212,000; opened Nov. 29, 1829; architect, W. Mountague.

Fellowship Porters' Hall, St. Mary-at-Hill.

Fishmongers' Hall, at the foot of London Bridge; erected in 1830, architect, Henry Roberts; of the Ionic order, with three fronts, all of which are separate compositions; a building of great merit.

Fleet Prison, Farringdon Street:—originally built in the time of Richard I. for Star Chamber prisoners; burnt down in the riots of 1780, after which the present prison was erected; it is used for debtors, and for persons committed for contempt of the Court of Chancery.

Founders' Hall, Lothbury; was used as a dissenting meeting house for more than a century; and has been taken by the French Congregation, removed from their old church in Threadneedle Street.

Foundling Hospital, Guildford Street, began by Captain

Thomas Coram, about 1722 ; charter granted 1739 ; building began 1742; its founder died supported by charity in 1751, aged 82, and was buried in its vaults.

Free Hospital, Greville Street, Hatton Garden.

Freemasons' Hall, in Great Queen Street, Lincoln's Inn Fields; foundation stone laid with masonic rites May 1, 1775, and opened May 23, 1776, architect, Thomas Sandby ; its length is 92 feet, breadth 43 feet, and height upwards of 60 feet; and is decorated by full-length portraits of illustrious Grand Masters ; cost, with the rebuilding of the Tavern, £30,000.

Furnival's Inn, Holborn, so named from the residence of one William le Furneval, temp. Richard II., appendage to Lincoln's Inn ; rebuilt 1820, by Mr. Peto ; handsome range of buildings.

Garrick Club, King Street, Covent Garden.

Garrick Theatre, Goodman's Fields, opened October 1830.

Geographical (Royal) Society, Regent Street.

Geological Society, instituted in 1807, to encourage the investigation of the formation and structure of the earth; incorporated 1826.

Gerard's Hall, Basing Lane, some interesting vaults of the 13th century.

Giltspur Street Compter, adjoining Newgate, built in 1791 ; used for confinement of persons previous to trial.

Girdlers' Hall, Basinghall Street, handsome and convenient, erected 1681.

Globe Fire, Life and Annuity Assurance Offices, Cornhill and Pall Mall ; established 1803.

Goldsmiths' Hall, Foster Lane, erected in 1833, on the site of the old hall, which was pulled down in 1829 ; in the Italian style; very handsome ; 159 feet in length by 100 in breadth ; architect, Hardwicke,

Gray's Inn, north side of Holborn, bequeathed to some students of the law temp. Edward III. by one of the family of Lords Grey of Wilton. In the hall is a curiously carved oak screen, and some portraits. The garden is spacious, and a great ornament.

Greencoat Hospital, or St. Margaret's Hospital, Tothill Fields, founded in 1633, by King Charles I.; rebuilt in 1700 by Dr. Busby and Charles Twitty, esq.

Greycoat Hospital, or School, Tothill Fields, instituted 1698; and letters patent obtained in 1706; 67 boys and 33 girls are here maintained, clothed, and educated.

Grocers' Hall, Poultry, on site of mansion of the Lords Fitzwalter, of whom the Company purchased it in 1411; built between 1798 and 1802; architect, Leverton.

Grosvenor House and Gallery of Pictures, Park Lane; architect, Cundy.

Guards (Royal) Club, 49, St. James's Street.

Guildhall, King Street, Cheapside, the public hall of the city; originally built in 1411; repaired after the fire of London; and refronted in 1789; the hall is 153 feet long, 48 broad, and 55 in height, and will contain about 7,000 people. Besides the Hall is the Aldermen's Room; a Common Council Chamber, decorated with very fine paintings; and the Courts of Law. The present front, except the archway, is modern; east and west windows, magnificent, and filled with painted glass; at west window are gigantic figures of Gog and Magog, supposed by some to represent an ancient Briton and a Roman, and by others to be a relic of druidic rites. The present figures were made in 1708. The old crypt is in excellent preservation, and a fine specimen, extending the whole length of the hall; height about 13 feet.

Guildhall, Westminster, near to the Abbey, erected in 1805, on site of the old Sanctuary; architect, S. P. Cockerell.

Haberdashers' Hall, Staining Lane, brick, large.

Hanover Square Rooms, for concerts, public meetings, &c.

Haymarket Theatre, first erected in 1720-1, by a builder named Potter, and opened with French comedies, under the patronage of the Duke of Montague ; pulled down in 1820; rebuilt, at a cost of £18,000, and opened July 4, 1821 ; architect, John Nash ; handsome Corinthian portico.

Heralds' College, St. Bennet's Hill, St. Paul's, a quadrangular brick building, where the records of the descent of families are preserved. It contains a large apartment for the Earl Marshal's Court.

Historical Society of Science, established 1840, for the publication of works showing the progress of the sciences.

Horse Guards, Whitehall, begun in 1751, by Vardy, after designs by Kent; cost more than £30,000. The archway is much too low; the park front is a rather handsome elevation ; the turret inelegant and heavy.

Horticultural Society, Regent Street, instituted in 1804, for improving the growth of fruit trees, &c. The Society has very extensive gardens at Chiswick, and their shows are visited by many thousands of the most distinguished people in the country.

House of Lords ; Royal entrance, and staircase, &c. to the old one, erected by Sir John Soane in 1822-3 ; and the Royal Gallery in the next year; most elaborately ornamented.

Houses of Parliament, in the Pointed style, now in the course of erection from designs by Barry ; foundation stone of the river wall laid in March 1839. Upwards of 80 different designs were sent in for the undertaking, and all were publicly exhibited after the decision of the Commissioners.

Hungerford Market, Strand, begun by Sir Edward Hungerford temp. Charles II. ; rebuilt by a Company in 1832 ; handsome and convenient ; architect, C. Fowler. A Suspension Bridge for foot passengers to the Surrey shore is now in the course of erection.

Hudson's Bay Company, Fenchurch Street.

Hyde Park, Grand Entrance, very noble and effective, designed by Decimus Burton; the Triumphal Arch, opposite to it and leading into St. James's Park, down Constitution Hill, is an elegant structure by the same architect. It was erected in 1827, and called George the Fourth's Gate.

Imperial Life and Fire Office, Sun Court, Cornhill; established 1803.

Innholders' Hall, College Street, Upper Thames Street, ancient brick edifice.

Insolvent Debtors' Court, Portugal Street, Lincoln's Inn Fields, erected in 1824 by Sir John Soane.

Ironmongers' Hall, Fenchurch Street, elegant building, erected 1748 ; designed by T. Holden.

Italian Opera House, Haymarket, first built on the present site in 1704, by Sir John Vanbrugh, who employed his interest and fortune to its advancement, and opened 1705, under the name of the Queen's Theatre ; improved by Adam and Novosielski ; burnt down 1789 ; rebuilt by Novosielski ; external façade erected in 1820, by Nash and Repton, of the Roman Doric order ; the basso-relievo of the centre, executed by Mr. J. G. Bubb in 1821, is of lithargolite or artificial stone, and represents the progress of music from the earliest attention to sound, to its then degree of perfection ; length from the curtain to the back of boxes 102 feet; width from the back of boxes 75 feet; projection of stage from the curtain 24 feet; width of the curtain 40 feet; and height from floor to ceiling, at the highest part over the pit, 56 feet.

k

Joiners' Hall, Upper Thames Street.

Judges' Chambers, Clifford's Inn, erected 1837 instead of old ones in Serjeants' Inn.

King's College, Strand, commenced Sept. 1829, and opened 1831 ; neat arch of entrance; it adjoins Somerset House, and the house of the Principal, &c. forms the eastern part of the river front; architect, Sir Robert Smirke; consists of a spacious chapel and hall, lecture rooms, library, &c.

King's College Hospital, Portugal Street, for accidents and diseases, established 1839.

Law Institution, Chancery Lane, erected by shares, and incorporated by royal charter, very fine Ionic portico ; architect, Vulliamy.

Leadenhall Market, for country killed meat, poultry, skins, and leather ; partly rebuilt in 1730 ; again in 1814.

Leathersellers' Hall, St. Helen's Place, Bishopsgate, erected 1820-2.

Lincoln's Inn, Chancery Lane, on the site of the house of the Lacys Earls of Lincoln, founded 1310. The Stone Buildings erected by Sir Robert Taylor ; the hall, a noble and well-proportioned room, erected in the time of Henry VII. is used for the sittings of the Lord Chancellor ; the gateway in Chancery Lane was begun in the 23d year of Henry VII. but not finished till the 12th of Henry VIII.: the chapel was rebuilt by Inigo Jones, 1620, at a cost of £2,000, and repaired by Wyatt in 1791, at a cost of £7,000, and has a tablet to the memory of Spencer Perceval, and a statue of Lord Erskine ; the Vice Chancellor's Court, erected in 1816; the library is good; the MSS. were bequeathed by Sir Matthew Hale.

Linnæan Society, Soho Square, instituted in 1788, by Sir J. E. Smith, for the encouragement of botany and natural history ; their house was bequeathed to them by Sir Joseph Banks ; incorporated in 1802.

Linwood Gallery, Leicester Square, formed by Miss Linwood for the exhibition of copies in needlework of some of the finest pictures.

Literary Fund Society, 72, Great Russell Street, Bloomsbury, instituted 1790, and incorporated 1818, to relieve authors and their widows and orphans.

Lock Hospital, Grosvenor Place, for syphilitic maladies.

London Assurance Corporation, Birchin Lane, established by royal charter in 1720.

London Bridge, one of timber, erected by order of King Ethelred in 1002; rebuilt by William Rufus 1097; another in 1165; one of stone and rubble in 1176, by Peter of Colechurch, curate and architect, and finished in 1209, being a work of 33 years. It had a drawbridge in the middle, and till the middle of the 18th century was covered with houses, gates, and a chapel. It was 930 feet in length, 20 in width, and 40 in height; it had 19 pointed arches, and the span of the centre was 70 feet; its waterway surface above the starlings was 540 feet, and below them 273 feet; and the space of the solids or piers in the width of the river was, above the starlings 396 feet, and below them 657 feet. It was altered by Mr. Dance and Sir R. Taylor, in 1759, and widened to 48 feet; many alterations were afterwards made, but nothing satisfactory. At length, a new one, of five semi-elliptic arches, of granite, designed by J. Rennie, was commenced 180 feet higher up the river by driving the first pile on March 15, 1824; the foundation stone was laid with great ceremony on June 15, 1825; finished July 31, 1831. It was opened by the king on the first of August. In length it is 920 feet, in width 56, and in height 55; the span of the centre arch is 150 feet, the

waterway 690, and the span of piers 92 feet. The quantity of stone used was 120,000 tons.

London Docks, between Ratcliffe Highway and the Thames;
opened 1805; covers 20 acres of ground; a branch dock
opened 1828; a magnificent jetty, affording a quay front-
age of 1,600 feet, 62 feet wide, erected 1839; cost
£60,000.

London, Edinburgh, and Dublin Life Assurance, Charlotte
Row, Mansion House.

London Hospital, Whitechapel road, established in 1740;
present edifice erected 1760, and subsequently enlarged.

London Institution, Moorfields, containing library, reading
rooms, theatre, &c., instituted 1805; present building
erected 1815-19, William Brooks, architect; front 100 feet
wide; magnificent Corinthian portico; the library is 97
feet by 42 in width, and 28 in height; the theatre will
accommodate about 600 persons.

London Maritime Institution, for alleviating the distress
of Master Mariners and their families; founded Oct. 12,
1790.

London Ophthalmic Infirmary, Moorfields, instituted in 1804
by the late John Cunningham Saunders, for the preven-
tion and cure of blindness; removed hither from Charter-
house Square in 1821, the present building being erected
at an expense of £8,000, by legacy of Harry Sedgwick,
Esq.

London University College, Gower Street, building commenced April 30, 1827; foundation stone laid by Duke of
Sussex; architect William Wilkins; the portico of ten
columns is most magnificent; and the whole exterior im-
posing and elegant; not completed, but opened for the
reception of students in 1828; new charter granted 1838.

Lowther Arcade, from the Strand to St. Martin's Church;

length 245 feet, width 20, height 35; erected in 1832; a double range of houses for shopkeepers with a covered walk.

Lyon's Inn, Wych Street, Strand, an appendage to the Inner Temple; handsome hall.

Mansion House, erected pursuant to a resolution of the Common Council in 1734; first stone laid Oct. 25, 1739; architect, George Dance, who was originally a shipwright, finished in 1753. It is of Portland stone, is solid and massive, dark and heavy; the sculptures consist of figures representing the presiding genius of the city; a Roman lictor and boy holding a cap of liberty; Neptune; emblems of commerce and plenty. They were designed and executed by Taylor; the whole building has been likened to "a deep-laden Indiaman, with her stern galleries and gingerbread work. The stairs and passages within are all ladders and gangways; and the superstructure at top, answers pretty accurately to the idea we usually form of Noah's Ark;" repaired 1840.

Marine Society, Bishopsgate Street, for training boys for the sea service, founded by Jonas Hanway, 1756; incorporated 1772; first stone laid April 30, 1773; in the front of the building is a figure of a female taking a helpless boy to her care.

Masons' Hall, Basinghall Street.

Masters in Chancery Office, Southampton Buildings, Holborn.

Mathematical Society, Crispin Street, Spitalfields, formed in 1717 by journeymen mechanics; lectures are delivered here.

Mechanics' Institution, Southampton Buildings, Holborn, established in 1823, by Dr. Birkbeck; there is a theatre capable of holding 1000 persons, and class rooms, reading rooms, library, laboratory, &c.

Medical Society, Bolt Court, Fleet Street, formed in 1773; their house given to them by Dr. Lettsom in 1788; an extensive library.

Medico-Chirurgical Society, Lincoln's Inn Fields, founded 1805; extensive professional library.

Mercers' Hall, Ironmonger Lane, Cheapside, on the site of the mercery where the father of St. Thomas à Becket had a mercer's shop, and where the archbishop was born; rebuilt after the fire of 1666; enriched entrance; the piazzas very noble and spacious.

Merchant-Taylors' Hall, Threadneedle Street, erected 16th century.

Merchant-Taylors' School, Suffolk Lane, Cannon Street, founded in 1561 by Sir Thomas White; the present building, erected in 1666 after the fire of London; has a chapel and library.

Meteorological Society, 20, Bedford Street, Covent Garden; established 1823; revived 1836.

Metropolitan Church Building Society, for building new Churches in the Metropolis. Numerous have been the churches erected through the aid of this Society.

Mews, on site of Old Sanctuary and Market, Prince's Street, Westminster, erected 1828; architect, Decimus Burton.

Microscopical Society, 21, Regent Street; established 1840.

Middlesex Hospital, Charles Street, Berners Street, instituted 1745; a ward appropriated in 1747 to parturient married women, and another ward in 1792 to cases of cancer; enlarged 1834; Medical School annexed in 1836.

Middlesex House of Correction, Cold Bath Fields, built on plan of Howard the philanthropist; opened 1794, and cost about £80,000.

Milton Literary Institution, Fore Street, Cripplegate, established 1836.

Mint, Tower Hill, large, commodious, and handsome building, for the coinage of monies; architect, Sir Robert Smirke.

Monument, Fish Street Hill, a Doric column, erected by Act of Parliament, from designs by Sir Christopher Wren, to commemorate the Fire of London, which in 1666 broke out near that spot; height of pedestal 40 feet; diameter at base 15 feet; height of shaft 120 feet; the cone at top and blazing urn of gilt brass 42 feet; total 202 feet; begun 1671, and completed 1677; cost £14,500; there are inscriptions, in Latin and English, descriptive of the fire and the rebuilding of the city; it is higher than the celebrated columns of Trajan and Antonine at Rome, and Theodosius at Constantinople; the staircase is of black marble, and contains 345 steps.

National Debt Redemption Office, Old Jewry; architect, Sir John Soane.

National Gallery of Paintings, Charing Cross; began 1832; opened April 9, 1838; architect, Wilkins. The pictures now (Jan. 1841) number 177; and some of them are of the very highest order. In the hall is the Waterloo Vase, executed in marble by R. Westmacott, and without doubt the largest and most splendid vase in the world. In this building the Royal Academy have rooms for their annual exhibition of Works of Art, and for their collection of casts and models.

Naval (Royal) Club, 160, Bond Street.

Nelson Memorial, Trafalgar Square, the foundation stone, being a block of Dartmoor granite weighing 14 tons, was laid Oct. 1840, of a column designed by Railton, and to be surmounted by a statue of the hero of Trafalgar, by Baily, and flanked by four colossal lions by Lough.

Newgate Prison, originally one of the City Gates; a prison

as early as 1218; one of the largest structures in the Metropolis; architect, George Dance, first stone laid by Alderman Beckford 1770; interior destroyed by fire in the riots of 1780; completed about 1782; principal front 300 feet in length, depth of building 192 feet; the walls of massive rustic stone work, 50 feet high; the prison consists of three differently sized quadrangles; the principal wards and rooms in all the stations are each about 38 feet in length, and 15 feet wide, the others about 24 feet by 15; interior arrangements much improved in 1837.

New Inn, Wych Street, Strand, an appendage to the Middle Temple.

Numismatic Society, Tavistock Street, Covent Garden; founded 1836.

Olympic Theatre, Wych Street; opened 1806, as an equestrian theatre, by P. Astley.

Ordnance Office, Pall Mall.

Oriental Club, Hanover Square.

Ornithological Society's Buildings, St. James's Park; designed by Watson in the Swiss style, erected 1840. On the ornamental water are a number of curious water-fowl belonging to the Society. The offices of the Society are in Regent Street.

Oxford and Cambridge Universities' Club House, Pall Mall; erected in 1837-8 from the designs of Sir Robert Smirke and his brother Sydney Smirke, of Corinthian order; the bas-reliefs in the panels above the windows of the principal floor were executed in Roman cement by Mr. W. G. Nicholl, from designs by R. Smirke, esq. The centre panel represents Minerva and Apollo presiding on Mount Parnassus, a female figure personifying the river Helicon pours from an urn sacred to the god of verse, and the Muses surround them at the foot of the mount. In one of the extreme panels Homer is represented singing to a warrior, a female, and a youth; in the other is Virgil reciting his Georgics to a group of peasants. The four other panels represent Milton reciting his verses to his daughter, inspired by a superior agency hovering over him ; Shakspere attended by Tragedy and Comedy ; Newton explaining his system; and Bacon recommending his philosophy. The interior is spacious and elegant.

Painter Stainers' Hall, Little Trinity Lane, Thames Street.

Pantechnicon, Belgrave Square, for the sale of carriages, works of art, &c.; the extensive premises are fire proof.

Pantheon, Oxford Street ; originally erected by James Wyatt; afterwards fitted up as a theatre; and now a bazaar of great beauty and extent, as altered by Mr. Sydney Smirke in 1834.

Parish Clerks' Hall, Wood Street, Cheapside.

Parthenon Club, St. James's Square.

Pelican Life Office, Lombard Street, architect, Sir Robert Taylor, and pronounced to be his masterpiece ; the emblematic group in front of the building was designed by Lady Diana Beauclerk, and executed at Coade's manufactory, by M. de Vááre.

Penitentiary, Milbank, Westminster, for the reformation of offenders; erected partly on the plan of Jeremy Bentham; external wall encloses eighteen acres of land, on which are several pentagonal buildings, with the Governor's house in the centre ; cost about £500,000; partly opened in 1816.

Pewterers' Hall, Lime Street, solid brick building, enclosing a small court, built 1678; much damaged by fire in February 1840.

Phrenological Institution, 7, King William Street, West Strand, founded in 1840.

Phrenological Society, Exeter Hall, established 1824.

Philomathic Society.

Pinmakers' Hall, Broad Street.

Plasterers' Hall, Addle Street, Cheapside.

Plumbers' Hall, Dowgate Hill.

Polytechnic Institution, Regent Street, incorporated by royal charter in 1838, for the exhibition of mechanical and scientific novelties, and works of art.

Portman Street Bazaar, a very large and convenient structure, containing riding-house, repository for 300 carriages, extensive stabling, and a ladies' bazaar of 2000 feet in extent.

Post Office, St. Martin's le Grand, Act passed 1815; first stone laid in May 1824; and opened September 1829; architect, Sir Robert Smirke; the principal front 380 feet in length, relieved by three Ionic porticos. The Grand Public Hall is 80 feet by 60, and is divided into three colonnades by two rows of six Ionic columns. The offices are very conveniently arranged. The old Post Office in Lombard Street was originally the house of Sir Robert Vyner, Lord Mayor in 1675. There is a branch establishment at Gerrard Street, Soho, for the London district, and receiving houses at Lombard Street and Charing Cross.

Prince's Theatre, King Street, St. James's; erected in 1836 . by Beazley, for Mr. Braham; the façade is of pure Roman architecture.

Princess's Theatre, see Queen's Bazaar.

Privy Council Office, Board of Trade, &c. at Whitehall, commenced in February 1824, and part of it completed in October 1825; of the Corinthian order, from the temple of Jupiter Stator at Rome; architect, Soane; part of an unfinished plan, the other wing to be on the other side of Downing Street, and connected by a triumphal arch.

Queen's Bazaar, Oxford Street; Princess's Theatre (now closed).

Queen's Theatre, Tottenham Court Road.

Red Cross Street, Library, founded for Protestant Dissenting Ministers about 1716, by Dr. Williams; very extensive collection of theological books.

Reform Club House, Pall Mall, adjoining the Travellers' Club House; architect, Barry; opened 1841.

The Rolls, Chancery Lane, wherein the rolls in Chancery, &c. have been deposited since 1483; there is a small and ancient chapel attached, in which the rolls are kept. In the gardens have recently been built Chambers for the Judges.

Roman Catholic Chapel, Moorfields, foundation stone laid Aug. 5, 1817, and covered in about the end of the following November; architect, John Newman, Esq.; consecrated April 20, 1820; the ceiling and altar are finely painted in fresco, representing the Crucifixion, Assumption of the Virgin, and many other scriptural subjects, by Signor Aglio; the sanctuary is very splendid, and is lighted without the means employed for the admission of light being discovered; there are six fluted Corinthian columns, of Como marble, each of one piece, 18 feet in height and 2 in diameter; and a richly sculptured altar of Carrara marble, all executed by Signor Comolli of Milan; the situation of the altar is unusual, being in the west; the cost of the erection and decorations was £26,000. A superb chalice and patina of fine gold, valued at 5,000 Roman crowns, was presented by Pope Pius VII.; and the pulpit was the gift of Lord Arundell of Wardour.

Royal Academy of Music, Tenterden Street, Hanover Square, for the instruction of persons of both sexes in the art of music; incorporated by George IV. 1822.

Royal British Scientific Institution, Pall Mall.

Royal Exchange, Cornhill, first stone of a bourse, after the model of that at Antwerp, laid by Sir Thomas Gresham, June 7, 1566, on ground given him by the city; proclaimed the Royal Exchange by Queen Elizabeth, Jan. 23, 1570-1; destroyed by the fire of London in September 1666; rebuilt 1667-8; architect, Edward Jerman; cost £58,962, defrayed in equal moieties by the City and Mercers' Company; repaired in 1767 and west side rebuilt, towards which Parliament granted £10,000; destroyed by fire in 1838; commenced rebuilding in 1840 from designs by Tite; to afford additional room the church of St. Bartholomew was pulled down, and the tower of the church of St. Benedict Fink was removed. The funds for the rebuilding to be mainly raised under an Act of Parliament by a tax on coals.

Royal Gallery of Practical Science, Lowther Arcade, Strand, incorporated 1834.

Royal Harmonic Institution, corner of Little Argyle Street, Regent Street.

Royal Humane Society, for the recovery of persons apparently drowned, Trafalgar Square; established in 1774, by Dr. Cogan and Dr. Hawes.

Royal Institute of British Architects, Lower Grosvenor Street, founded in 1834.

Royal Institution, Albemarle Street, originated mainly through the celebrated Count Rumford in 1799, for the encouragement of useful inventions, and for lectures on philosophical science; it consists of a news-room, a reading library, a mineral cabinet, apparatus-room, théatre capable of accommodating 700 persons, a library, and repository of models of machines, &c.; incorporated by charter of George IV.

Royal Society of Literature, St. Martin's Lane, founded

1823, by George IV., chiefly by the exertions of Bishop Burgess.

Royal Society of Musicians, Lisle Street, Soho, established April 1738.

Royal Society, Somerset House, founded 1648; incorporated 1662.

Royal Westminster Ophthalmic Infirmary, Charing Cross, for diseases of the eyes; founded in 1816.

Russell Institution, Great Coram Street, Russell Square, originally for concerts and dancing, purchased in 1808 for a literary institution at a cost of 5,000 guineas.

Saddlers' Hall, Cheapside, erected 1823.

Sailors' Home, for the reception of sailors on their return ashore; on the ruins of the Brunswick Theatre, Goodman's Fields, which was built 1827-8, and fell down on the morning before the first night of performance, through the weight of the iron roof being too great for the walls. Several persons were killed.

St. Anne's Society's Schools, near the Post Office, and at Brixton Hill, Surrey, for educating, clothing, and providing for children from all parts. The asylum at Brixton Hill holds 100 boys and 50 girls; architect, J. H. Taylor.

St. Bartholomew's Hospital, West Smithfield, given to the corporation of London on the suppression of Monasteries by Henry VIII.; rebuilt in 1730 from designs by Gibbs; but the entrance from Smithfield, with figures of Lameness and Sickness, and a statue of Henry VIII. was erected in 1702. The grand staircase was gratuitously painted by Hogarth, and in the great hall are several portraits.

St. George's Hospital, Hyde Park Corner, established 1733, by subscription; rebuilt 1830-1; architect, W. Wilkins; grand front 200 feet in length; contains 160 beds.

St. James's Palace, St. James's Park, built by Henry VIII. on site of a hospital for lepers; its ancient character remains only in portions, in consequence of repeated alterations; but its interior arrangements are magnificent, and the most convenient for purposes of state of any in the Metropolis.

St. Katharine's Docks, by the Tower, first stone laid May 3, 1827, and opened October 25, 1828; 2,500 men were constantly employed during the eighteen months; to provide the ground 11,300 persons were obliged to remove, and 1,250 houses were pulled down; the area of the docks is twenty-four acres, of which eleven and a half are devoted to wet docks, into which ships may enter at any time in perfect safety; engineer, Telford; lock-gates, &c. manufactured by Bramah; cost nearly one million and a half.

St. Luke's Hospital, Old Street, established as an asylum for lunatics in 1732; present building commenced 1751, and completed 1786; cost £55,000.

St. Paul's School, St. Paul's Churchyard, founded in 1509, by Dr. John Colet, Dean of St. Paul's; taken down and rebuilt 1822, from designs by G. Smith.

Salters' Hall, Cannon Street, rebuilt by Henry Carr, Esq. 1823, and opened in May 1827; Ionic portico of four columns; interior tastefully decorated.

School of Design, Somerset House, established 1837.

Scottish Hospital, Crane Court, Fleet Street, founded by James Kinnier in 1665.

Serjeants' Inn, Chancery Lane, has a hall and chapel, with seats for the Judges.

Sessions' House, Old Bailey, and New Court adjoining.

Sion College, London Wall, founded by will of the Rev. Dr. Thomas White, Vicar of St. Dunstan's in the West, dated Oct. 1, 1623, for the clergy of London. There is a hall, library of about 25,000 books, and almshouses for twenty poor persons.

Six Clerks' Office, Chancery Lane.

Skinners' Hall, Dowgate Hill, handsome structure, elegant
façade, and grand apartments; architect, Robert Adam.

Small Pox Hospital, Battle Bridge, erected in 1767, and
removed hither from a house in Windmill Street, Tottenham Court Road, where it was established in 1746; vaccination introduced by Dr. Woodville in 1799, and the
original purpose of the hospital has been since superseded.

Soane's Museum, 13, Lincoln's Inn Fields, collected by the
late Sir John Soane, architect, and placed in a house built
by himself in 1812. It contains a good library, many antique vases and sculptures, the Belzoni Egyptian Sarco-
phagus, for which Sir John Soane paid £2,000; several
pictures, particularly the Rake's Progress, and the Elec-
tion, by Hogarth; bequeathed to the public on the death
of the proprietor in 1833, and opened to the public every
Thursday and Friday in April, May, and June.

Society of Arts, originated March 1754, house in John Street,
Adelphi, erected for them by the Messrs. Adams, four en-
terprising brothers and architects, in 1772-4; decorated
with a series of six paintings, analogous to the purposes
of the institution, by James Barry, Esq. R.A. being intended to demonstrate that the "attainment of happiness,
both individual and public, depends on the cultivation of
the human faculties." They are equally an honour to
the British school, and an ornament to the capital.

Soho Bazaar, opened in 1815 by Mr. Trotter; the first of
the kind in the Metropolis; of great extent.

Somerset House, Strand, so named from the protector
Edward Seymour Duke of Somerset, who here, in 1549,
built a palace from the designs of John of Padua.
On the attainder of the Duke it was granted by
Edward VI. to his sister the Princess Elizabeth; and
Anne of Denmark, James the First's queen, kept a splen-

did court here. It was subsequently the palace of Henri-
etta-Maria, Charles's queen, who had a convent of capu-
chin friars here, a circumstance which contributed to
aggravate the unhappy differences of the period. In
April 1659 the Commons ordered Somerset House to be
sold; but on the Restoration it was again inhabited by Hen-
rietta-Maria, who is reported to have said, " Had I known
the temper of the English some years past as well as I do
now, I had never been obliged to leave this house." It
was subsequently occupied by royalty or the foreign ambassadors, till appropriated by Act 1775 for public offices,
when the present building was commenced from designs
by Sir William Chambers. The first stone laid in 1776.
The front to the Strand, which has a chaste and elegant
façade, is 135 feet wide and 61 deep, and is embellished by
sculptured figures and masks; the quadrangular court is
240 feet wide and 296 deep, surrounded by buildings 54
feet deep; the Thames front 800 feet long, (completed by
the addition of King's College in 1834), is one of the
boldest architectural objects in the Metropolis; the terrace
promenade is 46 feet wide, and is erected on a series of
lofty arches. Many departments of Government have
offices here.

South Sea House, Threadneedle Street, for the Company of
Merchants trading to the South Seas, incorporated in 1710.
A substantial brick building, in which is one room large
and elegant.

Southwark Bridge, from Queen Street, Cheapside, of three
colossal cast iron arches; commenced September 23, 1814,
and opened in April 1819; J. Rennie, engineer; cost
£800,000. In length it is 700 feet, in width 42, and in
height 53; the span of central arch is 240 feet; the surface of waterway 660 feet, and the space of piers 48 feet;
the arches are of the largest span of any known to exist,

the centre being four feet wider than the famous iron bridge at Sunderland. The total weight of iron is about 5,780 tons, and many of the solid castings weigh 10 tons each ; the whole was cast at the works of Messrs. Walker and Co. at Rotherham, co. York. The settling of the centre arch at the vertex was only one inch and seven-eighths, which was exactly one-eighth of an inch less than what had been allowed for in putting it together.

Staple's Inn, Holborn, an appendage to Gray's Inn. In the hall are busts of the twelve Cæsars on brackets.

State Paper Office, St. James's Park, erected in 1833 ; architect, Sir John Soane.

Stationers' Hall, Ludgate Hill, on site of a residence of John Duke of Bretagne, temp. Edward II. ; rebuilt after the fire of 1666, when their loss, with property, was £200,000 ; modernized in 1800 ; hall window of painted modern glass, the work of Egginton, and the gift of Alderman Cadell, the bookseller, Sheriff of London in 1801.

Statistical Society, St. Martin's Place, established 1834.

Stock Exchange, Capel Court, erected by subscription in 1801, for conducting the business of Stockbrokers, who alone are admitted ; handsome interior ; architect, Mr. James Peacock.

Sun Fire and Life Insurance Office, established in 1710 ; Office in Bartholomew Lane, now erecting ; will cost £20,000.

Symond's Inn, Chancery Lane, formerly the residence of the Masters in Chancery.

Tallow Chandlers' Hall, Dowgate Hill, handsome building, erected 1672.

Temple Bar, commenced in 1670, and finished in 1672 ; architect, Sir Christopher Wren ; it is of Portland stone, and has statues of Charles I. and II. in Roman costume, and of Elizabeth and James. Over this gateway it was customary to place the heads of those executed for treason. Those of the Lords concerned in the Pretender rebellion 1745, were the last here placed.

Thames Tunnel, suggested by Mr. Brunel in 1823 (one commenced near the spot in 1809 having been abandoned); foundation stone laid 2d of March 1825; on May 18, 1825, when a distance of 400 feet had been advanced, the water burst in from above while 120 men were at work, but no lives were lost; the works were recommenced in September, and a second irruption took place Jan. 12, 1828, when six men were drowned; the tunnel was at length completed in 1841, and opened in 1842; it consists of two passages, each 16 feet wide, with carriageway and footpath ; it leads from Wapping to Rotherhithe.

Thavies' Inn, Holborn, appendage to Lincoln's Inn.

The Temple, Inns of Court, are an extensive range of buildings between Fleet Street and the Strand and the River. There are two Societies, the Inner Temple and the Middle Temple. The buildings consist of halls, chapels, libraries, and chambers. The hall of the Middle Temple, built 1562-72, is spacious, and has a fine timber roof; the library was built 1822-4, Hakewill architect. Inner Temple hall, rebuilt 1816, library 1819. The Middle Temple Gate was built by Wren 1684-8.

Tilers' and Bricklayers' Hall, Leadenhall Street.

Tothill Fields Prison, Westminster, rebuilt in 1836; architect Abrahams.

Tower, surrounded by a ditch, the circumference of which is 330 yards ; there is a double line of walls inclosing an area of 12 acres ; the White Tower was the Norman citadel or keep ; it now contains Record Offices, and armoury; Ordnance Office, erected in 1788, extensive edifice; Grand Store

House, finished in the time of William and Mary, containing the artillery; Small Armoury; New Horse Armoury; Spanish Armoury; Jewel Tower; Governor's House; Chapel of St. Peter ad Vincula; Record Office or Wakefield Tower; and Bloody Tower.

Travellers' Club House, Pall Mall, adjoining the Athenæum, erected in 1832; architect, Barry; resembles a Roman palace.

Treasury, St. James's Park, erected by Kent; of three stories, displaying the Tuscan, Doric, and Ionic orders; the Whitehall front was originally the Chapel of Wolsey's Palace of Whitehall.

Trinity House, Tower Hill, for the Corporation of Trinity of Deptford Strond, in whom are vested the appointment of pilots, erection of lighthouses, and sea marks, &c. on the British coasts and seas; first stone laid by William Pitt, Sept. 18, 1793, architect, Samuel Wyatt; opened 1795. Here are shown many portraits, and models.

Vaccine Institution, Providence Row, Finsbury, for gratuitous vaccination, and supply of vaccine lymph.

Vauxhall Bridge, of cast iron, nine arches of equal span; commenced in May 1811, opened in August 1816; designed by James Walker, but Mr. Ralph Dodd, Sir James Bentham, and Mr. Rennie were also employed; cost about £300,000; length 809 feet, width 36, span of each arch 78 feet, height 29; the piers are of stone.

Vintners' Hall, Upper Thames Street, rebuilt by Sir Christopher Wren; handsome; the interior of the hall very elegant.

Union Fire and Life and Annuity Assurance Company, Cornhill.

Union Club House, Charing Cross, erected 1824; adjoins the College of Physicians; architect, Sir Robert Smirke; contains some of the finest rooms in Europe.

United Service (Senior) Club House, Pall Mall, erected 1828; architect, Nash.

United Service (Junior) Club House, corner of Charles Street, Regent Street.

United Service Institution, Whitehall, established 1831 ; contains a library, model room, mineralogical, geological, antiquarian, and numismatic collections ; easily accessible to the public, by an introduction from a member.

University Club House, Suffolk Street, for gentlemen of both Universities ; the number is limited to 500 from each ; commenced in 1822, and opened Feb. 13, 1826; architects, William Wilkins and J. P. Gandy ; cost £26,500.

Upholders' Hall, Crane Court, St. Peter's Hill.

Water Colour Painters' Society, Suffolk Street, Pall Mall East, formed in 1804, to encourage this branch of the Arts; gallery erected 1823, and opened 1824. The New Society has its gallery at 53, Pall Mall.

Waterloo Bridge, in the Strand, of nine semi-elliptical arches, of Cornish granite ; Act obtained in 1809 ; commenced in October 1811, and opened in June 1817, by the Duke of Wellington ; projected by Ralph Dodd ; architect, J. Rennie ; cost £1,000,000; in length it is 1,326 feet ; width 42, height 54 ; the span of each arch 120 feet ; the surface of waterway is 1,080 feet ; and the space of the piers 160 feet ; the roads or approaches to either end of this bridge are 70 feet in width, except at the entrance from the Strand. They are carried over a series of semi-circular arches, each 16 feet in span. The approach on the Surrey side is formed by 39 of these arches, besides an elliptical arch of 26 feet span, over the Narrow-wall Road, and a small embankment about 165 yards long ; the whole length of the brick arches in the Surrey approach is

766 feet, of those in the Strand approach 310; length of bridge from the ends of the abutments 1,380 feet; making a total of 2,456 feet. It is one of the most stupendous works of modern times.

Watermen's Hall, St. Mary Hill, Thames Street. Here is a portrait of Taylor the Water Poet.

Wax Chandlers' Hall, Maiden Lane, modern building, handsome.

Weavers' Hall, Basinghall Street, of brick; in the interior is an Ionic screen.

Wesleyan Centenary Hall, Bishopsgate Street. The Society in 1839, with a portion of the money subscribed to mark the centenary of Methodism, purchased the disused City of London Tavern, to convert into Missionary Offices, &c. and a new and handsome façade of the Corinthian order has been put to it from designs by W. T. Pocock.

Western Exchange Bazaar, Bond Street, established in 1817.

Western Literary and Scientific Institution, Leicester Square, established in 1825; and is held in the house formerly inhabited by Sir Joshua Reynolds; a Lecture Room, &c. built at the back, in Princes Street, in 1839; architect, Godwin.

West India Club, 60, St. James's Street.

Westminster Bridge, of Portland stone, fifteen arches; Act passed 1736, commenced in January 1739, and finished in 1750, being 11 years and nine months; it cost £389,500; architect, Monsieur Labelye, a native of Switzerland; length 1,066 feet, width 42, height 58; the span of centre arch 76 feet; surface of waterway 820; space of piers 246. There is always under water materials to the value of £40,000.

Westminster Hall, a building of great scientific skill, erected

in 1097-8, by William Rufus, as the great hall of the
palace he designed to rebuild; it was repaired and re-
modelled by Richard II. in 1397, to such an extent as to be
almost a new building; the alterations were completed in
1399, and the original contract for them is still preserved
in the office of the Clerk of the Pells. Within the last
few years it has been entirely renovated and restored. It
is one of the finest vaulted rooms in the world unsup-
ported by pillars; originally divided into three ailes.

Westminster Hospital, by the Abbey, founded originally in
1719 at James Street, Buckingham Gate; the present
edifice begun 1832, opened in 1834; architect, Inwood;
cost £39,000; the oldest hospital in London supported
by voluntary subscriptions.

Westminster Literary, Scientific, and Mechanics' Institution, Smith Street, Westminster, established in 1837;
building erected 1840.

Westminster School, or St. Peter's College, Dean's Yard,
founded in 1070; refounded by Queen Elizabeth in 1560
for 40 boys; but the boarders have generally been far
more numerous.

Whitecross Street Prison, for debtors, built between the
years 1813 and 1815, in consequence of the crowded state
of Newgate Prison, where debtors and criminals had been
previously indiscriminately confined.

Whitehall Chapel, originally built for the banqueting house
to the new palace of James I. by Inigo Jones; it was begun in 1619, and executed in two years, by Nicholas
Stone, Master Mason to the King, at the cost of £17,000.
It was pronounced in 1685, by Mons. d'Azout, the famous
French architect, to be "the most finished of the modern
buildings on this side the Alps." The ceiling, painted on
canvass by Rubens and his pupil Jordaens, is esteemed

one of the finest in the world. It represents the apotheosis of James I. The artist received £3,000 for it; and in 1778 Cipriani had 2,000 guineas for cleaning it. The whole building has been extensively repaired, and the interior cleaned and retouched within a few years.

White's Club, 38, St. James's Street.

Windsor Club, 6, Waterloo Place.

York Stairs Water Gate, Buckingham Street, Strand, designed and erected by Inigo Jones about 1626; originally connected with the house of the Duke of Buckingham on this site; of Portland stone, and rustic work.

Zoological Society, established 1826; this Society has a museum, containing an extensive collection of specimens of mammalia, birds, reptiles, and fishes, testacea and crustacea, and insects; and delightful and extensive gardens, with a large collection of living animals, birds, &c. in the Regent's Park; where also they are about to erect buildings for the reception of their museum.

STATUES.

Achilles, Hyde Park, colossal, of bronze, by Westmacott;
18 feet high; copied from one of two figures found on
the Quirinal at Rome grouped with horses; erected in
1822, by a subscription among the ladies of England,
in honour of the Duke of Wellington; said to have cost
£30,000.

Anne, Queen, in front of St. Paul's Cathedral, with figures
of the four quarters of the globe at her feet; by Francis
Bird. This group cost £1180.

—— another Statue in Queen Square, Westminster.

Bedford, Francis Russell, Duke of, Russell Square; in
bronze, by Westmacott; figure 9 feet high; put up
1809.

Canning, George, Palace Yard, Westminster; pedestrian,
colossal; of bronze, by Chantrey; likeness good; drapery
heavy.

Cartwright, Major, Burton Crescent; bronze, by Clarke of
Birmingham; sitting figure, larger than life.

Charles I. at Charing Cross; bronze, equestrian, cast in
1633 by Hubert le Sueur, and erected at the expense of
Thomas Howard, Earl of Arundel; ordered by the Parliament to be destroyed, when it was bought by John
River, a brazier, in Holborn, who hid it till the Restoration of Charles II. when in 1678 it was re-erected on a
pedestal ornamented by Grinling Gibbons; the likeness
most perfect.

Charles II. Soho Square; pedestrian, in marble, with figures representing the rivers Thames, Severn, Trent, and Humber at his feet; erected by his son the unfortunate Duke of Monmouth.

———— in the area of the late Royal Exchange by Spiller; a fine work, and will probably be re-erected. The series of statues of Sovereigns round the building, by Cibber, Rysbrack, Wilton, &c. were much injured at the fire in 1838, and sold with the materials. That of Sir Thomas Gresham was destroyed; but one of Sir John Barnard escaped.

Cumberland, William Duke of, Cavendish Square; equestrian; erected 1770.

Edward VI. at Christ's Hospital, opposite Christ Church Passage.

Elizabeth, above the entrance to the parochial schools, adjacent to St. Dunstan's Church in the West.

Fox, Charles James, Bloomsbury Square; colossal, holding a roll of Magna Charta; in bronze, by Westmacott, likeness admirable, and figure good; erected 1816.

George I. on horseback, Leicester Square; of gilt bronze, modelled by C. Buchard for the Duke of Chandos; brought hither from Canons.

———— on horseback, Grosvenor Square; erected by Sir Robert Grosvenor in 1726; the work of Van Nort.

———— on the top of the steeple of Bloomsbury church.

George III. Pall Mall East; an admirable likeness of the monarch, mounted on his favourite charger; in fine bronze by Mr. Matthew Cotes Wyatt; is between ten and eleven feet high, and stands on a pedestal of Portland stone, twelve feet high; erected 1836; cost £4,000.

James II. Whitehall; pedestrian, bronze, cast by Grinling Gibbons in 1687; considered a good likeness; attitude easy and graceful.

Kent, Duke of, son of George III. and father of the Queen, erected by public subscription, at the top of Portland Place; pedestrian, in bronze, by Gahagan ; good likeness; wants altitude.

Nelson, Horatio Viscount, on top of a column in Trafalgar Square, designed by Railton, now in the course of erection, the statue by Baily.

Pitt, William, Hanover Square ; pedestrian, colossal, of bronze, by Chantrey ; erected 1831.

Victoria, Queen, pedestrian, in Victoria Square, Pimlico.

William III. St. James's Square; in a Roman habit, on horseback, by Bacon ; the horse modelled from a favourite horse of George III.

———— in the Great Hall of the Bank of England; pedestrian.

York, Duke of, son of George III. at top of a Doric column of Scotch granite, Carlton Terrace ; pedestrian, bronze, by Chantrey; cost £7,000, independent of column; height of column 123 ft. 6 in. ; of figure 13 ft. 9 in. ; fine and extensive panoramic view from the summit of the column.

CHURCHES.

St. Alban, Wood Street, originally founded by King Athelstan; rebuilt in 1634 by Inigo Jones; destroyed by fire in 1666; and rebuilt 1685, in Pointed style, architect, Wren; cost £3,165; height of tower 85 feet; richly ornamented altar-pieces; finely carved pulpit; to the right of the reading desk is an hour-glass and enriched brass frame.

Allhallows, Barking, Tower Street, belonged to the Abbey of Barking in Essex; the steeple built 1659; escaped the fire.

Allhallows, Bread Street, erected in 1684; architect, Wren; tower 86 feet high; pulpit finely carved.

Allhallows the Great, Thames Street, rebuilt by Wren in 1683; cost £5,641; in the interior is a beautiful screen made at Hamburg, and presented by the Hanseatic merchants in 1670.

Allhallows, Lombard Street, built in 1694 by Sir Christopher Wren, on site of one erected before the year 1053, and rebuilt 1516; cost £8,058; the carving of the door cases is very beautiful.

Allhallows, London Wall, escaped the fire; present church built by Dance, jun. in 1767.

Allhallows Staining, Mark Lane, fell down 1669, and soon rebuilt; part as old as the time of Henry III.

All Saints, King's Cross, consecrated July 5, 1838; will accommodate 1,000 persons; cost £3,200, to which the Metropolitan Churches Fund contributed £1,000.

All Saints, Skinner Street, belongs to Bishopsgate parish; first stone laid in June 1838; architect, Meredith.

St. Andrew by the Wardrobe, built in 1692; architect, Wren; cost £7,060.

St. Andrew, Holborn, erected in 1687, under the direction of Sir Christopher Wren; 105 feet in length, 63 in breadth, and 43 in height; the tower is 110 feet high, and was not completed till 1704; the altar-piece and roof are richly ornamented.

St. Andrew Undershaft, Leadenhall Street, rebuilt 1525, at the expense of William Fitzwilliam, an ancestor of the present noble house; completed 1532, one of the latest specimens of genuine Pointed architecture.

St. Anne and St. Agnes, St. Anne's Lane, built by Wren in 1683; plain, with square tower.

St. Anne, Dean Street, Soho, built 1685, of brick; the organ was the gift of William III.

St. Anthony, Budge Row, of the Tuscan order, built by Cartwright, from designs by Sir Christopher Wren, in 1682; it has one of the finest of his steeples.

St. Augustin, Watling Street, erected in 1695; architect, Wren; repaired in 1829, at cost of £2,400.

St. Bartholomew, Bartholomew Lane, erected by Wren in 1679; singular finish to the tower; the altar-piece and pulpit richly adorned; taken down, in 1841, to make room for the approaches to the new Royal Exchange.

St. Bartholomew the Great, Smithfield, belonged to the priory founded by Rahere, about 1102; partly rebuilt about 1410; some fine remains of Norman architecture; a curious timber roof, with the rafters exposed to view; a minstrel gallery, and a singular altar-piece.

St. Bartholomew the Less, of unknown erection, but before

the 15th century; partly rebuilt in 1823 under the direction of Mr. Hardwick.

St. Bennet, Gracechurch Street, rebuilt in 1685; architect, Wren; cost £3,583.

St. Bennet, Paul's Wharf, first built in 1181, rebuilt after the fire by Wren in 1682; cost £3,328.

St. Bennett Fink, Threadneedle Street, founded by one Robert Fink; erected by Wren in 1670-3; cost £4,129; towards the fittings up, which are handsome, Mr. Holman, a catholic, contributed £1,000; tower taken down in 1840 to make additional room for the new Royal Exchange.

Berwick Street, Soho; first stone laid 1838 by Earl de Grey; pointed style, very large; will accommodate 1,800 persons; cost £14,000, of which £10,000 was raised by voluntary subscriptions; consecrated July 22, 1840; architect Blore.

St. Botolph, Aldersgate, in Little Britain; repaired about 1779, at a cost of £12,000. Here is a monument to Daniel Wray, scholar and amiable man.

St. Botolph, Aldgate, rebuilt in 1741-44, of brick; the steeple lofty and well proportioned; architect, Dance.

St. Botolph, Bishopsgate Street, rebuilt, 1725 of brick; handsome steeple.

St. Bride, Fleet Street, erected by Sir Christopher Wren, after the destruction of the ancient fabric (which must have been erected anterior to 1362, and was much enlarged about 1480) by the great fire of London; completed about 1680 at an expense of £11,430; additionally embellished in 1699, and generally repaired in 1822-3; the spire is 226 feet high (24 feet higher than the monument), and for its elegance and scientific construction is deserving high encomium; its original height before struck by lightning in 1764, was 234 feet; no spire in the kingdom, designed after the Roman orders, equals it in elevation, and except those of Salisbury, Norwich, and Lichfield, no one in the Pointed style.

Burghley Street, St. Martin-in-the-Fields, erected by the Commissioners; cost £7,478; architect, Savage.

St. Catharine Coleman, Fenchurch Street, escaped the fire of London, but rebuilt in 1734; a very plain building.

St. Catharine Cree, Leadenhall Street; gothic building, rebuilt in 1630, and consecrated by Archbishop Laud with so many ceremonies that it was made an article of impeachment against him. It is a very interesting building.

Christ Church, Newgate Street, belonged to the Grey Friars, and was consecrated in 1325; burnt down by the fire of London, and the choir rebuilt and a tower added; architect, Wren; elegant and commodious; here the Spital sermons are preached.

Christ Church, Spitalfields, erected between 1723 and 1729; very good Doric portico, ascended by a flight of steps; steeple is 234 feet high; length of church 125 feet, breadth 55, height 50; architect, Hawksmoor.

St. Clement Danes, Strand, of stone, of the Corinthian order, erected by Sir Christopher Wren in 1680; the tower raised to its present height of 116 feet by Mr. Gibbs in 1719.

St. Clement, Eastcheap, built in 1686, plain but neat; architect, Wren; cost £4,365.

Curtain Road, Shoreditch, will accommodate 1,200 persons; consecrated July 4, 1839; architect, Vulliamy.

St. Dionis Back Church, Lime Street, Fenchurch Street, rebuilt by Wren in 1674-84, of stone and brick; cost £5,737.

St. Dunstan's in the East; the tower the work of Sir Christopher Wren between 1667 and 1669; who also repaired the church after the ravages of the fire of London. The tower is in general much admired, and is altogether pleasing ; but it sinks in comparison with that of others attached to ancient churches in the Pointed style, especially with that of St. Nicholas at Newcastle. The church was taken down in 1817, and a new edifice erected from designs by Mr. D. Laing, who preserved the tower. and spire of Sir Christopher Wren.

St. Dunstan's, Fleet Street, rebuilt in 1832; architect, Shaw. The form is octagonal in the interior. A fine painted window by Williment.

St. Edmund the King, Lombard Street, erected by Wren in 1690 ; cost £5,207.

St. Ethelburga, Bishopsgate Street, erected about 1420; Pointed architecture ; very small edifice.

St. Giles, Cripplegate, erected 1546, on site of one of Norman architecture, burnt down the year previous; light Gothic.

St. Giles in the Fields, built on site of the church of Queen Matilda's hospital, 1730 ; architect, Flitcroft ; cost £10,000. Over the north-west gate is a sculptured representation of the Crucifixion, removed from the old church of the hospital.

St. George, Hart Street, Bloomsbury, stands north and south ; union of Tuscan and Corinthian ; architect, Hawksmoor ; on a pyramidal steeple is a statue of George I. thus alluded to, " the Pope only made Henry VIII. head of the church, but King George's good loyal people made him head of the steeple;" the vaults are particularly spacious. Walpole calls the church " a master-piece of absurdity."

St. George, Botolph Lane, erected by Wren in 1674; Grecian style; small and neat; cost £5,207.

St. George, Hanover Square, one of Queen Anne's new churches; foundation laid 1712; completed 1724; length 100 feet, breadth 60, height 45; portico of six Corinthian columns, only inferior to that of St. Martin in the Fields; steeple very fine; interior bad; architect, Gibbs.

St. George the Martyr, Queen Square, erected by subscription in 1706; originally a chapel of ease to St. Andrew's, Holborn; made parochial 1723; plain exterior, but tasteful interior.

Hanover Chapel, Regent Street, chapel of ease to St. George's, Hanover Square; first stone laid June 6, 1823; consecrated June 20, 1825; cost £16,180; architect, Charles Robert Cockerell, Esq.; it is built of Bath stone, and will accommodate nearly 1,500 persons; the order of the interior, which is much admired, is Corinthian, from the decorations of the Golden Gate of Justinian at Constantinople; the organ is placed over the communion table; the order of the exterior is the Asiatic Ionic, chiefly from the Temple of Minerva at Priene; and the proportions from the tetrastyle portico of Minerva Polias at Athens.

St. Helen's, Bishopsgate, dedicated to the mother of Constantine the Great; belonged to the priory founded before the reign of Henry III; tower built 1669.

St. James, Duke's Place, Aldgate, very small; built of brick in 1622, on site of Trinity Priory.

St. James, Garlick Hill, rebuilt by Wren in 1683; 75 feet long, 45 feet broad, 40 feet high to the roof, steeple, composed of turret and spire, 98 feet high; cost £5,357.

St. James, Piccadilly, erected in the time of Charles II. by the gallant Earl of St. Alban's, &c. at a cost of £8,000, as a chapel of ease to St. Martin in the Fields; made parochial by James II. The exterior is brick and ill-shapen, but it incloses, says Mr. Gwilt, " one of the choicest and most elegantly formed interiors which this Metropolis can boast; one which displays, in the highest degree, the extraordinary talents of Wren." It is an example of Wren's love of harmony in proportions; the breadth being half the sum of its height and length; its height half its length; and its breadth the sesquialtera of its height; the numbers being 84, 63, and 42 feet. The font, of white marble, carved by Grinlin Gibbons, has representations of the Fall of Man, the Preservation of Noah, the Baptisms of Christ and the Eunuch, &c. Over the altar is some exquisite carving in wood, of a pelican feeding its young, between two doves, some foliage, fruit, &c. by the same admirable artist.

St. John's Street Chapel, Charles Street, Berkeley Square.

St. John the Baptist, Strand, part of the old palace of the Savoy, erected in 1245; the roof is very fine, divided into pannels, and carved with religious and heraldic devices.

St. John the Evangelist, Milbank; begun 1721, finished 1728; architect, Archer; the two Doric porticoes are good, and the entire structure not deserving of that obloquy which has been attached to it. It has been pronounced to resemble an elephant on his back.

King Street Chapel, Golden Square; built 1702.

St. Lawrence, Jewry, rebuilt in 1671 by Wren; cost £11,970; handsome interior; on the spire is a gridiron, the emblem of the Saint; over the altar is a fine painting of his martyrdom; in the church is a monument to Archbishop Tillotson, who died in 1694.

St. Leonard, Shoreditch, erected 1735; architect, Dance

m

the elder; 75 feet long and 66 broad; spire 70 feet in height; Doric portico of four columns.

St. Magnus, London Bridge, erected by Wren in 1676; cost £9,579; interior very elegant; it contains a modern monument to Bishop Coverdale, once Rector.

St. Mark's Chapel, North Audley Street; architect, Gandy; Grecian Ionic.

St. Margaret, Lothbury, rebuilt 1690, architect Wren; cost £5,340; handsome church; length 60 feet, breadth 64; beautiful font with carved work by Grinlin Gibbons. The parish of St. Christopher le Stocks, when the church was taken down by the Bank, was united to this parish.

St. Margaret Pattens, Rood Lane, Little Tower Street, rebuilt in 1687, by Sir Christopher Wren; cost £4,986.

St. Margaret, Westminster, originally built in the south aisle of the Abbey; removed by Edward the Confessor in 1064; rebuilt by the Woolstaplers in the time of Edward I.; a very neat and elegant interior; the altar piece and pulpit among the richest in London. The magnificent painted window was made at Dort, as a present to Henry VII.; was first set up in Waltham Abbey, and after the dissolution removed to New Hall, in Essex; and was bought by the parishioners in 1758, for 400 guineas. This is the place of worship for the House of Commons.

St. Martin in the Fields, began 1721, finished 1726; cost £36,891; architect, James Gibbs; the portico is elegant and august, the steeple very good; it was rebuilt, after being struck by lightning, in 1842. The whole church deserves much praise; length 140 feet, breadth 60, height 45. The organ was the gift of George I. On its site there had been a church before 1222.

St. Martin, Ludgate, rebuilt in 1684 by Wren, on site of one built in 1437; cost £5,378.

St. Martin Outwich, Threadneedle Street; rebuilt in 1797; architect, Cockerell.

St. Mary, Abchurch Lane, erected in 1686 by Wren; cost £4,922; has an hemispherical roof.

St. Mary, Aldermanbury, erected by Wren, in 1676, on site of an old church which had stood for five centuries; cost £5,237. In it is a handsome monument to Samuel Smith, Esq. by Domenico Cardelli, of Rome.

St. Mary Aldermary, Bow Lane; fine tower of Pointed order, restored in 1681. It is one of the finest specimens of Wren's efforts in the Pointed style; built by a legacy of £5000, of Henry Rogers, Esq. 1681; 100 feet in length, 63 in breadth, and 45 in height; steeple 135 feet, with highly ornamented tower.

St. Mary at Hill, near Lower Thames Street, repaired after the fire in 1670 by Wren; plain square brick tower.

St. Mary-le-Bow, Cheapside, built by Sir Christopher Wren on a Roman causeway; finished in 1677; cost £8,071; unlike most others in London, it is nearly square in its plan; the steeple, combining the five orders of architecture, is highly celebrated for its scientific arrangement and mechanical skill, is 225 feet high, and is terminated by a spire; the steeple has been skilfully restored by George Gwilt, Esq. F.S.A.; there is an ancient Norman crypt, part of the original edifice built in 1087.

St. Mary-le-Strand, foundation laid 1714; steeple finished 1717; architect, Gibbs; consecrated 1723; a handsome edifice, both exterior and interior.

St. Mary Magdalen, Old Fish Street, erected 1685; architect, Wren; cost £4,291.

St. Mary Somerset, Upper Thames Street, first erected about 1335; rebuilt 1695; architect, Wren; cost £6,579.

St. Mary's, Vincent Square, Westminster, in the parish of

St. John; erected partly by subscription and partly by the Church Commissioners in 1837 ; architect, Blore.

St. Mary Woolnoth, Lombard Street, an exquisite example of the Italian style, commenced in 1716 and completed in 1719; architects, N. Hawksmoor and Gibbs; "the interior, in some respects, is unrivalled by most of those by Sir Christopher Wren, the master and instructor of its architect." On this spot there was a church in 1355; rebuilt 1496; restored 1620; damaged by the fire of London 1666, and restored 1677.

St. Matthew, Friday Street, rebuilt 1669, very plain; architect, Wren; cost £2,301.

St. Michael Bassishaw, Basinghall Street, erected by Wren 1676-79; cost £2,822; repaired 1697.

St. Michael, Cornhill, designed by Wren, completed by Gibbs in 1723; cost £4,686; admired for its tower, in the Pointed style, and the combination of the various orders of architecture; the tower was built by Gibbs in 1722.

St. Michael, Paternoster Royal, College Hill ; rebuilt by Wren in 1694; cost £7,455.

St. Michael, Queenhithe, built by Wren in 1677; 71 feet long, 40 broad, and 39 high; the steeple and spire 130 feet high.

St. Michael, Wood Street, erected in 1669 by Sir Christopher Wren; of the Ionic order; cost £2,554.

St. Mildred, Bread Street, erected in 1683; architect, Wren; cost £3,705; handsome pulpit and altar-piece.

St. Mildred, Poultry, re-built by Wren in 1676 ; cost £4,654; the interior handsome; the vane on the cupola is a ship half rigged.

St. Nicholas Cole Abbey, Old Fish Street, re-erected by Wren 1676 ; cost £5,580 ; a plain stone building, with a square tower.

St. Olave, Hart Street, Crutched Friars ; antient, with many monuments.

St. Olave, Old Jewry, erected by Sir Christopher Wren after the fire of 1666; highly decorated interior.

St. Paul, Bunhill Row, pointed style, handsome and substantial ; site given by the Artillery Company ; consecrated July 10, 1839 ; architect, Good.

St. Paul, Covent Garden, designed and built by Inigo Jones about 1631, at an expense of £4,500, which was defrayed by Francis 4th Earl of Bedford ; it is the most complete specimen of the Tuscan order, as described by Vitruvius, no ancient building of the kind now remaining, either in Italy or elsewhere. Walpole relates this anecdote on the authority of Speaker Onslow : " When the Earl sent for Inigo, he told him that he wanted a chapel for the parishioners of Covent Garden ; but added, he would not go to any considerable expense ; ' In short,' said he, ' I would not have it much better than a barn.' 'Well then,' replied Jones, ' you shall have the handsomest barn in England.' " It was reduced to a shell by fire in 1795; restored 1798, by Hardwick.

St. Peter ad Vincula, a Royal Chapel in the Tower of London.

St. Peter, Cornhill, said to have been first founded about 179, by Lucius the first Christian British king ; rebuilt immediately after the fire by Wren ; cost £5,647 ; very plain exterior, but a handsome interior, with screen, the work of Gibbons ; and a monument to Mr. Woodmason's seven children, all destroyed by fire in Leadenhall Street 1782.

St. Peter-le-Poor, in Broad Street, begun about 1788, and completed in 1791, at a cost of more than £4,000 ; architect, Jesse Gibson ; built on a circular plan ; façade simple and elegant; the altar at the west side of the church; there are no side windows.

St. Peter, Eaton Square, architect, Hakewell; Ionic order; handsome hexastyle portico; nearly destroyed by fire Dec. 30, 1836; restored by Gerrard.

St. Peter's, Saffron Hill, chapel of ease to St. Andrew Holborn; built 1832; of pointed style, 100 feet long, 64 broad, and 60 high; will hold 2,000 persons; cost £9,523; architect, Barry.

St. Philip's Chapel, Regent Street; first stone laid May 15, 1819; opened July 1820; architect, G. S. Repton; cost £15,000; the tower is a copy from the Choragic monument of Lysicrates at Athens; the interior about 70 feet square.

Rolls Liberty, Bream's Buildings, Chancery Lane, Norman Style, erected 1842 from designs by Messrs. C. Davy and J. O. D. Johnson.

St. Sepulchre, Skinner Street, almost rebuilt by Wren in 1670; the tower is about 140 feet in height; the interior is elegant, and has twelve columns of the Tuscan order, supporting a vaulted ceiling.

St. Stephen, Coleman Street, rebuilt by Wren in 1679; cost £4,020; very extensive roof supported without pillars; over the entrance gate to the churchyard is a representation of the Resurrection, cast in lead.

St. Stephen, Walbrook, built by Wren, first stone laid Oct. 16, 1672, and completed 1679; cost £7,652; justly reputed the master-piece of the architect, as it is the admiration of all beholders; it is unfortunately obscured by Dance's Mansion House.

> "Behind proud Dance's palace, in disgrace,
> Retiring Walbrook hides her blushing face;
> Perhaps St. Stephen thinks this pile of stones
> Again may rattle round his batter'd bones."

The roof is supported and the area divided by sixteen Corinthian columns, eight of which sustain an hemispherical cupola, adorned with caissons, and having a lantern light in the centre.

St. Swithin, Cannon Street, built by Wren 1680, on some very old ruins; cost £4,687 ; small but elegant; in front of it is the "London Stone," supposed to have been a Roman miliary.

Temple, circular part erected 12th century; the body, in Pointed style, built 1240; suffered injury from fire in 1695; repaired in 1742 on a very extensive scale.

Tennison's Chapel, Regent Street, belongs to St. James's, Piccadilly; founded by Archbishop Tennison.

Trinity, Minories, partly rebuilt 1706, at a cost of £858, of brick, very small and plain, but containing some curious monuments.

Trinity, near Gough Square, in St. Bride's parish ; foundation stone laid Oct. 3, 1837 ; consecrated June 21, 1838 ; cost £5,000 ; ground presented by the Goldsmiths' Company ; architect, Shaw.

Trinity, Gray's Inn Lane, in the parish of St. Andrew, Holborn ; of brick, with small stone steeple; will accommodate 1,500 persons; and has catacombs for 1,000 coffins; cost £7,200; consecrated Dec. 13, 1838; architect, Pennethorne.

Trinity, Little Queen Street, Holborn, in the parish of St. Giles in the Fields ; pointed architecture of the fifteenth century ; opened 1831 ; contains 2,000 sittings ; cost about £8,600; architect, Francis Bedford.

St. Vedast, Foster Lane, rebuilt in 1698 by Wren; the tower and spire very elegant; pronounced one of the best efforts of this great artist; the altar screen is in Gibbons's best style.

Peerage. Westminster, Marquisate to Grosvenor, 1831.

Baronetage. Blakiston, 1763. Blunt, 1720. Brown, 1731-2.
  Chamberlain, 1828. Clarges, 1674. Colleton, 1660.
  Fludyer, 1759. George, 1809. Glyn, 1759; and 1800.
  Hammick, 1834. Harnage, late Blackman, 1821. Hayes,
  1797. Heathcote, 1732-3. Hulse, 1739. Hunter, 1812.
  Nelthorpe, 1666. Pepys, 1801. Robinson, 1660. Shaw,
  1665. Whichcote, 1660.

Representatives returned to Parliament. For the City of
  London 4; City of Westminster 2.

Manufactures.   There are many establishments in and
  near London, the extent of which would excite no little
  surprise in those who for the first time visited them.
  Indeed, in the densely packed masses of buildings of the
  Metropolis, especially in the eastern districts on both
  sides of the Thames, are many individual establishments
  which would appear like little towns, if isolated, but
  which scarcely meet the eye of the passer-by.

POPULATION IN 1841.

The Population of the Parishes for 1841 not having been
published at the time of printing this sheet, the following
Abstract of the Population Returns for the Districts of the
several Superintendant Registrars in the County of Middlesex, is here substituted.

MIDDLESEX.

Superintendent Registrar's Districts.	Houses Inha- bited.	Uninha- bited.	Build- ing.	Persons.
Barnet (part of) . .	1,467	93	11	8,210
Bethnal Green . . .	11,774	391	171	74,087
Brentford . . .	6,735	480	78	37,054
Clerkenwell . . .	6,943	207	79	56,709
Edmonton (part of) .	7,086	353	59	43,009
St. George-in-the-East	5,985	244	24	41,351
St. George, Hanover Square	7,628	342	187	66,433
St. Giles and St. George .	4,970	189	29	54,250
Hackney. . . .	7,197	317	187	42,274
Hendon	2,453	189	11	15,444
Holborn . . .	4,098	448	8	39,720
Islington	8,511	284	317	55,720
St. James, Westminster .	3,596	116	5	37,407
Kensington . .	16,628	659	751	114,952
Kingston (part of) .	1,116	80	6	5,907
London, East .	4,796	236	7	39,655
London, City of .	7,923	582	79	55,967
London, West . .	3,332	162	9	33,629
St. Luke . . .	6,371	242	24	49,982
St. Martin-in-the-Fields .	2,440	70	4	25,195
Marylebone . .	14,178	576	193	137,955
St. Pancras . . .	14,750	581	322	129,711
Poplar	5,068	180	121	31,091
Shoreditch . . .	12,737	458	192	83,552
Staines . . .	2,552	197	11	13,216
Stepney . . .	14,364	554	124	90,657
Strand	4,532	747	9	43,894
Uxbridge . . .	3,246	174	42	18,889
Westminster . . .	6,439	206	52	56,718
Whitechapel . . .	8,755	493	44	71,758
Metropolitan Police on Duty	—	—	—	2,220
Total in 1841	207,670	9,850	3,156	1,576,616
Houses & Population in 1831	180,493	14,413	3,919	1,358,330

SUMMARY OF LONDON.

London is the largest and richest city in the world; occupies a surface of thirty-two square miles, thickly planted with houses, mostly three, four, and five stories high. It consists of London city, Westminster city, Finsbury, Marylebone, Tower Hamlets, Southwark, and Lambeth districts. The two latter are on the south side of the Thames. It contains 300 churches and chapels of the Establishment; 364 Dissenters' chapels; 22 foreign chapels; 250 public schools; 1,500 private schools; 150 hospitals; 156 almshouses, besides 205 other institutions; 550 public offices; 14 prisons; 22 theatres; 24 markets. Consumes annually 110,000 bullocks, 776,000 sheep, 250,000 lambs, 250,000 calves, and 270,000 pigs; 11,000 tons of butter, 13,000 tons of cheese, 10,000,000 gallons of milk, a million quarters of wheat, or 64 millions of quartern loaves, 65,000 pipes of wine, 2,000,000 gallons of spirits, and 2,000,000 barrels of porter and ale. Employs 16,502 shoemakers, 14,552 tailors, 2,391 blacksmiths, 2,013 whitesmiths, 5,030 house-painters, 1,076 fish-dealers, 2,662 hatters and hosiers, 13,208 carpenters, 6,822 bricklayers, &c. 5,416 cabinet-makers, 1,005 wheelwrights, 2,180 sawyers, 2,807 jewellers, 1,172 old clothesmen (chiefly Jews), 3,628 compositors, 700 pressmen, 1,393 stationers, 2,633 watch and clock makers, 4,227 grocers, 1,430 milkmen, 5,655 bakers, 2,091 barbers, 1,040 brokers, 4,322 butchers, 1,586 cheesemongers, 1,082 chemists, 4,199 clothiers and linen-drapers, 2,167 coachmakers, 1,367 coal merchants, 2,133 coopers, 1,381 dyers, 2,319 plumbers, 907 pastrycooks, 869 saddlers, 1,216 tinmen, 803 tobacconists, 1,470 turners, 556 undertakers. [The above are all males above twenty years of age.] 10,000 private families of fashion, &c. About 77,000 establishments of trade and industry, 4,400 public houses, 330 hotels, 470 beer shops, 960 spirit and wine shops. There are six bridges over the Thames at London. London Docks cover

20 acres; 14 tobacco warehouses, 14 acres ; and the wine cellars 3 acres, containing 22,000 pipes. The two West India Docks cover 51 acres. St. Katharine's Docks cover 24 acres. The Surrey Docks, on the opposite side, are also very large. There are generally about 5,000 vessels and 3,090 boats on the river, employing 8,000 watermen and 4,000 labourers. London pays about one-third the window duty in England, the number of houses being about 120,000, rated at upwards of five millions sterling. The house rental is probably seven or eight millions.—*(Knight's London.)*

HISTORY.

A. D.

61. London depopulated by the troops of Boadicea.

497. Ambrosius, successor of Vortigern, captured London from Hengist, who had taken it about two years before.

532. Mordred, the base nephew of King Arthur, crowned at London after his treacherous usurpation of his uncle's dominions.

644. London ravaged by a plague.

798. London almost wholly burnt down, and numbers of the inhabitants perished. It had greatly suffered by fire in 764 ; and did so again in 801.

833. A wittenagemot, or meeting of wise men, held at London, to consult on the best means of repelling the Danes, whose incursions had become formidable.

839. The Danes obtained possession of the city, gave it up to pillage, and committed unheard-of cruelties and massacres.

851, or 852. The Danes having landed from a fleet of 350 sail, laid waste London by fire.

860. The Danes, renewing their invasion, obtained a permanent settlement in England.

A. D.

872. The Danes garrisoned London.

884. Alfred compelled the Danes to surrender London after a short siege.

945. A wittenagemot, or parliament, held by Edmund the First.

961. A malignant fever raged, and St. Paul's Cathedral burnt.

982. London almost wholly destroyed by fire.

992. Ethelred fitted out a numerous fleet at London to prevent the landing of the Danes.

994. Anlaf and Sweyn, kings of Norway and Denmark, arrived before the city with a fleet of 94 ships, but were vigorously repulsed by the citizens.

1008. Ethelred and Olaf attacked and destroyed London bridge.

1013. Sweyn invested London, where the cowardly Ethelred had taken refuge, but was obliged to retire. He shortly after made a second and successful attack.

1016. Canute, the son of Sweyn, made three unsuccessful attempts to possess London, being gallantly met by Edmund Ironside.

1017. The whole kingdom awarded to Canute by a council in London.

1041. Edward the Confessor was chosen king by a general council of the clergy and people held in London.

1052. Earl Godwin sailed with his fleet through London Bridge to attack the royal fleet, then consisting of fifty sail, lying at Westminster. An accommodation was effected.

1067. William I. was received into London with a magnificent procession of clergy, magistrates, and citizens.

1077. A fire happened in London which destroyed the greatest part of it.

A. D.

1086. A fire began at Ludgate which consumed a great part of London, including the Cathedral of St. Paul.

1091. Upwards of 600 houses and many churches were blown down in London on November 16, and London Bridge, being of timber, was destroyed.

1092. Another fire happened, which destroyed a great part of London.

1099. William Rufus kept his Whitsuntide at his new Hall at Westminster, built in 1097.

1100. Henry I. crowned king of England at London.

1136. A great fire happened near London Stone, which extended eastward to Aldgate, and west to St. Erkenwald's shrine, in St. Paul's, which it destroyed, together with London Bridge, then of wood.

1139. King Stephen obliged the citizens to pay one hundred marks of silver for a right to choose their own sheriffs.

1152. King Stephen held a council in London for the purpose of securing the accession of his son Eustace.

1176. A new bridge of stone was commenced over the Thames at a short distance west of the wooden one at London.

1189. A massacre, by the populace, of the Jews at the coronation of Richard I.

1191. Longchamp, Bp. of Ely, regent in the absence of Richard, summoned to attend a council of the nobility, held in St. Paul's Church Yard; but refusing, was besieged in the Tower by Prince John, and compelled to relinquish his castles and retire to the continent.

1194. Richard I. on his return to England, after his avaricious imprisonment by Henry VI. of Germany, received with great pomp and magnificence by the citizens.

1196. A sedition headed by William Fitz-Osbert, caused a

A. D.

good deal of trouble to the authorities, but the rebel was smoked out of Bow Church, which he had fortified, and was beheaded near Smithfield.

1210. John summoned a parliament to meet him at his palace at St. Bride's. The same year the king was excommunicated by Pope Innocent.

1212. A dreadful fire, originating in Southwark, burnt down St. Saviour's Church and a great part of the bridge, to the destruction of about three thousand persons who had congregated as spectators.

1214. Baynard's Castle destroyed by King John.—The Crown of England rendered subservient to the Pope of Rome in a full assembly at St. Paul's.

1215. The Barons, admitted secretly into the city at Aldgate, May 24, compelled John to consent to meet them at Runnimede.—The Tower garrisoned by the Barons, and held till that event, and subsequently till it was given up to Louis the Dauphin.

1220. Henry III. kept his Lent at the Tower with his Court.

1222. Disputes arising between the Londoners and Westminster men at two wrestling matches, the king punished the city by severe fines.

1224. A parliament held at London.

1236. Henry and his queen Elianor made a public entry into London on the day appointed for the queen's coronation, new year's day, when 6,000 poor people were entertained in Westminster Hall.

1241. A grand feast at Westminster Hall by the king, in honour of the legate; and in the same hall was another still more splendid in 1243, in honour of the nuptials of his brother Richard Earl of Cornwall.

1244. A riot in the church of the priory of St. Bartho-

A. D.

lomew, occasioned by the visit of Boniface, Archbishop of
Canterbury, in opposition to the canons, several of whom
were nearly killed.

1247. A great earthquake about London.

1256. Henry III., the king and queen of Scotland, and a
great number of the nobility, entertained at Tothill Fields,
by John Mansel, priest, and a minister of state, high in
the King's favour.

1258. Baldwin, the Greek Emperor, received in a very
pompous manner by the mayor. This year 20,000 persons are said to have died in London, from a scarcity of
grain.

1263. Prince Edward, at his return from Wales, broke
open the treasury of the Templars, and took £10,000 of
the citizens there deposited. This produced a rebellion.

1264. In Passion Week upwards of five hundred Jews were
cruelly massacred, and their houses and synagogues destroyed by the populace.

1267. Gilbert de Clare, Earl of Gloucester, fortified London.

1269. A frost from November to Candlemas stopped all
merchandize, and goods were brought from Sandwich by
land.

1272. Henry III. died at Westminster, and buried in
the abbey.

1274. Edward I. and his queen received with great rejoic-
ing and pomp.

1278. The Jews, to the number of 210, executed in the
city by order of the king, being accused of clipping the
king's coin.

1282. The head of Llewellin Prince of Wales, brought in
triumph to the city, stuck on the pillory in Cheapside, and

A. D.

then fixed upon the Tower.—In the severe winter five of the arches of London Bridge borne down and carried away by the ice.

1305. Sir William Wallace condemned for high treason in Westminster Hall, and executed at Smithfield.

1306. Prince Edward knighted at Westminster.

1317. Edward III. kept his Whitsuntide with great state at Westminster Hall.

1320. The parliament of the White Bands, or partizans of the barons, met at Westminster, and marched their army to London.

1328. Philippa of Hainault received with great pomp and magnificence by the mayor and citizens.

1340-2. Edward III. chiefly kept his court at the Tower.

1347. David King of Scotland conducted in procession a prisoner to the Tower.

1349. 50,000 people buried of the plague on the site of the present Charter-house, which was purchased for that purpose. Of this plague, which is thought to have originated in India, Stowe says it so wasted and spoiled the people of England that scarce the tenth person of all sorts was left alive. The pestilence did not subside till nearly ten years after.

1357. Great justing at Smithfield before the king.

1359. Edward the Black Prince, and his royal prisoner, John King of France, with a numerous cavalcade, received in the city with such ostentation as was never before seen.

1362. On the first five days of May justs were held at Smithfield, before the king and queen.

1363. Henry Picard, lord mayor, entertained the kings of England, Scotland, France and Cyprus, the Prince of Wales, and most of the nobility.

A. D.

1369. A grand tournament at Smithfield, in honour of Alice Pierce, Edward's mistress, whom he dignified with the appellation of Lady of the Sun.—This was also a plague year.

1377. A remarkable mummery was made by the citizens, for the disport of the young prince, Richard son of the Black Prince, which went from Newgate to Kennington. —The Savoy Palace attacked by the Londoners, in consequence of John of Gaunt upholding the tenets of Wycliffe.

1380. The mob under Wat Tyler destroyed the Savoy Palace in the Strand; brake open the Fleet and set the prisoners free; and did a great deal of mischief all over the city. It was suppressed by Sir William Walworth striking the ringleader on the head with his mace, and so killing him, in Smithfield, in the presence of the King.

1382. Anne of Luxembourg, sister to the Emperor Wenceslaus, conducted in the greatest pomp through the city to Westminster, where she was married to the young King, Jan. 14.

1390. A great "passage of arms," took place on London Bridge between the Earl of Craufurt, and Lord John de Wells.

1393. The Scotch Earl of Mar challenged the Earl of Nottingham to joust at Smithfield, in which the former was severely wounded.

1399. Henry Duke of Lancaster was declared King in place of the deposed Richard, and crowned Oct. 13.

1400. The Grecian Emperor, John Emanuel Palæologus, arriving to solicit succour against the Turks, was received with great pomp by the corporations.

1401. Richard II. kept his Christmas at Westminster Hall,

A.D.

entertaining on each day 10,000 guests. This year was
passed the statute for the "burning of obstinate heretics,"
and a London priest was the first who suffered.

1407. A plague carried off 30,000 inhabitants ; and on
Oct 12, three tides occurred in the Thames within twenty-
four hours.

1413. Henry IV. died in the Jerusalem Chamber at Westminster, March 20. A prophecy, it is said, foretold his
death in Jerusalem. It is alluded to in Shakspere's play.

1430. A battle fought in Smithfield between a knight of
Arragon and one of the King's squires, in which the latter
was victorious, and knighted by the King.

1445. Queen Margaret conducted with great pomp through
the city.

1447. July 2, Jack Cade entered the city, and coming to
London Stone said, " Now is Mortimer lord of this city."
After the dispersion of the insurgents and the death of
Cade, Henry, on the 4th of December, marched his army
through the city.

1455. The king being taken prisoner at St. Alban's, was
brought to the Bishop's palace, "where they kept their
Whitsontide with great joye and solemnitie."

1460. Lord Scales demanded admittance into the city with
an army in favour of Henry VI. but was refused. He
then took possession of the Tower ; but the Earl of
March, coming with an army of 25,000 men, left the Earl
of Salisbury to besiege the Tower. Scales, in attempting
his escape by water, was recognized and killed by the
ferrymen, who landed him dead at St. Mary Overy's.

1461. Edward IV. dined at Baynard's Castle. The day
after his coronation at Westminster he went crowned to
St. Paul's, and " there an angel came down and censed
him."

A. D.

1467. Lord Scales, brother to the queen, met the Bastard of Burgundy at Smithfield before a great company.

1470. Henry, released from his captivity in the Tower by the Earl of Warwick, was proclaimed King, and went crowned to St. Paul's. Edward, however, having procured assistance, marched to the capital, and was admitted with great joy.

1471. Edward IV. met by the mayor, aldermen, and citizens on the 21st of May, between Shoreditch and Islington.—The Bastard Falconbridge, under pretence of releasing King Henry, attacked London Bridge, but was repulsed.

1472. PRINTING INTRODUCED BY CAXTON, AND THE ART EXERCISED IN WESTMINSTER ABBEY.

1483. Edward IV. died at Westminster, April 9; and his executors met at the house of Cicely Duchess of York in Paul's Wharf, to issue a commission for the care of the royal property.—Edward V. received into the city with great pomp and joy.—Richard resided at Crosby Place and Baynard's Castle, where the citizens went to beseech him to take the crown.

1486. Henry VII. united the rival claims of York and Lancaster by marrying Elizabeth, dau. of Edward IV. at Westminster.

1497. Perkin Warbeck exposed for a whole day in the stocks at Westminster, again at the Cross, Cheapside, and conveyed to the Tower, whence he endeavoured to escape.

1499-1500. The plague carried off upwards of 30,000 citizens.

1501. May 2, a Royal jousting at the Tower.— Prince Arthur married to Katharine of Spain on the 12th of November, with very great pageantry.

1510. Henry VIII. and his Queen came to the city to see

A. D.

the march of the City Watch, which took place every year on the vigils of St. John Baptist and St. Peter and St. Paul.

1511. A sumptuous tournament at Whitehall, in honour of the Duke of Anjou.

1513. A plague year.

1515. So hard a frost that carriages of all sorts passed over the river between Westminster and Lambeth.

1517. An insurrection against foreigners on May-day, since called Evil May-day, which did very great mischief before it was quelled. The houses were plundered and lives lost, and it was with difficulty appeased.

1522. The Emperor Charles V. conducted by the King to London, which was decorated with processions, &c. He was lodged at the Blackfriars.

1524. A parliament held at the Blackfriars.

1525. A plague year.

1529. The Cardinals Campejus and Wolsey sat at the Blackfriars to consider of the lawfulness of the King's marriage with Catharine, which ended in the sentence of divorce.— And in the same year the parliament which condemned Wolsey in a *præmunire*, assembled there.

1531. Richard Rose, cook to the Bishop of Rochester, boiled to death in Smithfield for poisoning sixteen persons with porridge.—Henry VIII. and Queen Katharine of Arragon, with the foreign ambassadors, dined at Ely House, Holborn.

1533. Anne Boleyn conveyed in state through the city to Westminster for her coronation. Three years afterwards she was condemned and beheaded at the Tower.

1542. Catharine Howard, queen, beheaded at the Tower.

1548. A plague year.

1554. The proposed marriage of Queen Mary with the

A. D.

King of Spain produced a rebellious movement. Sir
Thomas Wyat, at the head of a party of rebels, endeavoured to enter London, but was compelled to retire. He
then crossed the Thames near Kingston, went to Westminster, and at Charing Cross was met by Sir John Gage,
whom he repulsed, and then proceeded on to Ludgate.
Being unable to effect an entrance, he surrendered to Sir
Maurice Berkeley.

1558. Jan. 14. Elizabeth went from the Tower to Westminster to be crowned with great pomp and state. Pa-
geants and speeches met her everywhere.

1563-4. 20,000 persons died of the plague.

1570. Queen Elizabeth sumptuously entertained at Gresham
House by Sir Thomas; and proclaimed the new Exchange to be a Royal Exchange.

1571. A great jousting at Westminster before the Queen on
the three first days of May.

1574. A plague year.

1579. Stubbes and Page each lost a hand in the Market-
place, Westminster, for writing against the talked of
marriage of Elizabeth with the Duke of Anjou.

1582. Nearly 7,000 died of the plague.

1588. After the defeat of the Spanish Armada, the Queen
rode in great state to St. Paul's Cathedral to return
thanks.

1592. More than 11,000 persons died of the plague.

1601. Feb. 7. The Earl of Essex held a conference with
his partisans, on the plan of seizing Elizabeth in her
palace at Whitehall. On the following morning he went
to the city, but not meeting with any aid, and the Queen's
friends being abroad, he returned by water to Essex
House, Strand, which he fortified. He was seized, and
beheaded on the 19th.

A. D.

1603. April 28. Elizabeth buried at Westminster.—May 7, James made his public entry into London; entertained four days at the Charter-house by Lord Thomas Howard; thence to Whitehall, and to the Tower.—Between 30 and 40,000 persons died of the plague.

1605. The Gunpowder Plot to blow up the King and Parliament, at the opening of the Parliament at Westminster, discovered. Guy Faukes seized and with others of the conspirators suffered.

1606. Christian IV. King of Denmark, treated with extraordinary magnificence and revelling.

1607. James I., his son Henry, and very many of the nobility, splendidly entertained by the Merchant Taylors' Company.

1610. Henry, eldest son of James, created Prince of Wales, at Whitehall, June 12, with great shows and feasting.

1618. In October, the brave, the gallant, generous, and learned Sir Walter Raleigh beheaded in Old Palace Yard, Westminster, at the instigation of Spain, to the eternal disgrace of the pusillanimous James. He had been imprisoned on the charge for which he suffered nearly fifteen years.

1623. Nov. 5, 94 persons killed by the falling in of a floor at Blackfriars during the sermon of a Jesuit priest.

1625. The plague carried off upwards of 35,000 persons.

1634 The four Inns of Court entertained their Majesties with a most splendid masque at the Banqueting House, Whitehall; the masquers and their company came in gorgeous procession from Ely House, Holborn.

1636. The plague carried off 11,000 persons.

1642. Jan. 4. Charles went to the parliament guarded, and made a rash attempt to seize five members and Lord Kimbolton, which produced the first warlike steps on the

A. D.

part of the Commons. The breach then became every day wider; Charles thought it advisable to leave the city; which then became completely under the Parliamentary influence, and numerous are their ordinances for its regulation and fortification.

1643. Westminster Abbey, in July, converted into barracks for the soldiers, who broke down the rails about the altar, placed forms round the communion table, from off which they dined and supped, drinking ale and smoking tobacco as they sat; they demolished the organ and pawned the pipes at the neighbouring pothouses for sale; and, dressing themselves in the surplices, &c. turned every thing religious into ridicule.—Sept. 25. The solemn league and covenant taken in St. Margaret's Church Westminster, by both houses of Parliament, the Assembly of Divines, and Scottish Commissioners. Within a few days it was also taken by all the principal citizens and inhabitants of London.

1644. In January, the city gave a splendid entertainment to both houses of Parliament at Merchant Taylors' Hall.

1645. June 14. Both houses attended a thanksgiving sermon at Christ Church, Newgate Street, and were sumptuously entertained at Grocers' Hall, in consequence of the battle of Naseby.

1649. Jan. 6. An ordinance passed to bring the King to trial; on the 8th the High Court of Justice assembled in the Painted Chamber; but removed on the 20th to Westminster Hall, which had been properly fitted up. The King having been removed from Windsor to St. James's, and thence to Sir Robert Cotton's, was placed at the bar; but denying the legality of the Court, the Court adjourned to the Painted Chamber to hear witnesses on the charges. On the 27th, in the Hall, the King was brought up and

A. D.

received that sentence which was too cruelly executed on the 30th, before his palace of Whitehall.—March 9. Several noblemen beheaded in Palace Yard.

1651. Sept. 16. Cromwell, after the battle of Worcester, conducted from Acton with great state, and feasted at Guildhall.

1653. April 20. Cromwell dissolved the Long Parliament by military force.—In December, he was sworn as Lord Protector, in the Chancery Court at Westminster.

1657. June 26. Cromwell solemnly inaugurated in Westminster Hall, with great magnificence.

1658. Several conspirators against Cromwell seized at their house of rendezvous in Shoreditch, Feb. 4—Sept. 3, the Protector died at Whitehall.

1660. After General Monk had prepared everything favourable for the King's return, Charles, after landing at Dover, advanced to town and made his public entry into the Metropolis on the 29th of May, the anniversary of his protection by the oak-tree, and also of Oliver Cromwell's triumphant entry on his return from Ireland, after the King's death.—July 5. The King and royal family sumptuously entertained at Guildhall.—In October the regicides were executed at Charing Cross.

1661. Jan. A desperate insurrection of a fanatical sect called Fifth Monarchy Men, which destroyed many lives before it was suppressed.—April 23. Charles crowned at Westminster, and revived the ancient custom of going in procession from the Tower.—May 22, the solemn league and covenant burnt in Cheapside; and on the 28th the acts for the trial of Charles, &c. burnt in the midst of Westminster Hall.

1664-6. This was the period of the great plague, which began at the top of Drury Lane in the winter of 1664,

A. D.

and continued to ravage London with unparalleled seve-
rity till February 1666. It was at its height in September 1665, when as many as 12,000 persons died in one
week, and of them 4,000 in one night. Defoe, the interesting historian of this awful visitation, declares that
100,000 persons perished. It was, at the commencement,
the general opinion of the people that to resist it was
to insult the Deity; and at the end it was thought that all
would die, and therefore it was not to be shunned. Fires
were burnt in the streets to purify the air, but the rain
put them out. It ceased in the beginning of the year
1666, and this severe affliction was followed in a short
time afterwards by the " great Fire of London," which
lasted four days and nights, and destroyed nearly the
whole city. It began on Sunday Sept. 2, in Pudding
Lane, near New Fish Street, and extended to Holborn
Bridge, Pye Corner, Aldersgate, Coleman Street, lower
end, Basinghall Street, Leadenhall Street, Mincing Lane,
and Tower Dock. It consumed 400 streets, 13,200 dwelling houses, St. Paul's Cathedral, 89 churches, besides
chapels, four of the city gates, and a vast number of public and stately edifices. The total loss of property was
estimated at nearly ten millions. The Monument was
erected to perpetuate the event, which was falsely ascribed
to the malignity of the Catholics. It was the result of ac-
cident, and in its effects ought to be viewed as a blessing
of the Almighty. The re-building brought into operation the great talents of Wren. London was rebuilt in
four years.

1667. Charles II. laid the foundation-stone of the Royal
Exchange, Oct. 23, and was magnificently entertained on
the spot. In 1671, and the six following years, and again
in 1681, the King was present in Guildhall, at the Lord
Mayor's feast.

A. D.

1673. The desperate attempt of Colonel Blood to obtain possession of the regalia took place.

1680—1684. These years were distinguished by gross violations of the laws of the country, through the medium of a series of plots, as false as destructive. The names of Russell and Sydney, among the sufferers, will ever be endeared in the memories of their countrymen.

1685, Feb. 6. Charles II. ended a reign of tyranny and licentiousness at Whitehall, not without suspicion of poison.—April 23. James II. and his Queen crowned at Westminster. Then came the day of retribution. Some of the merciless persecutors in the preceding reign now experienced an excess of cruelty in themselves.

1687. The King was entertained at Guildhall on Lord Mayor's day.

1688. James quitted Whitehall in disguise on the night of Dec. 10.

1689. King William and Queen Mary were present at the Lord Mayor's feast in Guildhall, as they were again in 1692, and the King in 1697.

1702. Queen Anne dined with the Lord Mayor, Nov. 9, and on the 12th, accompanied by both houses of Parliament, went in great state to St. Paul's to attend a solemn thanksgiving for the success of the Duke of Marlborough in the Low Countries. During her reign there were frequent thanksgivings at St. Paul's.

1703. A great storm commenced on the night of Nov. 26, which destroyed property to the amount of two millions sterling in the city alone. Several persons were killed, and nearly 200 wounded.

1710. Numbers of meeting-houses destroyed by the Sacheverell, or High Church mob.

1714. King George the First dined at the Lord Mayor's feast.

A. D.

1715. 120 houses destroyed by fire in Thames Street, Jan. 15.

1720. This year was memorable for the bursting of the "South Sea Bubble." A company of merchants trading to the South Sea, having increased their wealth, proposed to Government to take into their fund all the debts of the nation incurred before 1716. This was accepted, and stock rose rapidly till it reached 1100 per cent. The directors then selling their stock, an alarm was created, and such a sudden reduction took place as to bring it down to 86 per cent. A vast many persons were entirely ruined, and the greatest misery and distress for a long time prevailed. A Parliamentary investigation took place, and the estates of the directors were confiscated, to the amount of £2,014,000.

1727. King George the Second and his Queen, the Duke of Cumberland, and the three eldest Princesses, dined at Guildhall on Lord Mayor's day.

1739-40. From Christmas Day to Feb. 17, the frost was so intense that the Thames was frozen over, and games and recreations were carried on on its surface. It is known as "the Great Frost."

1746. Lords Kilmarnock and Balmerino were executed, Aug. 18, on Tower Hill, for aiding in the attempt to restore the House of Stuart; and April 9, 1747, Simon Lord Lovat shared the same fate. At this execution, the falling of a scaffold killed as many as twenty persons, and injured a great many more.

1747. A dreadful fire at Cornhill, March 25, destroyed nearly 100 houses.

1751. Two shocks of earthquake were felt. They did some damage, and created great alarm.

1761. King George the Third and Queen Charlotte, with the Royal Family, dined at the Lord Mayor's feast.

A. D.

1768. Mr. Wilkes being confined in the King's Bench prison, a riot occurred, in which several persons were killed by the military.

1780. Lord George Gordon, M.P. at the head of a body of 50,000 men, members of a Protestant Association, marched from St. George's Fields to Westminster, to present their petition to the Commons against the Catholics. The mob attempted to gain admittance to both Houses of Parliament, but without success. They then separated into parties, and proceeded to destroy the houses and chapels of all Catholics. The excesses continued for several days. They attacked Newgate Prison, set it on fire, and released the prisoners. They then attacked the two prisons in Clerkenwell, liberated the prisoners, and destroyed the offices and houses of several Magistrates. They twice unsuccessfully attacked the Bank, and did much other mischief for several days. The civil authorities were so paralysed, that they appeared to give up the city to the wild fury of the mob. At length a strong arrival of military awed them into quiet. Several hundred lives were lost; and a vast number of houses burnt down.

1786. As George the Third was stepping out of his carriage at St. James's, Margaret Nicholson, an insane woman, under the pretence of presenting a petition, struck at him with a knife. The blow was warded off by a page, and the woman seized.

1788. A severe frost from Nov. 25, for exactly seven weeks.

1789. George the Third having recovered from his mental indisposition, their Majesties went to St. Paul's in great state on April 23, and the day was celebrated as one of general thanksgiving throughout the kingdom.

1791, Feb. 2. The Thames overflowed its banks to a very great extent.

A. D.

1792, May 8. An attempt made to set the House of Commons on fire.

1794. A large fire, July 23, at Cock Hill, Ratcliffe Highway, consumed more houses than any fire since the fire
of London in 1666. It originated from the boiling over
of a pitch kettle at a boat builder's. 700 houses were destroyed, and about 400 families lost all they possessed.

1797. The King and royal family went in procession to
St. Paul's to celebrate the three great victories under
Howe, St. Vincent, and Duncan.

1799. The French having repeatedly threatened an invasion,
a Volunteer Corps, above 12,000 strong, was raised and
reviewed by their Majesties in Hyde Park. A similar
threat in 1803 increased the corps to 30,000 strong.

1800, May 15. At Drury Lane Theatre an attempt made
to assassinate his Majesty by one James Hatfield, a
lunatic, by firing a pistol.

1806, Jan. 8. The body of Lord Nelson carried in great
state to St. Paul's Cathedral, for interment.

1809. The celebrated O. P. riots, produced by raising the
price of admission, occurred at the Theatre Royal, Covent
Garden.

1810. Sir Francis Burdett committed to the Tower by the
House of Commons. London was in a riot for several
days, and he was obliged to be conducted by the military.

1812, May 18. Mr. Perceval, Chancellor of the Exchequer,
shot in the lobby of the House of Commons by a man
named John Bellingham.

1813-14. A dense fog, great fall of snow, and a frost severe
enough to render the river Thames capable of supporting
booths, &c. and great crowds of visitors, produced a very
distressing winter.

A. D.

1814. Louis XVIII. of France, the Emperor Alexander of Russia, the King of Prussia and his two sons, Marshal Blucher, &c. &c. entertained with great pomp and state, by the City, the Merchant Taylors' Company, &c.

1815. The Metropolis was illuminated throughout for three nights to celebrate the victory at Waterloo.—On the 1st Aug. the grand celebration of peace was observed by a display of fire-works in the parks, upon a scale of great magnificence. Every entertaining amusement was provided for the crowds of people who attended.

1816. The first steam-boat seen on the Thames, was one fitted up by Mr. George Dodd, at Glasgow; and which had come from that port in 121 hours.

1820. The Cato Street conspiracy, to assassinate the whole of the Ministry, was discovered Feb. 23. Arthur Thistlewood and four others were executed.—Queen Caroline returned, June 6, to England after a long absence, and was most enthusiastically welcomed by the country; on July 5, a bill of pains and penalties was introduced into the House of Lords against her. The hearing of evidence was commenced on August 17, and continued till Nov. 10, when the Bill was abandoned. On the 29th her Majesty went to St Paul's to return thanks for the defeat of these proceedings; and the Metropolis was most brilliantly illuminated.

1821, July 19. George IV. crowned. The procession was a walking one on a platform from Westminster Hall to the Abbey. Queen Caroline went to the Abbey and demanded her admittance as Queen Consort of England, but was refused. On this pageant, witnessed but by few, an immense sum of money was expended.—August 7. Queen Caroline died at Brandenburgh House, Hammersmith, and on the 14th her remains were conveyed through the

A. D.

Metropolis on their way to Germany. The people were desirous that the procession should go through the city; the Government was opposed to it; some riots occurred, and the soldiers fired, but the people conducted the procession through the city.

1824-5. The bubble year. Upwards of 300 schemes were projected this year; and the amount of money requisite to carry them into operation was three hundred and fifty millions sterling. By the end of the year upwards of fifty millions had been paid, when the bubble burst, and thousands were reduced to poverty and ruin. Several banks stopped payment, and the panic was awful. To afford relief, Government issued one and two pound bank notes, and 150,000 sovereigns per day for one week. The panic soon subsided.

1830. The city made great preparations to entertain William the Fourth and his Queen at the Lord Mayor's festival. His Majesty, however, on the advice of his Ministers, a few days before the day fixed, declined to attend, a letter having been received from the City, by the Home Secretary, announcing fears that an attack would be made on the Duke of Wellington, and the occasion taken for a general riot. The great unpopularity of the Duke was occasioned by his declaring, in his place in Parliament as Prime Minister, that no Reform in the Representation of the people was at all needed. The excitement of the people was increased; meetings were held, the Ministry condemned, and many affrays between the police and the mobs took place. On the 16th the Duke of Wellington's Ministry resigned, and that of Earl Grey was appointed, pledged to Reform.

1831. On the first of March, Lord John Russell submitted to the House of Commons the plan of the Government for

A. D.

Reform. The debate lasted for six nights, when the Bills were ordered to be brought in. On the 19th of April the Ministers were defeated by a majority of eight in Committee on the English Bill, and Parliament was dissolved. On the 21st of June the new Parliament met, and on the 20th of September passed the Reform Bill by a majority of 113 to 58. The Bill was thrown out in the Lords on the 7th of October, by a majority of 199 to 158. On the 20th Parliament was prorogued; and then followed public meetings, the formation of political unions, and many serious riots, and incendiary fires. Parliament met again December 6, again the Reform Bill was passed by the Commons, and thrown out in Committee by the Lords. Lord Grey resigned, and the Duke of Wellington was called upon to form a ministry, but failing to do so, Earl Grey was restored, with an assurance from the King of the success of the Reform Bill. On the 4th of June 1832, it passed the House of Lords, and on the 7th it received the Royal Assent by Commission.

1833. The first Reformed Parliament met on the 29th of January.

1834, Oct. 16. The two Houses of Parliament, with nearly all their various offices, &c. were destroyed by fire. The old Painted Chamber was subsequently fitted up for the temporary House of Lords; and the White Hall, late the House of Lords, for the temporary House of Commons.

1837. Queen Victoria paid a visit to the citizens of London, and dined at the Guildhall on Lord Mayor's Day. Her reception exceeded that of any previous monarch. In the evening the Metropolis was brilliantly illuminated.

1840, February 10. Her Majesty was married at St. James's Palace, to Prince Albert of Saxe Coburg; and on the 21st of November the Princess Royal was born at Buckingham Palace.

EMINENT NATIVES.

Adair, James, partisan of Wilkes, Recorder of London, and afterwards Chief Justice of Chester; died 1798 at Lichfield.

Adams, John, Provost of Queen's College, Cambridge; died 1719.

Albricius, physician and philosopher of the eleventh century.

Alcock, John, Mus. Doct. musical composer; born in 1715; died 1806.

Aldrich, Henry, eminent scholar and divine; born in Westminster 1647; died 1710.

Alford, Michael, jesuit, and author on ecclesiastical history; born 1587; died at St. Omer's 1652.

Allestrey, Jacob, poet; died 1686.

ALLEYNE, EDWARD, "the Proteus for shape, and Roscius for a tongue," actor, founder of Dulwich College; born in St. Botolph's, Bishopsgate, 1556; died in 1626, and buried in the chapel of his own college at Dulwich.

Andrewes, Lancelot, Bp. of Winchester, greatly esteemed by Elizabeth, James, and Charles; learned, able, and beneficent; wit and author; born in All Hallows Barking, 1555; died 1626.

Anspach, Elizabeth Margravine of, accomplished author; born in Berkeley House, Spring Gardens, 1750 ; died 1828.

Anthony, Francis, noted empyric and chemist; born 1550.

—— John, his son and successor ; died 1655.

Argall, John, writer and disputant ; died 1606.

Arnald, Richard, divine and commentator ; died 1756.

Arnall, William, political writer, author of the "Free Briton," in defence of Walpole ; received £11,000 from the Treasury in four years ; committed suicide from want, in 1741, aged 26.

Arne, Thomas Augustine, Mus. Doct. eminent musical composer; author of the opera of Artaxerxes and burletta of Tom Thumb, &c.; King Street, Covent Garden, 1710; died in 1778.

Arnold, John, ingenious mechanic, watch-maker; born 1744; died 1799.

—— Dr. Samuel, musician, and composer of the opera of The Maid of the Mill, the oratorio of the Prodigal Son, &c.; born about 1739 ; died Oct. 22, 1802, in Duke Street, Westminster.

Arnolde, Richard, merchant, author of a work called "The Customes of London ;" died 1521.

Ashwell, George, divine and loyalist; author of treatises in defence of the Church of England; St. Martin, Ludgate, 1612.

Bacon, Francis, Viscount St. Alban's, Lord Chancellor of England; philosophical writer; fined £40,000 for accepting bribes as Chancellor; generally esteemed "the glory and ornament of his age and nation," and "the father of experimental philosophy;" York House, Strand, Jan. 22, 1560-1 ; died at Highgate in April 1626.

Baker, Henry, ingenious and diligent naturalist; instructor

of the deaf and dumb ; author of poems; Chancery Lane, 1698; died in 1774.

Barnes, Joshua, learned divine, and Greek Professor at Cambridge; educated at Christ's Hospital; so charitable that he was known to give away his only coat to a beggar at the door ; 1654; died in 1712.

BARROW, ISAAC, eminent mathematician and divine; educated at the Charter House ; Greek and Mathematical professor at Cambridge ; so eloquent a preacher that Charles II. called him an unfair one, for leaving nothing to be said after him ; born 1630 ; died May 1677.

Basire, James, celebrated engraver; born 1730; died 1802. His father Isaac, and his son and grandson, both named James, were also eminent engravers.

Bathurst, Allen Earl, distinguished nobleman ; the friend of Bolingbroke, Addison, Pope, Swift, Gay, &c.; born in St. James's Square, Westminster, 1684; died in 1775, aged 91.

Baynes, Paul, divine; died 1617.

BECKETT, St. THOMAS à, Archbp. of Canterbury; haughty churchman; born on site of Mercers' Hall, 1119; martyred at the altar of Canterbury Cathedral, Dec. 29, 1170; canonized in 1172; and the pilgrims to his shrine outnumbered those to any other in the kingdom.

Berkeley, George, D.D. divine, printed a few political sermons; born in Grosvenor Street, 1733; died in 1795.

—— Sir William, royalist; Governor of Virginia, of which place he wrote a description ; and dramatic author; died in 1677.

Berriman, William, pious and learned divine; born 1688.

Betterton, Thomas, celebrated tragic actor, much esteemed in private life; born in Tothill Street, Westminster, 1635; died in 1710, and buried in Westminster Abbey.

Birch, Thomas, D.D. divine; industrious historian and biographer; voluminous author; born a quaker, 1705; died Jan. 9, 1765, from a fall from his horse.

Bird, Francis, sculptor; executed Busby's monument in Westminster Abbey, and the Conversion of St. Paul in the pediment of St. Paul's Cathedral, &c.; born 1667; died 1731.

Birkhead, Henry, Latin poet; born near St. Paul's, 1617.

Blackhall, Offspring, Bp. of Exeter, born 1654; died 1716.

BLACKSTONE, SIR WILLIAM, illustrious lawyer; lecturer at Oxford; Justice of Common Pleas; author of the Commentaries; born in Cheapside, 1723; died 1780.

Bolton, Robert, learned Dean of Carlisle, 1697.

Boulter, Hugh, Archbishop of Armagh; educated at Merchant Taylors' School; active, charitable, and public-spirited; born in 1671; died 1742.

Bourgeois, Sir Francis, painter, to whom Mr. Desenfans bequeathed his pictures, and who again bequeathed them, with the bulk of his property, to Dulwich College; pupil of Loutherbourg; born in 1756; died 1811, and buried at Dulwich College.

BOWYER, WILLIAM, "the most learned English printer;" born in Dogwell Court, Whitefriars, 1699; died in 1777.

BOYCE, WILLIAM, Mus. Doc. composer of sacred music, and organist, but so deaf as to be almost insensible to sound; born at Joiners' Hall, 1710; died 1779.

Bromfield, William, surgeon; founded the Lock Hospital; born 1712; died 1792.

Broughton, Thomas, learned divine and biographer; born in Holborn, 1704; died in 1774.

Browne, Sir Thomas, physician and antiquary; author of "Religio Medici;" born in St. Michael, Cheapside, 1605; died 1682.

Buckingham, George Grenville Chandos Temple, first Duke, so created by Geo. IV. as a mark of personal friendship, and he was the only peer elevated to ducal rank during that reign; patron of the arts; born 1776; died 1839.

Bulkley, Charles, dissenting Minister, born 1719; died 1797.

Burton, William, B.C.L. author of a commentary on the Roman Itinerary of Antoninus in Britain; died 1658.

Byrne, Anne Frances, artist in water colours; chiefly of fruit and flowers; died 1837.

—— William, landscape engraver; died 1805, aged 62.

Calamy, Edmund, presbyterian divine; declared himself a nonconformist on the publication of the Book of Sports; one of the writers of "Smectymnuus," &c.; born in 1600; died 1666.

Cambell, Sir James, Lord Mayor of London in 1629; born in Aldgate Ward.

Cambridge, Richard Owen, ingenious writer; author of the "Scribleriad," &c.; born in 1717; died 1802.

Camden, William, antiquary and historian; educated at Christ's Hospital and St. Paul's School; Master of Westminster School; founded a professorship of history at Oxford; called by foreigners "the Pausanias of England;" born in the Old Bailey, 1551; died 1623, and buried in Westminster Abbey.

Campion, Edmund, Roman Catholic divine; employed by Pope Gregory XIII. to make converts in England; born 1540; hanged and quartered at Tyburn in 1581.

Carter, John, draughtsman, architect, and antiquary; born in 1748; died 1817; buried in Hampstead churchyard.

Caryl, Joseph, nonconformist divine; learned commentator on the book of Job; born in 1602; died in 1673.

Cecil, Richard, divine, and author of sermons and biographies; born in Chiswell Street, 1748; died 1810.

CHALONER, SIR THOMAS, gallant soldier; able statesman and diplomatist, and learned writer; born about 1515; died 1565.

Charnock, Stephen, nonconformist divine, scholar and theologian; author of "Discourse on Providence;" born in 1628; died 1680.

CHAUCER, GEOFFREY, "the father of English poetry;" follower of Wickliffe, for which he fled the country, but returning was imprisoned, and obtained liberty by disclosing the designs of his party; born 1328; died 1400 in London, and was buried in Westminster Abbey.

CHURCHILL, CHARLES, divine, poet, and satirist; educated at Westminster School; became a party writer and reckless man; Vine Street, Westminster, 1731; died 1764.

CIBBER, COLLEY, poet laureate to George II.; dramatic writer and actor; autobiographer; born in Southampton Street, 1671; died 1757, aged 87.

Cibber, Susanna Maria, eminent actress; wife of Theophilus Cibber, sister of Dr. Arne; born in Covent Garden; died 1766, and was buried in the cloisters of Westminster Abbey.

Cockburn, Catharine, author of the tragedy of "Fatal Friendship," &c. and of some pamphlets in vindication of Locke's "Essay on the Understanding;" born 1679; died 1749.

Cocker, Edward, a name proverbial in the school of arithmetic; very skilful in calligraphy; born 1631; died 1677.

Colechurch, Peter of, builder of the first London bridge of stone (12th century).

Colet, John, learned Dean of St. Paul's, and founder of St. Paul's School; born in St. Antholin's parish, 1466; died 1519.

Conybeare, John Josias, ingenious critic and divine; educated at Westminster School, where he became usher; professor of Anglo-Saxon literature and poetry at Oxford; antiquary, chemist, mineralogist, &c.; died 1824.

COOKE, GEORGE FREDERICK, actor of great talent, but very intemperate habits; originally a printer; Westminster, 1756; died 1812.

Cooper, Anthony Ashley, Earl of Shaftesbury; celebrated author of the "Characteristics;" born in Exeter House, 1671; died at Naples, 1713.

—— Samuel, eminent miniature painter; born 1609; died 1672.

COWLEY, ABRAHAM, poet and wit; educated at Westminster School; loyalist; became a physician; born 1618; died 1667, and buried in Westminster Abbey.

Coxe, William, Archdeacon of Wilts, traveller, biographer, and topographer; Dover Street, Piccadilly, 1747; died 1828.

Crashaw, Richard, divine and poet; became a Catholic; died 1650.

Croft, Sir Herbert, Bart. left the law for the church; lexicographer; author of "Love and Madness;" died 1816.

Croke, Richard, classical scholar; Greek professor at Cambridge; died in London in 1558.

Crowther, Rev. Samuel, amiable divine; born in New Boswell Court, Carey Street, 1769; died 1829.

Culpepper, Nicholas, physician, astrologer, and herbalist; born in 1616; died 1653-4.

Cumberland, Richard, learned Bishop of Peterborough; writer on divinity and archæology; St. Anne, near Aldersgate, 1632; died 1718.

Davenant, John, Bishop of Salisbury; Watling Street, 1641.

Davies, John, D.D. divine and learned critic; Master of Queen's college, Cambridge; born 1679; died 1732.

Day, John, divine and author; Aldersgate Street, 1566.

Day, Thomas, poetical and miscellaneous writer, educated at the Charterhouse; tried to educate two young girls on a principle of his own, in order to make one his wife, but the plan failed; eccentric but benevolent man; author of "Sandford and Merton;" Wellclose Square, 1748; died from a fall from a young horse, which his benevolence would not allow to be trained in the usual manner, 1789.

Dee, Dr. John, mathematician and astrologer; visited by Queen Elizabeth; born 1527; died 1608.

De Foe, Daniel, author of "Robinson Crusoe," and a voluminous and very ingenious political and miscellaneous writer; pilloried by order of the Commons for a libel; born 1663; died 1731.

Denne, Samuel, antiquary and divine; historian of Rochester, Lambeth, &c.; born in Westminster deanery, 1730; died 1799.

Dennis, John, poet, political writer, and critic; one of the heroes of the "Dunciad;" born 1657; died 1733-4.

Devereux, Robert, third Earl of Essex, husband of the infamous Countess; commanded the parliament army, and gained many great victories over the royalists; Essex House, Strand, 1592; died 1646, buried in Westminster Abbey, with a public funeral.

Dobson, William, painter of history and portraits; patronized by Vandyck; born 1610; died 1646.

Doddridge, Dr. Philip, eminent dissenting divine and schoolmaster; author of "The Family Expositor;" born 1702; died at Lisbon, 1751.

Dollond, John, optician, and inventor of the achromatic telescope; brought up a silk weaver; Spitalfields, 1706; died 1761.

Donne, John, divine and poet; educated for the law, but took orders at request of James I.; became Dean of St.

Paul's; founder of the metaphysical class of poets; born 1573; died 1631, and buried at St. Paul's.

Duncan, Mark, physician and author; died 1640.

Duncombe, William, miscellaneous writer, author of "Brutus," a tragedy; 1690; died 1769.

Dyer, George, barrister, biographer, bibliographer, and elegant poet; historian of the University of Cambridge; born 1755; educated at Christ's Hospital; died in Clifford's Inn, 1841, aged 85.

EDWARD V. King of England; Sanctuary at Westminster.

Edwards, Edward, A.R.A., painter of historical pictures, &c.; Castle Street, Leicester Fields, 1738; died 1806.

—— Thomas, critic and poetical writer; born in 1699; died in 1757, whilst on a visit to Richardson, at Parson's Green, Fulham.

Edwin, John, of great reputation as a burlesque comedian; 1749; died 1790.

Egerton, Daniel, comedian, born 1772; died July 23, 1835, at Chelsea.

Ellis, George, F.R.S., F.S.A. editor of "Early Metrical Romances," &c. and concerned in the political satire of "The Rolliad;" educated at Westminster School; died in 1815, aged 70.

—— John, F.R S., naturalist; writer on zoophytes; born about 1710; died 1776.

—— John, miscellaneous writer; St. Clement Danes, 1693.

Etherege, Sir George, courtier and wit; writer of plays of great popularity in the time of Charles II.; born about 1636; died through a fall down stairs in taking leave of a friend he had been entertaining.

Faithorne, William, very celebrated engraver; died 1691.

Farnaby, Thomas, learned grammarian; annotator on Juvenal, Persius, &c.; imprisoned for saying, during the ascendancy of the Parliament, that one King was better than 500 ; born about 1575; died 1647.

Fearne, Charles, lawyer; educated at Westminster School; writer on jurisprudence and metaphysical philosophy; died 1794, aged 45.

Fell, Samuel, learned and loyal divine; Dean of Christ Church; educated at Westminster School; born in St. Clement Danes, 1594; died 1648-9, it is said of a broken heart, occasioned by the execution of Charles I.

Felton, Henry, divine and author; St. Martin in the Fields, 1679.

Ferrar, Nicholas, pious enthusiast, and learned and ingenious gentleman; Mark Lane, 1592.

Flatman, Thomas, poet and painter; brought up to the law; Aldersgate Street, 1633; died 1688.

Fleetwood, William, learned and eloquent prelate; born in the Tower, 1656; became Rector of St. Austin's, Watling Street, Canon Residentiary of St. Paul's, and successively Bishop of St. Asaph and Ely; author; died 1723.

Fleming, Abraham, poet, translator of Virgil, &c. and editor of Holinshed's Chronicle (16th century).

Fletcher, John, dramatist; son of Dr. Fletcher, Bishop of London; "the inseparable partner of Beaumont;" born 1576 ; died of the plague, 1625.

Florio, John, "the resolute;" author; tutor to Prince Henry, son of James I.; died 1625.

Folkes, Martin, scholar and antiquary; author on the coinage; born in Queen Street, Lincoln's Inn Fields, 1690; died 1754.

Forbes, James, traveller, author of "Oriental Memoirs," &c. pleasing writer, and accomplished gentleman; 1749; died at Aix la Chapelle 1819.

Fulke, William, divine, and Master of Pembroke Hall, Cambridge; died 1589.

Gale, John, baptist divine of eminence, and author; 1680; died 1721.

—— Samuel, antiquary; author of "History of Winchester Cathedral;" educated at St. Paul's School; born in St. Faith's, 1682; died 1754.

Gataker, Thomas, learned divine and critic; one of the Assembly of Divines, at Westminster, and friend of episcopacy; St. Edmund the King, Lombard Street, 1574; died 1654.

Gellibrand, Henry, Professor of Astronomy at the Gresham College, and writer on trigonometry, navigation, &c.; St. Botolph, Aldersgate, 1597; died at his College in 1636, and buried in the church of St. Peter le Poor, Broad Street.

George the Third, King of England; Norfolk House, St. James's, 1738; died 1820.

Gibbon, John, herald at arms, astrologer, and author; 1629; died 1700.

Gibbons, Grinling, sculptor, and carver in wood, particularly of flowers; of which specimens may be seen in the choir at St. Paul's Cathedral, on the font in St. James's Church, Westminster, and on the bases of the statues of Charles I. at Charing Cross, and James II. at Whitehall; born in Spur Alley, in the Strand, of Dutch parents; died in 1721.

Gill, Alexander, Head Master of St. Paul's School, and preceptor of Milton; author of Latin poems; born 1597; died 1642.

Girtin, Thomas, ingenious young landscape painter; 1773; died 1802.

Glover, Richard, poet; author of "Leonidas," and other

poems; Member of Parliament for Weymouth; St. Martin's Lane, Cannon Street, 1712; died 1785.

Goad, John, divine; eminent as a classical teacher; Head Master of Merchant Taylors' School for twenty years; convert to Popery; Bishopsgate Street, 1615; died 1689.

Godwin, Mary Wolstonecraft, of singularly eccentric habits and opinions; author of "Vindication of the Rights of Women," and wife of the author of "Caleb Williams;" 1759; died 1797.

Golding, Arthur, poet, and translator from the Latin (lived in the 16th century).

Gomersal, Robert, divine and poet; 1600; died 1646.

GOUGH, RICHARD, learned antiquary and topographer; the Camden of the 18th century; Winchester Street, Austin Friars, 1735; died at Enfield, 1809.

Graunt, John, haberdasher; author of natural and political "Observations on the Bills of Mortality;" became a convert to Popery; Birchin Lane, 1620; died 1674.

GRAY, THOMAS, lyric poet, and writer of Latin verse; Professor of Modern History at Cambridge; born at No. 41, Cornhill, 1716; died 1771.

Green, Matthew, poet, author of "The Spleen," &c.; born 1696; died 1737.

Greene, Maurice, Mus. Doct. musician and composer; organist of St. Paul's and Chapel Royal; Professor of Music at Cambridge; one of the founders of the charitable fund for the support of decayed musicians; died 1755.

GRESHAM, SIR THOMAS, merchant; politician and benefactor; founder of the Royal Exchange and Gresham College; born 1519; died 1579.

Grey, Nicholas, learned schoolmaster; born 1590; died 1660.

Griffith, alias Alford, Michael, jesuit; 1587.

Grosvenor, Benjamin, pious dissenting divine; born 1675.

Hacket, John, Bishop of Lichfield and Coventry; educated at Westminster School; Rector of St. Andrew's, Holborn; Residentiary of St. Paul's; expended upwards of £20,000 in restoring his Cathedral after the injuries inflicted during the civil wars; author of a life of Lord Keeper Williams, and a Latin comedy, entitled "Loyola," acted twice before James I.; born at Exeter House, Strand, 1592; died 1670.

Hall, Edward, Serjeant at law and representative in Parliament; author of the Chronicle which bears his name; died 1547.

—— Henry, learned divine; born 1716.

Halley, Edmund. (Vide the Natives of Middlesex.)

Hamilton, William Gerard, statesman and orator, called "Single-speech Hamilton," from his opening speech being the only one he delivered in the English House of Commons; he was Secretary to the Viceroy of Ireland, and had the celebrated Burke for his secretary; the Letters of Junius have been attributed to him; born in Lincoln's Inn, 1729; died 1796.

HAMPDEN, JOHN, representative in Parliament; refused to pay the tax of ship-money, and defended himself against a crown prosecution for eight days, which, though not successful, obtained for him the title of patriot; one of the five members seized by the King in their places in the Commons; his talents and integrity have commanded the respect of all parties; born 1594; died of a shot wound in a skirmish against Prince Rupert's troop 1643.

Hare, Francis, Bishop of Chichester; preceptor of the great Duke of Marlborough; Dean of St. Paul's 1726; author; died 1740.

HARLEY, ROBERT, EARL OF OXFORD; commenced his parliamentary life by acting with the Whigs, but afterwards became a leader of the Tories; Secretary of State; Lord High Treasurer; tried for high treason temp. Geo. I. but acquitted; commenced collecting the MSS. now in the British Museum, which bear his name; characterised by Pope as

> " A soul supreme, in each hard instance tried,
> Above all pain, all anger, and all pride,
> The rage of power, the blast of public breath,
> The lust of lucre, and the dread of death."

Born 1661 ; died 1724.

Harpsfield, John, Dean of Norwich, Archdeacon of London, Rector of St. Martin Ludgate; a persecutor; Old Fish Street; died 1578.

————— Nicholas, catholic divine ; Greek Professor; brother of preceding ; Prebendary of St. Paul's ; imprisoned in Lambeth Palace ; died 1583.

Harrison, William, historian ; died 1592.

Hawkins, Sir John, a solicitor, and magistrate, friend of Dr. Johnson, to whom he acted as executor ; author of History of Music, Life of Johnson, &c. ; born 1719 ; died 1789.

Hearne, Samuel, traveller in North America ; died 1792.

Heath, James, loyalist ; historian of the Civil War ; educated at Westminster School; born 1629; died 1664.

Heberden, Wm. physician, scholar, and author ; 1710; died 1801.

Henderson, John, actor; apprenticed to a silversmith ; his representation of Falstaff is said never to have been equalled; born 1747 ; died 1785.

Henry, Philip, eminent nonconformist divine; educated at Westminster School; Whitehall, 1631; died 1696.

Herrick, Robert, poet of merit; 1591; died 1660.

Heywood, Eliza, voluminous novel writer; 1693; died 1756.

—— Ellis, jesuit; died 1573.

—— Jasper, brother, jesuit, and poet; 1535; died 1597.

Highmore, Joseph, portrait and historical painter, and author; St. James, Garlick Hithe, 1692; died 1780.

—— Anthony, son of the preceding, lawyer and author; born 1758; died 1829.

Hill, Aaron, poet and dramatist; translator; Beaufort Buildings, Strand, 1685; died 1750, buried in Westminster Abbey.

Hinchliffe, John, learned Bishop of Peterborough; Swallow Street, Piccadilly, 1731; died 1794.

HOADLY, BENJAMIN, physician and philosopher; author of the play of "The Suspicious Husband;" Broad Street, 1705-6; died 1757.

—— Dr. J. son of the above; divine; writer for the stage; Broad Street, 1711; died 1776.

Hodges, William, landscape painter, born 1744; died 1797.

HOGARTH, WILLIAM, painter of domestic life, of great power, truth, and originality; apprenticed to an engraving silversmith; engraved designs for books; clandestinely married a daughter of Sir James Thornhill; and then appeared the "Harlot's Progress," which reconciled Sir James to the match; appointed serjeant painter to the king; born at St. Martin, Ludgate, 1697; died 1764.

Holcroft, Thomas, dramatist, novelist, and miscellaneous writer; brought up a shoemaker; charged with Hardy, Horne Tooke, Thelwall, &c. in 1794, with treason, but not brought to trial; author of "the Road to Ruin;" Orange Court, Leicester Fields, 1744; died 1809.

HOLLIS, THOMAS, antiquary and virtuoso; politician; writer of republican principles; benefactor to literature; born 1720; died 1774.

Holloway, Thomas, engraver of the Cartoons of Raphael; born in Broad Street, 1748; died 1827.

Holman, Joseph George, comic writer and performer; died in America, of the yellow fever, in 1817, on the same day with his second wife, and only two days after their marriage.

Hoole, John, dramatic poet, and translator of Tasso's "Jerusalem delivered;" author of "Orlando Furioso;" Moorfields, 1727; died 1803.

HORSLEY, SAMUEL, Bishop of St. Asaph; born in the Churchyard of St. Martin's in the Fields, 1733; educated at Westminster School; Secretary to the Royal Society, and author on Mathematics; Prebendary of St. Paul's; opponent of Priestley and the Unitarians; Bp. of St. David's, in 1788; Bp. of Rochester, 1793; and St. Asaph, 1802; died 1806.

Horton, Thomas, learned and pious divine; died 1673.

How, William, botanist; educated at Merchant Tailor's School; author of the first "Flora;" born 1619; died 1656.

Howson, John, Bishop of Durham; born in St. Bride's, 1556; died 1632.

Hull, Thomas, actor; educated at the Charter House, and subsequently for the medical profession; author of "Richard Plantagenet," and other dramas, &c.; Strand, 1728; died 1808.

Ingulphus, Abbot of Croyland, in Lincolnshire, the church of which he rebuilt; educated at Westminster School; became prime favourite of William I. ; wrote a life of St. Guthlac, and a history of his abbey ; born 1030 ; died 1109.

Isaacson, Henry, author of a Chronology ; born in St. Catherine Cree, 1581 ; died in 1654.

Jackson, Joseph, letter founder ; born in Old Street, 1733 ; died 1792.

Jane, of the Tower, eldest daughter of Edward II. and wife to King David Bruce.

Jebb, John, divine, but gave up his clerical and academical appointments on conscientious grounds ; studied medicine, and became M.D. and a frequent speaker in popular assemblies in London, during the American war ; born in 1736 ; died 1786.

Jenyns, Soame, elegant and ingenious writer, wit, and companion ; Member of Parliament ; Great Ormond Street, 1703-4 ; died 1787.

JONES, INIGO, architect ; sent by Earl of Arundel to study in Italy, and studied the works of Palladio ; introduced to James I. by Christian IV. of Denmark, when on a visit to England in 1606 ; revived classic architecture ; designed the Banquetting House, Whitehall, &c.; in repairing Winchester Cathedral and other edifices in the pointed style, he did not at all succeed ; Roman Catholic loyalist and sufferer ; born (near St. Paul's) 1572; died 1652.

—— John, benedictine monk, 1575.

—— SIR WILLIAM, accomplished scholar and linguist ; barrister ; Judge of the Supreme Court, Bengal; founded at Calcutta a Society similar to the Royal Society of London ; friend of the native Indians ; author of many works, original and translated ; his knowledge of the Eastern languages has scarcely ever been surpassed ; born 1746

p

died 1794; monument in St. Paul's Cathedral, erected by the East India Company.

JONSON, BEN, dramatist, cotemporary with Shakspere; born in Hartshorn Lane, Charing Cross, 1574; educated at Westminster School; employed by his father-in-law as a bricklayer; enlisted as a private soldier; became actor at the Curtain Theatre; killed a brother actor in a duel, and suffered a long imprisonment; became an author, and for a satire on the Scottish nation was condemned to lose his ears in the pillory, but saved them by submission; wrote many plays and masques; and was made laureate; died 1637, and was buried in Westminster Abbey, in a perpendicular position. The spot is indicated by a small square stone, inscribed "O Rare Ben Jonson."

Jortin, Dr. John, learned and amiable divine; born in St. Giles's, 1698; educated at the Charter House; Vicar of Kensington, Rector of St. Dunstan in the East, and Prebendary of St. Paul's; voluminous author; died at Kensington, 1770.

Keats, John, "a young poet of extraordinary promise, and almost as extraordinary performance;" born in Moorfields, 1796; died 1820.

Keble, Joseph, lawyer; for nearly half a century made reports of the causes in the King's Bench, and of 4000 sermons delivered at Gray's Inn Chapel; born 1632; died 1710.

Kent, Edward Duke of, 4th son of George III.; soldier; father of Her present Majesty; born 1767; died 1820.

Killigrew, Anne, beautiful and virtuous Maid of Honor to the queen of James II.; poet and painter; celebrated by Dryden, and characterised by Wood, as "a Grace for beauty, and a Muse for wit;" born 1660; died a victim to the small pox, in 1685, and lies buried in the Savoy Chapel.

King, Thomas, theatrical performer and dramatic writer; born 1730; died 1805.

—— William, Judge of the Admiralty in Ireland; learned and witty author; educated at Westminster School; born 1663; died 1712, of disease brought on by intemperance.

—— Dr. William, Principal of St. Mary Hall, Oxford; ingenious and humorous writer; born 1685; died 1763.

Kitchiner, William, physician; "another Crichton;" born 1777; died 1827.

Klose, F. J. musical composer and performer; died 1830.

Knight, Samuel, divine; biographer of Dean Colet and Erasmus; antiquary; educated at St. Paul's School; born 1674; died 1746.

Langhorne, Nathaniel, divine, historian, and antiquary; died 1681.

Lawrence, Thomas, physician; born in St. Margaret's, Westminster, 1711; died 1783.

Lee, Samuel, nonconformist divine and learned antiquary; died 1691.

Leighton, Robert, pious and much beloved Archbishop of Glasgow; born 1613; died 1684.

Leland, John, divine; antiquary, to whom Henry VIII. gave the title of "Royal Antiquary," with power to visit monastic libraries, &c.; educated at St. Paul's School; born in the time of Henry VII.; died 1552, insane, from immense study.

Lemon, Robert, Keeper of the State Papers; intelligent and industrious; died July 29, 1835, at the new State Paper Office, St. James's Park.

Levi, David, mechanic and Jew; author of a Hebrew Lexicon, &c.; born 1740; died 1799.

Lewis, Matthew Gregory, "Monk Lewis;" Member of Parliament; author of romances and dramas, distinguished for the licentious, the marvellous, and the terrific; educated at Westminster School; born 1773; died 1818.

Lillo, George, tragic poet; by trade a jeweller; author of "George Barnwell," &c.; born in Moorgate, 1693; died 1739.

Lisle, Sir George, gallant but unfortunate royalist officer; knighted at Naseby, and shot by the Parliamentarians, 1648, after being compelled to surrender Colchester Castle.

Lloyd, Robert, ingenious poet; friend of Churchill; born in Westminster, 1733; died a prisoner for debt, in the Fleet, in 1764.

Lowman, Moses, learned dissenting divine and author on Biblical literature and criticism; born 1680; died 1752.

Lowth, William, learned divine, father of Bishop Lowth; educated at Merchant Tailors' School; born, St. Martin's, Ludgate, 1661; died 1732.

Maddox, Isaac, active and learned prelate; originally placed with a pastrycook, who dismissed him for his love of books; became Vicar of St. Vedast, Foster Lane, Bishop of St. Asaph, and then of Worcester; author of a defence of the Church of England; born 1697; died 1759.

Maittaire, Michael, learned critic and bibliographer; author of "Annales Typographici;" educated at Westminster School, of which he became second Master; born 1668; died 1747.

Maplet, John, physician and scholar; born in St. Martin's le Grand, 1615.

Marsham, Sir John, learned writer on history and chronology; son of Alderman Marsham; suffering loyalist; M.P. for Rochester; created a baronet by Charles II.;

educated at Westminster School; born in St. Bartholomew's, 1602; died 1685.

Martyn, John, Professor of Botany at Cambridge, and author of scientific and critical books; born in Queen
Street, 1699; died at Chelsea, in 1768.

Mary II. Queen of England, wife of William III. and
daughter of James II.; strongly attached to the Protestant religion and the Church of England; born in St.
James's Palace, 1662; died of the small pox at Kensington, in 1695.

Maskelyne, Dr. Nevil, mathematician and astronomer royal;
educated at Westminster School; born 1733; died 1811.

Masters, Robert, divine, antiquary, and topographer; author of histories of Corpus Christi College, Cambridge, of
the parish of Waterbeach, Cambridgeshire, &c.; born
1713; died 1798.

Matthews, Charles, comedian, monodramatist; educated at
Merchant Tailors' School; born No. 18, in the Strand,
1776; died June 28, 1835.

Mendez, Moses, poet, of Jewish parentage; author of the
" Chaplet," and other popular musical entertainments;
died very rich, in 1759.

Merry, Robert, poet of the Della Cruscan School; satirised
by Gifford in the " Baviad;" author of " Lorenzo," a
tragedy; born in 1755; died in 1798.

Mill, Henry, engineer to the New River Company; distinguished for his knowledge of hydraulics; born in Red Lion
Square, Holborn, 1680; died 1770.

Miller, Joseph, witty actor, whose jests have been published
under his name; born 1684; died 1738, and buried in
the churchyard of St. Clement's, Portugal Street, with an
epitaph by Stephen Duck, the poet.

Milton, John, one of the most illustrious of poets; author

of "Paradise Lost," &c. educated at St. Paul's School;
opened an academy in Aldersgate Street; became a political partisan, and wrote many powerful works; defended the execution of Charles; was appointed Latin
Secretary to the Council of State; became blind through
study; born in Bread Street, 1608; died in Artillery
Walk, 1674, and was buried in Cripplegate church, where
a monument, by Bacon, was subsequently erected by the
elder Samuel Whitbread.

Mitan, James, historical engraver; born 1776; died 1822.

Mitford, William, historian of Greece, born 1743-4; died
1827.

Monro, Alexander, physician and anatomist; born 1697;
died 1767.

More, Sir Thomas, Lord Chancellor; educated in Threadneedle Street; author of "Utopia," a political romance;
disinterested and upright man, but a bitter opponent of
the Reformation; refused to take the oath of Supremacy,
and was beheaded at Tower Hill in 1535; born in Milk
Street, 1480.

MORLAND, GEORGE, painter of rustic scenery and low life,
with which latter he became familiarly acquainted by his
habits of intemperance; many of his pictures were painted
while in confinement for debt, or in the midst of embarrassments occasioned by his imprudence; born in 1764;
died 1804 in prison, a victim to intemperance.

Mortimer, Thomas, voluminous writer; author of a Dictionary of Commerce; born 1730; died 1809.

Muffett, or Moufet, Thomas, physician, naturalist, and author; born in the 16th century; and died towards the
close of the reign of Queen Elizabeth.

Munday, Anthony, continuator of Stowe, and ballad poet;
born 1553; died 1633.

Munden, Joseph Sheppard, comedian ; Brook's Market, Holborn, 1758; died 1832.

Neal, Daniel, dissenting divine, and historian of the Puritans; educated at Merchant Tailors' School; minister of a congregation in Aldersgate Street; born 1678; died 1743, at Bath.

Needham, John Tuberville, Roman Catholic divine; professor of natural philosophy in the English College at Lisbon ; author on microscopical discoveries, and on the Chinese Empire ; born 1713; died 1781, at Brussels.

Neele, Henry, poet, lawyer, and lecturer on poetry; born in the Strand, 1798 ; died by his own hand in 1828.

Nelson, Robert, distinguished by the epithet of "the pious," for his devotional writings, and his works of benevolence and charity; educated at St. Paul's School; born 1656; died at Kensington, 1715.

Newton, John, Rector of St. Mary Woolnoth, and author of discourses on the passages forming Handel's Oratorio of the Messiah; originally a dissipated slave trafficker; then a dissenting preacher, and subsequently entered the church ; became the intimate friend of the poet Cowper, with whom he jointly published a volume of hymns; born 1725 ; died 1807.

Nichols, Frank, physician and anatomist ; educated at Westminster School; elected Gulstonian Reader by the College of Physicians ; author ; born 1699; died 1779, at Epsom.

—— Richard, poet of elegance and imagination ; 1584.

Nicholson, William, writer on mathematics, chemistry, and natural philosophy ; born 1758; died 1815, in poverty.

Nollekens, Joseph, R.A., sculptor; eccentric and avaricious; born in Dean Street, Soho, 1737; died in Mortimer Street, 1823, having amassed a fortune of £200,000.

North, George, divine, antiquary, and numismatist; educated at St. Paul's School; born 1710; died 1772.

—— Dr. John, divine; Greek professor at Cambridge, and Master of Trinity College; third son of Dudley Lord North; born 1645; died 1683.

Oglethorpe, General James Edward, soldier; founded the colony of Georgia; eulogised by Pope, Thomson, and Johnson; born 1698; died 1785.

Oldfield, Anne, comic actress and accomplished woman; born at Westminster, 1683; died 1730, and buried in Westminster Abbey.

Palmer, John, actor; erected a theatre at Goodman's Fields; born about 1742; died 1798, on the stage at Liverpool, while performing in the "Stranger," and having just exclaimed, in the words of the drama, "There is another and a better world!"

Palsgrave, John, divine; grammarian; compiled the first French grammar, and taught the sister of Henry VIII. the language on her marriage with Louis XII.; Prebendary of St. Paul's, and Rector of St. Dunstan in the East; died in 1554.

Paterson, Samuel, bookseller, auctioneer, and writer on bibliography and miscellaneous literature; born in St. Paul Covent Garden, 1728; died 1802.

Pearce, Zachary, Bishop of Rochester, distinguished for learning, munificence, and piety; educated at Westminster School; became Vicar of St. Martin in the Fields, and Dean of Westminster, which he resigned; author of a Commentary on the Gospels, &c.; born in Holborn, 1690; died 1774.

Peirce, James, dissenting minister and voluminous writer in defence of presbyterianism; born at Wapping, 1673; died 1726.

Pemberton, Henry, learned physician, mathematician, and mechanist; professor of physic at Gresham College; at the request of the College of Physicians revised their Pharmacopeia; author of numerous scientific books; born 1694; died 1771.

PENN, WILLIAM, founder of Pennsylvania; son of Admiral Sir William Penn; became Quaker, and was committed to the Tower for preaching against the established Church; became heir to his father, and obtained from the crown a grant of land in North America, to which he sailed in 1681, with a band of persecuted Quakers, and having established a code of laws, returned to England; born near the Tower, 1644; died 1718, at Ruscomb, in Berkshire.

Pengelly, Sir Thomas, learned judge; born in Moorfields, 1675.

Philips, Catherine, accomplished poetess and translator, on whose death Cowley wrote an ode; born 1631; died of the small pox, 1664.

Phillips, Edward, author of the "Theatrum Poetarum;" nephew of the poet Milton, by whom he was educated, and whose life he wrote; born 1630.

—— Sir Richard, schoolmaster and hosier at Leicester, where he established and edited the "Leicester Herald" Newspaper, and opened a bookseller's shop; he was imprisoned for selling Paine's "Rights of Man," in 1793; lost his stock in trade by fire, and then went to London, where he established in 1796, the "Monthly Magazine," and became an extensive publisher; High Sheriff of London in 1807, and knighted on going up with an address;

author of some political works and useful school books; born in London; died at Brighton, 1840, aged 72.

Phræas, or Freas, John, divine, lecturer in medicine and the belles lettres; appointed, in 1465, by Pope Paul II. to the Bishopric of Bath, but poisoned by a rival candidate previous to consecration; translator of Xenophon, &c.

Playford, John, writer on musical subjects, and much improved the art of printing music; born in 1613; died 1693.

POPE, ALEXANDER, poet, distinguished for correctness of versification, splendour of diction, and invention; Roman Catholic; vain and irascible; born in Lombard Street, 1688; died 1744.

Pott, Percival, surgeon, lecturer, and author; inventor of many new instruments; scientific operator; born in Threadneedle Street, 1713; died 1788.

Price, John, learned critic; educated at Westminster School; born 1600; died 1676.

Pridden, John, divine and antiquary; educated at St. Paul's School, Minor Canon of St. Paul's and Westminster; priest of the Chapel Royal, and Rector of St. George, Botolph Lane; compiled an Index to the Rolls of Parliament; born 1758; died 1825.

PRIOR, MATTHEW, poet, politician, and diplomatist; educated at Westminster School; born 1664; died 1721.

Pye, Henry James, poet laureat, and police magistrate; born 1745; died 1813.

Quick, John, comedian; born in Whitechapel, 1748; died 1831.

Quin, James, actor; eminent in tragedy and comedy; generous friend to the poet Thomson, whom he delivered from arrest by a spontaneous present of £100, though then unknown to him; born in King Street, Covent Gar-den, 1693; died in Bath, 1766.

Radcliffe, Anne, novelist and traveller; author of the "Mysteries of Udolpho," and other romances; born 1764; died 1823.

Rastall, John, printer, historian, polemist, and compiler of law books; married a sister of Sir Thomas More; convert from Popery to Lutheranism; died in 1536.

Rawlinson, Sir Thomas, Lord Mayor of London; father of Thomas, the book collector, and Dr. Richard, the founder of an Anglo-Saxon professorship at Oxford; born in St. Dionis Backchurch, 1647; died 1705.

Reed, Isaac, conveyancer; critic, intimate with early English literature; editor of Shakspere; book collector; born in Stewart Street, Old Artillery Ground, 1742; died 1807.

Reeve, John, comedian and mimic; Ludgate Hill, 1799; died 1838.

Ricardo, David, writer on finance and statistics; of a Jewish family; married a quakeress, and became an unitarian; Member of Parliament for Portarlington; born 1772; died 1823.

Ridgley, Thomas, dissenting divine; born 1667.

Riley, John, painter to the king, whose works afford, says Lord Orford, draperies and heads which would have done honor to Lely or Kneller, but whose reputation was impeded by his modesty; born 1646; died 1691.

Roberts, Barré Charles, ingenious writer and medallist; born in St. Stephen's Court, Westminster, 1789; died 1810.

Rogers, Charles, antiquary and virtuoso; born in Dean Street, Soho, 1711; died 1784.

Rousseau, Samuel, printer, linguist, author of several works on the Persian language and literature; died in 1820.

Rowlandson, Thomas, graphic humorist ; born in Old Jewry, 1756; died 1827.

Rowley, William, physician ; opponent of vaccination ; author on diseases of the eye, &c.; born 1743; died 1806.

Ryan, Lacy, actor ; from observation of whom Garrick is said to have derived his excellence in Richard III.; author of " the Cobbler's Opera ; " born in Westminster about 1694 ; died 1760.

Ryland, William Wynne, engraver, who introduced stippling, and whose principal pieces were after Angelica Kauffman; born 1732; executed 1783, for a forgery on the East India Company.

Sale, John, musical composer and singer ; born 1758 ; died 1828.

Seward, William, biographer and anecdotist; educated at the Charter House; born 1747 ; died 1799.

Schnebbelie, Jacob, architectural draughtsman ; born in Westminster, 1760 ; died 1792.

Sharp, William, engraver of great merit ; successively adopted the visionary ideas of Mesmer, Swedenborg, Brothers, and Southcote ; and changed from the principles of Horne Tooke to Toryism; born in Haydon Yard, Minories, 1740; died at Chiswick, 1824.

Sherley, Thomas, physician to Charles II.; author of a curious essay " on the probable causes whence stones are produced in the earth, &c. ; " born in Westminster; died 1678.

Sherlock, Thomas, Bishop of London ; Master of the Temple ; defended the Corporation and Test Acts against Bishop Hoadly, whom he succeeded in the Bishoprics of Bangor and Salisbury ; refused the primacy ; his sermons were very eloquent; born 1678; died at Fulham, 1761.

Shirley, James, divine ; convert to Popery ; dramatic writer and poet of deserved reputation ; educated at Merchant

Tailors' School; born in St. Mary Woolchurch, 1594; died in 1666, from fright, occasioned by the fire of London. His wife also died from the same cause within 24 hours.

Skinner, Stephen, physician and philologist; died 1667.

Smith, John Raphael, designer and mezzotinto engraver; drew portraits in crayons with great felicity; born about 1740.

—— Dr. Thomas, divine, orientalist; lost his livings for refusing to take the oaths to King William; author of many learned works; born in Allhallows, Barking, 1638; died 1710, in London.

—— Sir William Sidney, Admiral of the Red; successfully defended Acre against Buonaparte; Park Lane, Westminster; died at Paris 1840, aged 76.

—— William ("gentleman" Smith), performer in tragedy and comedy, in the latter of which he was almost without a rival; born about 1730: died 1819, at Bury St. Edmund's.

Spencer, Sir Richard, K.C.H. Governor of Western Australia, and a Captain in the Royal Navy, in which service he gallantly distinguished himself; inventor of a life boat; born 1779; died 1839.

SPENSER, EDMUND, poet of imagination, feeling, description, and versification; Secretary to Lord Grey de Wilton, when Lord Lieutenant of Ireland: patronised by Sir Philip Sydney and Sir Walter Raleigh; driven from Ireland by the cruelties of Tyrone, who burnt his house with one of his children in it; born near the Tower, about 1553; died in 1598-9, and buried in Westminster Abbey.

Spiller, John, sculptor of great promise, pupil of Bacon; executed statue of Charles II. for the Royal Exchange; born 1763; died 1794, of pulmonary disease, and his beautiful wife died of the same disease a few months afterwards.

Stanhope, Philip Dormer, 4th Earl of Chesterfield; statesman, diplomatist, wit, and man of letters; distinguished for the elegance of his manners; his celebrated letters to his son were not written with a view to publication; born 1694; died 1773.

Stanley, John, blind musician of great talent; organist at Temple Church, and conductor of Handel's Oratorios after the death of the composer; born 1713; died 1786.

Stepney, George, poet, political writer, and diplomatist; born in Westminster in 1663; died at Chelsea, 1707.

Stevens, George Alexander, strolling player; writer of songs, poems, and inventor of a popular droll amusement, called a " Lecture on Heads;" died 1784.

Stewart, John, commonly called " Walking Stewart," from having perambulated on foot nearly half the globe, during which he encountered many singular and dangerous adventures; walked from the East Indies across the desert of Arabia to Europe; born in Bond Street; died in Northumberland Street, 1822.

Storace, Stephano, composer of dramatic music, remarkable for fire and spirit; born 1763; died in 1796.

Storer, Thomas, poet; died 1604.

Stowe, John, tailor, antiquary, chronicler, and historian of great industry, integrity, and much talent, who, when 78 years of age, was *rewarded* by receiving a license from James I. "to repair to churches or other places, to receive the gratuitous and charitable benevolence of well disposed people!" born in St. Michael's, Cornhill, 1525; died 1605, afflicted by poverty and disease; monument in the church of St. Andrew Undershaft.

Strange, Sir John, able lawyer; died 1705.

Stuart, James, antiquary, architectural draughtsman, called "Athenian Stuart," from the publication of his "Antiquities of Athens;" born 1713; died 1788, of grief for the death of a child.

—— James Edward Francis, "the Pretender," eldest son of James II. landed in Scotland from France to claim the throne; but was soon obliged to return to France; born St. James's Palace, 1688; died 1766.

Sturt, John, writing engraver, celebrated for letters on a minute scale; born 1658; died 1730.

Suett, Richard, inimitable actor in ludicrous comedy and broad farce; chorister at St. Paul's Cathedral; died 1805, aged 47, buried in St. Paul's Cathedral.

Sykes, Arthur Ashley, divine; educated at St. Paul's School, and became one of its assistants; Preacher at King Street Chapel, Golden Square, and St. James's Church; controversialist in favour of Whig principles, &c.; born about 1684; died 1756.

Taylor, Jane, amiable and accomplished poetess and essayist; born 1783; died 1823, of a pulmonary disease.

—— Thomas, "The Platonist;" translator of Pausanias, and voluminous author; born 1758; died 1836.

Temple, Sir William, patriotic statesman and diplomatist, and popular writer; born in 1628; died at Moor Park, Surrey, in 1700.

Thicknesse, Anne, wife of Governor Thicknesse; beautiful, accomplished, and exemplary authoress; imprisoned in France, and escaped the guillotine through the death of Robespierre, who had sent an order for her execution; born near the Temple, 1737; died in the Edgware Road, 1824.

Thornton, Bonnell, miscellaneous and humorous writer;

educated at Westminster School; born in Maiden Lane in
1724; died in 1770.

Tooke, Andrew, Head Master of the Charter House School,
where he had been educated; Gresham professor of Geo-
metry; author of school books; born in 1673; died in
1731.

—— John Horne, divine, of literary and political celebrity; educated at Westminster School; defended Wilkes
and advised Mr. Beckford to make his celebrated reply to
his Majesty; began the publication of the Debates in
Parliament, and defeated the House of Commons on the
question; replied to Junius, and esteemed to be the victor; resigned his gown and studied for the bar; acquired
the name and fortune of Mr. Tooke of Purley, by de-
feating an Enclosure Bill; imprisoned for sedition; author of " the Diversions of Purley," a work of high rank
in philology; tried for high treason, but acquitted; became the nominee of Lord Camelford for Old Sarum;
born in Newport Street, 1736, where his father was a
poulterer; died at Wimbledon, 1812.

Toulmin, Joshua, bookseller, and baptist and unitarian
preacher and author; born about 1742; died 1815.

Townley, James, divine, and author of the farce of " High
Life below Stairs ;" died 1778.

Trusler, John, divine; bookseller and compiler; born in
1735; died 1820.

Tucker, Abraham, metaphysician; author of " the Light of
Nature pursued;" born 1705; died 1774.

Twining, Thomas, learned divine; born 1734.

Tye, Christopher, musician; born in Westminster 16th century.

Tyrrell, James, historian; political writer; born in Great
Queen Street, Westminster, 1642; died 1718.

Vernon, Edward, gallant Admiral, but struck off the list for his opposition to the then ministry; born in Westminster, 1684; died 1757.

Verstegan, Richard, ingenious historical and antiquarian writer; born in the precinct of St. Katharine by the Tower; died at Antwerp in 1635.

Vertue, George, eminent engraver, whose works are very numerous; born in St. Martin's in the Fields, 1684; died 1756.

Viccars, John, zealous puritan, distinguished for intemperance and fanaticism; satirised in Hudibras; educated at Christ's Hospital, where he became one of the Under Masters; born about 1582; died 1652.

Villiers, George, 2d Duke of Buckingham; soldier, statesman, wit, and poet; distinguished for levity, imprudence, and profligacy; born at Wallingford House, Westminster, 1627; died 1688.

Vincent, Thomas, nonconformist divine; tutor in a dissenting academy at Islington; zealous during the great plague, on which he published a tract; died 1678.

—— William, critic and divine; pupil, usher, and Head Master at Westminster School; Rector of Allhallows, Thames Street; Dean of Westminster; born 1739; died 1815.

Uvedale, Robert, learned botanist and schoolmaster; educated at Westminster School; born in St. Margaret's, Westminster, 1642; died 1722.

Walker, Thomas, dramatic performer; the original representative of Macheath; born 1698; died in 1743, in great distress, produced by intemperance.

Ward, John, philologist, classical scholar, and antiquary;

9

lecturer on law; author of "Lives of Gresham Professors;" born 1679; died at Gresham College, 1758.

Warren, Dr. Richard, physician to George III.; writer on Bronchial Polypus, &c.; born 1732; died in 1797.

Warner, John, learned and munificent Bishop of Rochester; born in St. Clement Danes, about 1585; died 1666.

Warwick, Sir Philip, historical and miscellaneous writer; M.P. for Westminster; born in St. Margaret's, Westminster, 1608; died 1682.

Watson, Sir William, physician and natural philosopher; educated at Merchant-Taylors' School; made some electrical discoveries; born 1715; died 1787.

Webber, John, artist of considerable talent; born 1751.

Wewitzer, Ralph, comedian, author of a jest book, and inventor of some pantomimes; born 1748; died 1824, in indigent circumstances.

Wheatley, Charles, divine; lecturer at St. Mildred's in the Poultry; author of sermons, &c.; born in Paternoster Row, 1686; died in 1742.

—— Francis, R.A. painter of rural and domestic subjects; born 1747; died 1801.

Whitbread, Samuel, active and able Member of Parliament; conducted the impeachment of Lord Melville; born 1758; died by his own hand, 1815.

White, Robert, engraver; born in 1645.

Whitehead, Paul, poet and satirist; born in Castle Yard, Holborn, 1709-10; died 1774.

Whitelocke, Bulstrode, Justice of the King's Bench, statesman and historian; Member of Parliament and parliamentarian soldier and Commissioner; declined a peerage from Cromwell; born 1605; died 1676.

—— Sir James, learned and eloquent Judge of the King's

Bench ; father of the preceding ; Member of Parliament ; educated at Merchant Taylors' School; born about 1570 ; died 1632.

Wilcocks, Joseph, ingenious writer, benevolent philanthropist, and traveller ; called by Pope Clement XIII. " the blessed heretic ; " born in Dean's Yard, Westminster, 1723 ; died 1791.

WILKES, JOHN, politician ; author of the " North Briton," for No. 45 of which he was prosecuted, but obtained a victory over the government ; printed an obscene poem called an "Essay on Woman," for which, and for blasphemy, he was tried, and, being abroad, was expelled the House of Commons and outlawed ; on his return his outlawry was reversed; he was elected M.P. for Middlesex, but again expelled, and declared ineligible to sit in Parliament ; became Alderman of Farringdon Without, Sheriff, and Lord Mayor; again elected for Middlesex, and sat in Parliament, and in 1779 chosen Chamberlain of London ; born 1727 ; died 1797.

Williams, Helen Maria, devotee of the French Revolution; died 1828.

Windham, William, eloquent senator and statesman ; Secretary at War in the administration of Lord Grenville and Fox; born 1750 ; died 1810.

Woolhouse, John Thomas, oculist to William III. and author.

Wray, Daniel, man of taste and learned writer ; born in St. Botolph, Aldersgate, 1701 ; died 1782.

Wren, Matthew, Bishop of Ely, imprisoned in the Tower for 18 years, having been impeached by the Commons for being connected with Archbishop Laud ; born in St. Peter Cheap, 1585; died 1667.

Wright, Abraham, divine, loyalist, and learned author ;

educated at Merchant-Taylors' School; born in Black
Swan Alley, Thames Street, 1611 ; died 1690.

York, Frederick Duke of, second son of George III. ;
Commander in Chief; able and active official man ; born
in Buckingham House, 1763; died 1827.

MISCELLANEOUS OBSERVATIONS.

London and Westminster contain above 8000 streets, lanes, alleys, and courts, and above 65 different squares. It has at least 246 churches and chapels, 207 meeting-houses for dissenters, 43 chapels for foreigners, and 6 synagogues for Jews—making 502 places of public worship. Thirty-five Churches burnt at the fire were not rebuilt, two have since been destroyed to make room for the Bank and Royal Exchange; and one for the new street to London Bridge. The churches remaining and rebuilt amount to 59; making a total of 97 churches within the city walls at the period of the fire. 22 churches were not burnt, and nine of them have been since rebuilt. The number of inhabitants during the sitting of Parliament is estimated at 1,250,000. In this vast city there are upwards of 4000 seminaries, public and private, for education, 10 institutions for promoting the arts and sciences, 122 asylums for the indigent, 17 for the sick and lame, 13 dispensaries, 704 charitable institutions, 58 courts of justice, 4040 professional men connected with the various departments of the law.

For lighting London and its suburbs with gas, there are eighteen public gas-works; twelve public gas-work companies; £2,800,000 in capital employed in works, pipes, tanks, gas-holders, and apparatus; £450,000 yearly revenue de-

rived; 180,000 tons of coals used in the year for making
gas; 134,300 private burners supplied to about 40,000 cus-
tomers; 30,400 public or street consumers; 380 lamp-
lighters employed; 176 gas-holders, several of which are
double ones, capable of storing 5,500,000 cubic feet of gas;
890 tons of coals used in the retorts, in the shortest day, in
twenty-four hours; 7,120,000 cubic feet of gas used in the
longest night, say 24th December; about 2500 persons employed in the metropolis alone in this branch of manufacture; between 1822 and 1827, the consumption was nearly
doubled; and between 1827 and 1837, it was again nearly
doubled.

The quantity of water *daily* supplied by the 8 different
water companies in 1833-4 was 21,110,555 imperial gallons.
By far the greatest portion of this was drawn from the
Thames, a small quantity from Hampstead, and the re-
mainder from the Lea and New Rivers. The capital expended on the works of these companies then amounted to
£3,170,000; and their gross rental to nearly £300,000.
The number of houses or buildings was nearly 200,000,
with an average (including manufactories and private dwellings) supply of about 180 gallons, at the rate of 10 gallons for every individual of the population, at an average
cost of about 30*s.* per annum for each house.

Coal was only partially used so late as 1640. The consumption of coals is now two million of tons annually.

The total value of butchers' meat sold annually in Smithfield Market, is stated at £8,500,000; 65,000,000 quartern
loaves are consumed per year; Vegetables and fruits
£1,000,000 per year; and Milk £1,250,000.

The Port of London, as actually occupied by shipping,
extends from London Bridge to Deptford, being a distance
of nearly four miles, and is from four to five hundred
yards in average breadth. It may be described as con-

sisting of four divisions, called the upper, middle, and
lower pools, and the space between Limehouse and Deptford; the upper pool extends from London Bridge to
Union Hole, about 1600 yards; the middle pool, thence
to Wapping New Stairs, 700 yards; the lower pool, from
the latter place to Horseferry Tier, near Limehouse, 1800
yards; and the space below to Deptford, about 2700 yards.
There are 13,300 vessels trading in the river Thames in
the course of a year, and 40,000 waggons going and returning to the metropolis in the same period. The amount
of exports and imports to and from the Thames is estimated
at £66,841,924 sterling annually, and the property floating
in the vast city every year is £170,000,000 sterling.

A penny post was first established in the year 1683, by a
person named Murray, an upholsterer.

Silk weaving was introduced into Spitalfields, Seven Dials,
Soho, &c. by Frenchmen, driven to find a refuge in this
country, through the revocation of the edict of Nantes,
in 1687.

Houses were principally built of wood and thatched with
reeds or straw, till the time of Richard I. In 1189 an
order was issued by the Mayor, that they should be of
stone to a certain height, and be covered in with slates or
tiles.

Shops were not inclosed as now till after 1710. They were
open, as are those of butchers and potatoe dealers in the
present day.

The King cannot legally enter the city without permission
of the Lord Mayor, and whenever Majesty deigns to do
so, it is customary to close the doors of Temple Bar, and
undergo the ceremony of knocking, asking for, and ob-
taining permission.

Londoners have for many centuries been spoken of reproachfully under the name of Cockneys. The origin of this term is uncertain, but many glossarists have variously attempted to explain it. It seems to have been meant to imply, one brought up in London, and ignorant of all the rest of the world.

The LONDON GATES were, *Aldgate*, one of the four original gates of the Roman city; rebuilt 1606; finally taken down in 1760. *Bishopsgate*, built by Bishop Erkenwald, in the 7th century; re-erected 1731, and finally taken down in 1760. *Moorgate*, erected in 1415, and was one of the most magnificent. *Cripplegate*, pulled down in 1760. *Aldersgate*, one of the four original gates; rebuilt 1617, and repaired after the fire 1670; pulled down in 1760. *Newgate*, rebuilt after the fire, with great magnificence, and used as a prison; pulled down in 1760. *Ludgate*, one of the original four gates; pulled down in 1760. *Posterngate*, on Tower Hill, erected soon after the Conquest.

In the *Adelphi Terrace*, at the centre house, Garrick the actor resided; and here resided his widow till her death in 1822.

Addle Street, Cripplegate, was formerly called King Adel Street, from the Saxon King Athelstan, who had a house in it, and built the church.

At No. 18, *Aldermanbury*, resided the infamous Judge Jeffreys.

In *Aldersgate Street*, the Marquesses of Dorchester and Earls of Westmorland had mansions.—The Half Moon Tavern was the resort of the wits temp. Charles II.—The Old Mourning Bush Tavern is said to have taken its appellation from the death of Charles I., when the landlord painted with black the bush that hung outside his inn.—In the Gate resided John Day, the early printer.

At *Allhallows, Barking*, were buried Fisher, Bishop of

Rochester; the accomplished Earl of Surrey; and Archbishop Laud, all of whom suffered death on Tower Hill.

Of *Allhallows, London Wall*, the Rev. William Beloe, translator of Herodotus, &c. and elegant poet, was rector. He died in 1817.

In the *Almonry*, Westminster, WILLIAM CAXTON, the first English printer, exercised his art under the patronage of the Abbot of Westminster (Billing), 1474.   Caxton's imprints speak of "*in* the Abbey of Westminster," and of the "Almonesrye." He died in 1492, and was buried in St. Margaret's Church, Westminster.

In *Angel Court*, Shoe Lane, the poet Chatterton committed suicide in 1778.

In the *Armourers' and Braziers' Hall*, Coleman Street, is the fine painting by Northcote, of the entry of Richard II. and Henry Bolingbroke into London.

Ashburnham House, in Little Dean's Yard, Westminster, was built by Inigo Jones. The principal staircase excites the admiration of all architects. In this house was deposited the Cottonian Library, here nearly destroyed by fire in 1731. The collection is now at the British Museum. In the garden is an alcove attributed to Inigo Jones, imitative of part of a small Roman temple. In the coal-cellar are remains of the conventual vaults; and in the wall may be seen a capital of the time of Edward the Confessor.

Bangor Court, Shoe Lane, pointed out the site of the residence of the Bishops of that see. It is now nearly covered by Bangor House, the printing office of Messrs. S. Bentley and Co.

In *Barbican* resided, in the time of Edward II, the Earls of Suffolk; and afterwards Peregrine Bertie, Lord Willoughby.

In *Bartholomew Close*, Smithfield, Dr. Franklin worked as a journeyman printer, with Mr. Palmer, in 1724, when he first came to London.

In *Beech Lane*, Barbican, the Abbots of Ramsey had a house, afterwards occupied by Prince Rupert.

Near *Beer Lane*, Great Tower Street, was the residence of Alderman Beckford; distinguished for his rejoinder, when Mayor, to the reply of George III. to an address from the city.

In *Bell Savage Court*, Ludgate Hill, Grinling Gibbons resided, and here carved a pot of flowers in so exquisite a manner that they became agitated by even the gentlest wind.

In *Bolt Court*, Fleet Street, was the residence of Dr. Samuel Johnson.

In *Bow Church*, Cheapside, are generally preached the Boyle Lectures, a series of eight sermons yearly in defence of natural and revealed religion, founded by the Hon. Robert Boyle. In this church the Bishops of London are consecrated. Here was buried Thomas Newton, Bishop of Bristol, and Dean of St. Paul's (formerly Rector), who died 1782.

In *Bread Street* resided the father of Milton, who was a scrivener. The house, in which the poet was born, still remains.

BROADWAY CHURCH, Westminster, was converted into a stable during the Civil War by the soldiers of the Parliament; rebuilt in 1842.—In the burial ground is a tablet to Margaret Patten, who died on June 26, 1739, aged 136. Her death took place in the parish workhouse in Dean Street, where her portrait is still preserved.

In *Brownlow Street*, Drury Lane, George Vertue, the eminent engraver, resided.

The site of *Buckingham Palace* was formerly the Mulberry Gardens. John Sheffield, Duke of Buckingham, who died 1720, built a house here, afterwards the town residence of Queen Charlotte, and where all her children but Prince

George was born. It was nearly pulled down in 1825, and the present palace commenced by Nash, and finished by E. Blore.

Bucklersbury was formerly inhabited by grocers and druggists, and the smell of the spices, &c. is supposed to have preserved the street from the ravages of the plague. Shakspere speaks of smelling like Bucklersbury in "simple time."

Budge Row was so named from having been the residence of persons dealing in budge or lambskin furs.—At the church of St. Antholin a sermon is preached every evening in the week, for which various legacies have been left.

Over the entrance of *Bull Head Court, Newgate Street*, is a stone representing William Evans, Charles the First's gigantic porter, who was seven feet and a half high, and the dwarf Jeffrey Hudson, his fellow servant, who, when 8 years old, and only 18 inches high, was served up in a cold pie, and presented therefrom to the Queen, by the Duchess of Buckingham, at Burley on the Hill. After thirty years of age he began to grow again, and reached 3 feet 9 inches. His dress is preserved in the Ashmolean Museum at Oxford.

Burlington House, Piccadilly, was erected by Lord Burlington, and designed to have been placed " so far out of town that no building should be raised beyond it ; " south façade designed 1717, and the entrance gateway and screen wall in 1718. Sir William Chambers says, "few in this vast city suspect, I believe, that behind an old brick wall in Piccadilly, *there is one of the finest pieces of architecture in Europe*." With the exception of the front elevation, the house has been rebuilt by the late Earl of Burlington, who (when Lord George Cavendish) purchased the property in 1815. The ceiling of the saloon was painted by Sir James Thornhill. Other ceilings were painted by Marco Ricci and his uncle Sebastian.

At the meeting house in *Bury Street*, Houndsditch, the celebrated Dr. Watts used to preach.

Castle Street, Holborn, was in 1619 the residence of Thomas Howard, Earl of Arundel, who first introduced uniformity of building into England.

In *Fleet Street*, near to Chancery Lane, Izaak Walton, angler, had his residence.

At *Charing Cross*, opposite the Admiralty, the poet Thomson wrote his "Winter."

In *Cheapside*, the house now occupied by Mr. Tegg, the bookseller, was erected by Sir Christopher Wren in 1668-9.

In *Chiswell Street* is Caslon's type-foundry, the first of the kind in the Metropolis.

In *Christ Church*, Newgate Street, was buried Mr. Burdett, ancestor to Sir Francis Burdett, who was tried and executed for wishing that the horns of a favorite white buck of his, which had been killed by Edward IV., were in the body of the King or his adviser. Richard Baxter, nonconformist divine, was also buried in this church.

At *Cloth Fair*, Smithfield, a court of *pied poudré* was held daily, during Smithfield Fair, for the trial of debts and contracts, and minor offences. Cloth Fair is a privileged place, and closed at a certain hour every night.

Coachmakers' Hall, Noble Street, Foster Lane, was formerly used as a Debating Society, and there Lord George Gordon used to speak. It was also occupied by the Cecilian Society, and there Mrs. Billington was accustomed to sing.

At *Coopers' Hall*, Basinghall Street, the Lotteries used to be drawn, after the drawing was not permitted in Guildhall. The last drawing took place in 1826.

In *Cock Lane*, Smithfield, in 1762, a female, by the aid of ventriloquism, acted the part of a ghost, and imposed on a great many reputable and learned people. She formed.

the subject of Churchill's satirical poem, entitled "The Ghost."

  Cornhill, or *Quern Hill,* was a favorite spot for the residences of the principal Romans in Britain. It was afterwards much noted for its dealers in old clothes and receivers of stolen goods.—Here Daniel De Foe, author of "Robinson Crusoe," &c. kept a hosier's shop, and here he stood in the pillory for writing a pamphlet entitled, "The shortest way with the Dissenters."

  "Earless on high, stood unabash'd Defoe."—Pope.

—On the site of the Pope's Head Tavern, King John had a royal palace, whither the great Hubert de Burgh was cited to appear before him.

Covent Garden was formerly an extensive garden belonging to the Abbot and Convent of Westminster, and thence named *Convent Garden.* It was granted by Edw. VI. to the ill-fated Edward Seymour, Duke of Somerset, on whose attainder it was granted to the Russells Earls of Bedford, who built a house for a town residence near the bottom of what is now Southampton Street.—In the church of St. Paul, Covent Garden, was buried Sir Peter Lely, the painter, who died Nov. 30, 1680, aged 63 ; his bust and monument was destroyed in the fire of 1795. Here is a tablet to Charles Macklin, the comedian, who died July 11, 1797, aged 107 years. He was buried in the churchyard, where many other theatrical performers of much eminence have been interred; and where also lie the remains of Samuel Butler, author of "Hudibras," and Dr. Wolcot, alias "Peter Pindar."

  In *Craven Street,* Strand, at No. 7, resided Dr. Franklin.

  In *Crooked Lane,* Edward the Black Prince is said to have resided.

  In *Crosby Place,* Richard Duke of Gloucester resided, and it is traditionally said that here he concerted his plots during the reign of the young Edward; and here the citizens came to beg his acceptance of the Crown; but these assertions are not supported by history. Here many Ambassadors have been lodged. In 1586 Henry Ramelius, Chancellor of Denmark; 1603, Monsr. de Rosny, great Treasurer of France; and here also were lodged the learned Barnevelt; the son of William Prince of Orange; and Mons. Fulke. In the 17th century it was the residence of the rich merchant Sir John Spencer and his heirs the Earls of Northumberland. It was used as a presbyterian meeting house from 1662 to 1769; and subsequently became a packer's premises. It has recently been restored, at the suggestion and under the auspices of Miss Hackett; and was fitted up in 1842 for a Literary Institution and Music-room.

At *Crutched Friars' Hall* was the first manufactory of Glass in England.

Devonshire House, Piccadilly, was erected by Kent, at the cost of £20,000. The old house was frequented by Waller, Denham, and most of the wits of the time of Charles II.

On the site of *Devonshire Square*, Bishopsgate, was Jasper Fisher's Folly, a magnificent structure, afterwards the town residence of the Cavendishes, Earls of Devonshire. It became a conventicle in the Civil Wars, and is alluded to by Butler in his "Hudibras."

The *Dissenters' Library*, in Red Cross Street, contains, among others, good portraits of the founder, Dr. Williams, Dr. Priestley, Isaac Watts, W. Tonge, A. Kippis, and A. Rees. Among the books is a copy of the Salisbury Liturgy, finely illuminated; and in the Library is a glass basin, said to have contained the water at Queen Elizabeth's baptism.

At the bottom of *Dorset Street*, or *Dorset Gardens*, Fleet Street, was the Duke's Theatre, designed by Wren, for Sir William Davenant, and pulled down in 1709

In *Duke Street*, Lincoln's Inn Fields, Dr. Franklin resided while engaged as a compositor in Watts's printing office.

In *Duke Street*, Westminster, the infamous Judge Jeffreys resided.

In *Eastcheap*, was an old inn, called the Boar's Head, celebrated by Shakspere. A house with a boar's head in the wall marked the site of it. The Street was pulled down to make the Approaches to New London Bridge.

In the Library of the *East India House* are Tippoo Saib's copy of the Koran; some hundred volumes of Chinese books; and in the Museum was the footstool of Tippoo's throne, of solid gold, in the form of a tiger's head; with eyes and teeth of crystal; &c. It has been removed to Windsor Castle.

At *Ely House,* on the site of Ely Place, Holborn, died John of Ghent, Duke of Lancaster ("time-honoured Lancaster,") in 1399. He went to reside there on the destruction by fire of the Savoy Palace by Wat Tyler.—It belonged to the see of Ely near 486 years, and was sold by the see about 1775. The present Ely House is in Dover Street.

At *Fishmongers' Hall* is preserved the dagger of Sir William Walworth, and a bust of the brave citizen by Pierce.

On *Fleet Bridge* was the first manufactory of knives in England, in 1563. The use of forks at table was not general till the time of James I.

In *Friday Street* is the Nag's Head Tavern, celebrated as the fictitious scene of the consecration of the Protestant Bishops in 1559; refuted by Strype in his Life of Archbishop Parker.

Garter Place, Barbican, takes its name from having been the residence of Sir Thomas Wriothesley, Garter king of arms, uncle to the first Earl of Southampton.

In the old *Gatehouse Prison*, Dean's Yard, Westminster, removed in 1777, were confined Sir Walter Raleigh, thence conducted to the place of his execution in New Palace

Yard ; Colonel Richard Lovelace, who presented to the House of Commons the celebrated Kentish petition for the restoring the King to his rights, and there "made that celebrated song, called "*Stone walls do not a prison make;*" Lady Purbeck, daughter of Chief Justice Coke, for adulterous intimacy with Sir Robert Howard; Sir Charles Lyttleton, characterized by Clarendon as one "worth his weight in gold," committed by the Parliament, and released at the Restoration; the Journalist Pepys, charged with being affected towards the abdicated James II. and many other persons of note.

In *Gerrard Street*, Soho, Dryden lived, and wrote his "Ode to St. Cecilia's Day." The house is now occupied by a tallow chandler.

At *Goldsmiths' Hall*, amongst much splendid plate, is preserved a gold and crystal cup, from which Queen Elizabeth is said to have drank to the success of her fleet in 1588.

At *Gray's Inn*, the elm trees on each side of the walk in the garden were planted by the illustrious Bacon.

In *Great Russell Street*, Covent Garden, at No. 17, was Tom's Coffee House, a fashionable resort at the beginning of the eighteenth century, for "playing at Picket," and for "the best conversation." Among the members of the club in 1768 were, besides many titled people, Foote, Murphy, Garrick, George Colman, Dr. Dodd, Sir Nathaniel Dance, Philip Francis, and in 1773, Dr. Goldsmith was admitted.

In *Great Windmill Street*, Dr. William Hunter resided.

In *Green Arbour Court*, Old Bailey, Oliver Goldsmith resided, in a wretched room in No. 12, and therein wrote his "Vicar of Wakefield," "Traveller," &c.

Grub Street, Cripplegate, was once noted for the residences of unfortunate authors; now for its asylum for the destitute. Here resided Henry Welby, who lived in perfect seclusion 44 years on account of a vow made on an attempt at his life by an ungrateful brother, and died October 29, 1636.

In the *Guildhall* are monuments to Alderman Beckford ;
Earl of Chatham, with an inscription by Edmund Burke ;
William Pitt, inscription by George Canning ; Lord Nelson,
inscription by Richard Brinsley Sheridan ; &c.   In the
Council Chamber are a statue of George III. by Chantrey,
and many pictures of historic interest, portraits, and busts.

In *Hanover Square*, Cripplegate, resided General Monk,
restorer of Charles II.

In *Hatton Garden* resided Sir Edward Coke, the lawyer;
Dr. Edward Stillingfleet, afterwards Bishop of Worcester ;
and Dr. Moor, Bishop of Norwich.

In *High Street*, St. Giles's, in 1837 were discovered, just
opposite the church, two elm trees in a high state of preservation, at a depth of about 15 feet under the surface of the
ground.   They are supposed to have belonged to a forest
which once covered the district.

In *Holborn*, John Gerard, the celebrated botanist, had his
garden, temp. Elizabeth.

The site of the *Horse Guards*, was the Tiltyard of
Whitehall Palace.

In *Ivy Lane* was held the *Hum-drum Club*, described in
the Spectator as consisting of honest gentlemen, of peaceable
dispositions, who used to sit together, smoke their pipes,
and say nothing till midnight.

In *Jewin Street*, Cripplegate, the poet Milton resided.

Leicester Place, Leicester Fields, stands on the site of
Leicester House, a seat of the Sydneys, Earls of Leicester.
Here resided, for a short time, Elizabeth, dau. of James I.
Queen of Bohemia, who died here in 1661.   George II.
when Prince of Wales, on quarrelling with his father, lived
here for several years.   His son, Frederick Prince of Wales,
on quarrelling with him, also came hither, and here he died.
It has been called " the pouting place of princes."   It afterwards held the museum of Sir Ashton Lever.   Leicester

r

House was pulled down, and Leicester Place now occupies the site.

In *Leicester Square* resided the patriotic Sir George Saville; and the celebrated painters, Sir Joshua Reynolds, Hogarth, and Northcote.

In *Leadenhall Street* stood the mansion of Leadenhall, which in 1309 belonged to Sir Hugh Neville, and in 1408 was purchased by the celebrated Whittington and presented to the city.—No. 46 was "Dirty Dick's," where an eccentric hardwareman of the name of Bentley resided, and obtained for himself and house the appellation of "Dirty."—The Old King's Head Tavern was the rendez-vous of Guy Fawkes and his city adherents.—No. 71 is on the site of the house in which Stowe, the antiquary and historian, died, poor, aged 80! Under the house No. 153, is a crypt, supposed to be the remains of part of the old church of St. Peter; and at the junction of Leadenhall Street, Aldgate High Street, and Fenchurch Street, near Aldgate Pump, is another crypt, the remains of the antient church of St. Michael.

In *Lincoln's Inn Hall* is a painting of Paul before Felix, by Hogarth; and an admirable marble statue of Lord Erskine, by Westmacott; cost 2300 guineas, subscribed by the barristers.—In the erection of the Chapel, Ben Jonson, the poet, is said to have assisted by working with his trowel.

In *Lincoln's Inn Fields*, the patriotic William Lord Russell and Algernon Sydney lost their heads in the year 1683.

Lombard Street takes its name from the Lombards, the great bankers of antient times. In this street and the neighbourhood, a majority of the banking establishments are still to be found.—On the site of the banking house of Messrs. Stone and Co. 68, Lombard Street, was the residence of Sir Thomas Gresham. — The husband of Jane Shore, concubine of the licentious Edward IV. was Mr. Matthew Shore, a goldsmith in this street.

Of the *London Institution*, then in Old Jewry, Professor Porson was the first librarian. He died in his apartments there of apoplexy in 1808. The present Institution in Finsbury Place, Moorfields, was erected in 1815.

In *Lovell's Court*, Fetter Lane, Richardson wrote his novels of Pamela and Grandison.

Of *Merchant Taylors' School* the first master was the learned philologist, Richard Mulcaster, appointed 1561. Among his successors were William Dugard, committed to Newgate, Feb. 1649, for publishing " Salmasius's Defence of King Charles I. ;" and John Goad, dismissed in 1681, for writing "A Comment on the Church Catechism." Among the most eminent scholars appear the names of Archbishops Juxon, Dawes, and Gilbert; Bishops Buckeridge and Wilcocks of Rochester ; Andrewes of Winchester ; Boyle of Waterford ; Thomas of Lincoln ; Henshaw of Peterborough ; the Lord Keeper Whitelock, &c. &c.

Milton Street, formerly *Grub Street,* was long proverbial as the abode of poor and hired authors. It was the residence of writers of A B C books, &c. before the introduction of printing. In it lived and died Fox the martyrologist ; and here resided Speed the historian ; Richard Smith, the antiquary ; and the poet Milton.

The Meeting-house in *Monkwell Street*, was the first in London, being opened by Mr. Doolittle in the reign of Charles II.; Dr. James Fordyce was subsequently a popular preacher here.

. From the *Monument* in September 1732 a sailor slid down a rope ; and on the following morning, as it hung perpendicular, a waterman's boy descended. Two young women and a boy have recently committed suicide by throwing themselves from the top of the Monument.

Moorfields, now thickly studded with elegant houses, was the general resort of the citizens for divers amusements. Here the well-meaning Whitfield long preached successfully.

Of *New Inn,* in the Strand, Sir Thomas More, Lord Chancellor, was a student before he entered as a member of Lincoln's Inn.

The number of visitors to the *National Gallery,* Trafalgar Square, has increased from 125,000 in the year 1837, to 397,649 in 1838 ; and in 1840 to upwards of 500,000.

Newcastle House, at the corner of Queen Street, Lincoln's Inn Fields, was built for the Marquess of Powis in 1686. It was subsequently the residence of Sir Nathan Wright, Lord Chancellor Somers, and Thomas Pelham Holles, Duke of Newcastle. To it might be applied Pope's lines on Hampton Court :

> " Here thou, great Anna, whom three realms obey,
>   Dost sometimes counsel take, and sometimes tea."

At the *New Court Meeting-house,* Carey Street, the eccentric Daniel Burgess, who preached with an hour-glass by his side, and his no less eccentric successor, Tom Bradbury, occupied the pulpit.

In *New Palace Yard,* Westminster, died on April 7, 1836, in his 81st year, William Godwin, author of "Caleb Williams," &c.

In the *Old Bailey,* Jonathan Wilde resided; as did also Peter Bales, celebrated penman, in the time of Elizabeth.

In *Old Jewry* resided the pious and patriotic Granville Sharp, whose father was a surgeon here.

In *Orchard Street,* Westminster, in 1757, resided Thomas Amory, an eccentric man and author of "Memoirs," &c.

The Chapel in *Oxenden Street,* Haymarket, was first built as a meeting-house by the celebrated Richard Baxter.

In *Painter Stainers' Hall*, Little Trinity Lane, are very many pictures, principally executed by members. Among them is a landscape by Lambert, with figures by Hogarth, representing the story of the "babe with bloody hands," from Spenser's Faërie Queen. There is also a portrait of Camden the antiquary, whose father was a Member of the Company, and gave them a silver cup and cover, still annually used on St. Luke's day. Sir Joshua Reynolds was also a Member.

In *Pannier Alley*, between Newgate Street and Paternoster Row, is a stone, with the figure of a boy sitting on a pannier, and this inscription:

When y^v have sough^t
The Citty rovnd
Yet still this is
the Highst Ground,
Augvst the 27,
1688.

Pardon Passage, Charterhouse Square, is named from the church, founded in 1348, called Pardon Church, which stood on the spot; and where it was customary to bury persons who had committed suicide, or had been executed. In the year of its consecration, in 1349, a great plague raged, and 50,000 bodies were buried here.

At *Paul's Cross* Jane Shore did penance; and here the project of Richard III.'s ascent to the throne was first broached by the celebrated Dr. Shaw. Elizabeth Barton, called the "Holy Maid of Kent," a pretended prophetess, was exposed upon a scaffold here, previous to her being hung at Tyburn, in 1534.

In *Petticoat Lane*, temp. James I. the famous Count Gondomar resided; it was then occupied by many pleasant houses of the citizens.

While the *Physicians' College* was in Amen Corner, Paternoster row, Dr. William Harvey, immortalized by the discovery of the circulation of the blood, erected a convocation room, and a museum in the garden, filled with choice books and chirurgical instruments, which in 1652 he gave to the college, at a splendid entertainment to which he had invited all the members.

In *Portugal Street*, Lincoln's Inn Fields, was formerly a theatre, built by the poet, Sir William Davenant, on the site of a Tennis Court. It is now the China warehouses of Messrs. Copeland and Co.—At Watts's printing office, Dr. Franklin worked as a compositor in 1725. His lodgings were in Duke Street, facing the Catholic Chapel.

Prescott Street, Goodman's Fields, was the only street which had numbers on the houses till the time of Queen Anne.

In *Printing House Square* was the office of Thomas Baskett, the King's printer; now the extensive premises for printing the Times newspaper.

In *Pudding Lane* began the fire of London in 1666.

Pye Corner was so called, says Dr. Howel, of such a sign, sometimes a fair inne for receipt of travellers. This place is alluded to in Ben Jonson's "Bartholomew Fair," where Littlewit, the proctor, thus addresses his wife, Win-the-fight: "Long to eat of a pig, sweet Win, i'th fair, do you see? i'the heart of the fair; not at Pye-corner." It was estimated in the year 1732 that the number of sucking pigs then annually consumed in the city of London amounted to 52,000.—This was the spot where the great fire of 1666 terminated.

On the site of the *Royal Exchange* was erected in 1282 a prison for offenders against morals, and called from its shape "the Tun Prison." It was removed, with a number of small alleys, to make room for Sir Thomas Gresham's Exchange, of which the first stone was laid in 1566, and it was proclaimed in 1571 as " the Royal Exchange," in the presence of Queen Elizabeth, who had previously honoured the munificent merchant with her company at dinner at his house in Broad Street. This building was destroyed in the fire of London, and its re-erection was commenced in 1667. The statue of Charles the Second, which occupied the centre of the Piazza, was the work of Spiller, a young and talented artist, whose enthusiasm was so great, that, though consumption was doing its fatal work, he persisted in labouring at it, in spite of earnest advice to the contrary. He was willing, he said, to die at the foot of the statue. It was completed, and raised to its destined site ; the young martyr to his profession gazed upon it there, returned home, and soon was known no more ! This statue escaped at the last fire, which occurred on the 10th Jan. 1838. The statues of Charles I. and II. (by Bushnell) on the south front, as also the modern statues by Bubb of the Four Quarters of the Globe, were likewise preserved. The latter have since been transferred to Nicholson's Wharf, near London Bridge. The statues of the Kings, round the area, previous to Charles II. were mostly by Cibber; those of George I. and II. by Rysbrach, and those of George III. and IV. by Bubb. These were all more or less destroyed, and sold among the old materials. Sir Thomas Gresham's statue, which escaped the fire of 1666, was destroyed in 1838, that of Sir John Barnard a second time escaped, together with a modern monument to Mr. Lyddeker, founder of the Merchants' Hospital Ship.—The first stone of the new Royal Exchange was laid Jan. 17, 1842, by Prince Albert. The Latin inscription on the stone was written by Dr. Blomfield, Bp. of London. The architect is William Tite, Esq. F.R.S. and F.S.A. — Under the Exchange, Alexander Cruden, author of the Concordance of the Scriptures, had a bookseller's shop. — In excavating the site of the new Royal Exchange, in 1841, an extensive gravel-pit was found, and amongst the *debris* were discovered large quantities of bones and other remains of animal and vegetable matter, with abundance of articles of domestic life, as shoes and sandals, knives and cutting instruments, on some of which were engraved the names of the makers; and some weaving instruments, in which part of the wool remained entwined, and which seemed to show the antiquity of this branch of staple manufacture. There were also found coins of Vespatian, Domitian, and Severus, but in the rubbish at top were coins of much later dates, showing this part of the city to be of comparatively recent formation. From the discovery within the last few years of tessellæ in the Bank of England, Cornhill, and the site of the French church in Threadneedle Street, where Roman villas doubtless stood, it would appear that Roman London was continually entrenching on the fields which surrounded it, and that the excavation alluded to was situate in fields, and was employed to furnish materials for the use of the Roman citizens.

At *St. Andrew's Church*, Holborn, was baptized the wretchedly unfortunate poet Savage, and in the parish were his early years very humbly spent. Here was married the great Sir Edward Coke to Lady Elizabeth Hatton; and here was rector the famous Dr. Sacheverel.—In the time of Henry VII. the rector was fined 4*d.* by the churchwardens, for driving a cart across the churchyard to the rectory.

Of *St. Andrew the Wardrobe* and *St. Anne Blackfriars*, was rector William Romaine, the popular preacher. He was, at different times, also lecturer at St. Dunstan's in the West; Assistant Morning Preacher at St. George's, Hanover Square; Curate of St. Olave's; Morning Preacher at St. Bartholomew's the Great; and Minister of Broadway Chapel, Westminster. In the church were buried Isaac

Oliver, unrivalled miniature painter, whose monument was destroyed during the fire of 1666; and its pious minister, the Rev. William Romaine, executed by Bacon, considered one of his best works, and erected by public subscription.—In the parish the painter Vandyck resided.

St. Andrew Undershaft was so named from a May-pole or shaft which used to be raised by it every year on the first of May, higher than the church steeple. After "Evil May Day," 1517, it was discontinued.

In *St. Anne's Churchyard*, Soho, was buried Theodore King of Corsica, with a stone erected by Horace Walpole in 1758.

In *St. Bartholomew the Great* are monuments to Sir Walter Mildmay, Chancellor of the Exchequer in the time of Queen Elizabeth, who died in 1576, and Edward Cooke, philosopher.

In *St. Bartholomew the Less* parish resided Sir Dudley Carleton.

At *St. Benedict*, Paul's Wharf, Lord Orford says Inigo Jones was buried.

In *St. Botolph's Church*, Bishopsgate, is a curious old and good picture of Charles I. emblematically describing his sufferings. Sir Paul Pindar's monument is here.

In *St. Bride's*, Fleet Street, were interred Wynken de Worde, the second English printer; Sir Richard Baker, author of "Chronicles;" and Samuel Richardson the printer, author of "Sir Charles Grandison," &c.

In *St. Catharine Cree Church* was buried, in 1554, the celebrated painter, Holbein, who died in Cree Church House; and Sir Nicholas Throgmorton.

In the Vestry-room of *St. Clement Danes*, is a picture by Kent, (formerly the altar-piece) some of the figures of which are said to be portraits of the wife and children of the Pretender. This painting was caricatured by Hogarth.

In *St. Dionis Backchurch* are preserved several syringes of brass, holding about a gallon of water, and resembling the garden syringe; the only instruments for putting out fires before the great Fire of London.

In the old Church of *St. Dunstan's in the West*, was an oval tablet to H. Judkin, "the honest solicitor of Clifford's Inn," who died June 30, 1818, erected by his clients! The lectureship was held by the popular preacher, William Romaine, who, in consequence of the opposition of the parish authorities, frequently lectured by the light of one candle, which he held in his hand.

In the church of *St. Edmund the King*, Lombard Street, is a monument to Dr. Jeremiah Milles (ob. 1784), Dean of Exeter, and President of the Society of Antiquaries.

Of *St. George the Martyr*, Queen Square, the antiquary, Dr. Stukeley, died rector in 1766.

In the church of *St. George*, Hanover Square, is an antient stained glass window, which formerly belonged to a convent at Malines, and was executed about the latter end of the 15th century. It represents the genealogy of Christ, as derived from Jesse, and was put up in its present situation in 1840.—The altar-piece is the Last Supper, painted by Sir James Thornhill.—Of this parish were Rectors, Dr. Moss, Bishop of Bath and Wells, 1774; and Bishop Courtenay, of Exeter.

In *St. Giles's in the Fields Church*, or Churchyard, were buried Andrew Marvell; Sir Roger L'Estrange; and Richard Pendrell, preserver of Charles II.

In *St. Giles's Church*, Cripplegate, is a bust of the poet Milton, by Bacon, erected at the expence of Samuel Whitbread, 1773, the celebrated brewer of this parish. Here was married Oliver Cromwell to Elizabeth Boucher; and here were buried Speed the historian; Fox the martyrologist; and the poet Milton.

St. Helen's Church, Bishopsgate, has an interesting relic on the north side, called the Nuns' Gate. There are memorials to Sir John Crosby and lady, builders of adjoining mansion, ob. 1475 ; Sir William Pickering, "finest gentleman of the age for his worth in learning, arts, and warfare," ob. 1574; Sir Thomas Gresham, bur. Dec. 15, 1579. Here may be seen the coffin, with a lock and key, of the usurer Bancroft.—The famous Italian Merchant and Ambassador, Sir Horatio Pallavicini, had a house in this parish, and there entertained Queen Elizabeth, April 1559.

St. James's Palace was built, on the site of a hospital for lepers, by Hen. VIII. His daughter Mary died here, and so did Prince Henry, the promising son of James I. Charles I. was imprisoned here, and here his body was for several days exhibited to the public. George IV. was born here, and here have been celebrated many royal births, baptisms, and nuptials. The state apartments are commodious and handsome. In one of the ante-rooms to the Presence Chamber is a looking-glass, formerly considered unequalled for size by any in the kingdom.

Of *St. James's*, Piccadilly, were Rectors, Archbishops Tennison and Wake; and Bishop Trimnell of Norwich. Here were buried Benjamin Stillingfleet, naturalist ; Dr. Akenside ; John Hunter; Tom D'Urfey ; and Sir Joshua Reynolds.

The burial ground of *St. John's the Evangelist,* in the Horseferry Road, contains the ashes of an Indian Chief, brought to England 1734, and buried in the presence of his Emperor Tomo, &c. according to the customs of the Karakee Chiefs.

In the church of *St. Lawrence*, Jewry, is a monument to Archbishop Tillotson.

In *St. Margaret's Church*, Westminster, was buried the body of SIR WALTER RALEGH, after his cruel execution in Old Palace Yard, in 1618; the only memorial to him is a painted tin or copper tablet put up by the Parish Clerk. Here are tablets to WILLIAM CAXTON, first English printer, lately erected by the Roxburghe Club; and Dr. Nares, musical composer, 1783; and busts of James Palmer, B.D. and Corn. Van Dun, in the costume of the guard of Queen Elizabeth, both founders of alms houses in the parish. Here is a beautiful painted window of the Crucifixion, made by direction of the Magistrates of Dort, as a present to Henry VII. for his chapel. It was not finished at the King's death, and fell into the hands of the Abbot of Waltham; was afterwards in the chapel of New Hall, Essex; and was purchased for 400 guineas for this church.

Of *St. Martin in the Fields* were rectors, Archbishops Lamplugh 1670, Tennison 1680, of Canterbury; Bishops Lloyd of Worcester 1676, Green of Ely 1717. The vestry has portraits of many of its vicars; of the architect; of Sir Edmund Berry Godfrey, whose murder was connected with Titus Oates's plot; and a fine model of the church.— The celebrated Nell Gwyn was buried in the churchyard. She left to the ringers of the church a sum of money to provide them with a weekly entertainment.—In 1727 Sig. Volante, an Italian, descended head foremost by a rope, with his legs and arms extended, from the top of the steeple over the houses to the furthest side of the Mews, a distance of about 300 yards.

Of *St. Martin*, Ludgate, was Rector, Samuel Purchas, author of the "Pilgrimages." He died in 1628.

In *St. Martin's Street*, Leicester Fields, resided Sir Isaac Newton, in the house on which has since been erected an observatory.

St. Martin's le Grand had a right of sanctuary. Persons not free of the city may carry on business here, being a liberty belonging to the Dean and Chapter of Westminster.

Of *St. Mary*, Aldermanbury, were ministers, Mr. Edmund Calamy; Dr. Stratford, Bishop of Chester; Ezekiel Hopkins, Bishop of Derry.—Here was married the great Earl of Manchester to his third wife, Essex, daughter of Sir Thomas Cheke; and here was buried the infamous Judge Jeffries.

In *St. Mary-at-Hill Church*, Billingsgate, is a monument to the ingenious author of "Popular Antiquities," Rev. J. Brand, ob. 1800.—Here on the Sunday after Midsummer Day, the Fellowship Porters meet, and during divine service approach the altar two and two, and make their offerings. They are generally followed by the congregation.—In 1485-6 the Boy Bishop ceremony was observed in this church.

Of *St. Mary Woolnoth*, Lombard Street, the Rev. John Newton, the friend of the poet Cowper, was rector.

Of *St. Matthew*, Friday Street, was rector, in 1647, Dr. Lewis Bayly, author of the "Practice of Piety," and afterwards Bishop of Bangor.—Here is a monument to Dr. Michael Lort, Greek Professor at Cambridge, and rector of this church.

In the old Church of *St. Michael Bassishaw*, Sir Thomas Gresham was buried.

In *St. Michael's Church*, Crooked Lane, was buried Sir William Walworth, who struck down Wat Tyler.

In *St. Michael*, Paternoster Royal, was buried the celebrated Sir Richard Whittington, thrice Lord Mayor of London, whose traditional history is still heard with great interest by youthful citizens, and has, doubtless, in many instances, stimulated a perseverance which has led to similar success in others. He here had a splendid monument, which was broken into by a priest in the hope of finding treasures. Being disappointed, he carried away the leaden coffin in which the body was inclosed.

Of *St. Michael*, Wood Street, was rector Dr. Thomas

Birch, historian and biographer.—In the old church the head of James IV. of Scotland is said to have been buried after the battle of Flodden Field.

In *St. Mildred's Church*, Poultry, was buried Tusser, the agricultural poet.

St. Olave, Hart Street, had for its rector, from 1760 to 1794, the learned Dr. Henry Owen, originally a physician.

ST. PAUL's CATHEDRAL. The first Bishop was Mellitus, the companion of St. Augustine in his mission to England. Among its Bishops appear St. Dunstan, ob. 988; Roger Niger, ob. 1241, canonized; Wengham, Lord Chancellor, ob. 1262; Chishull, Lord Chancellor, ob. 1280; Wentworth, Lord Chancellor, ob. 1339; Sudbury and Courtenay, Archbishops of Canterbury; Braybrooke, Lord Chancellor, ob. 1404; Kemp, successively Archbishop of York and Canterbury, and a Cardinal; Warham, Abp. of Canterbury; Edmond Bonner; Nicholas Ridley, martyr, 1555; Grindall and Sandys, Archbishops of York; Bancroft, Abbot, Laud, Juxon, and Sheldon, Archbishops of Canterbury; E. Gibson, ob. 1746; Sherlock, ob. 1761; R. Lowth, ob. 1787; Porteus, ob. 1809; and Howley, now Abp. of Canterbury.—The carvings in the choir are the matchless work of Grinlin Gibbons. Among the sculptors were Cibber and Bird. On the North front of the Church, directly opposite to Paul's Alley, the smoke and damp had in 1822, so discoloured one of the panels as to produce the appearance of an interesting moonlight picture.—Among the monuments are those to Howard the Philanthropist, by Bacon, cost 1300 guineas, and the first public monument erected in this Cathedral, 1796; Dr. Johnson, by Bacon, inscription by Dr. Parr; Lord Nelson, by Flaxman; Lord Heathfield, by Rossi; Earl Howe, by Flaxman; Lord Collingwood, by Westmacott; Sir J. Moore, by Bacon; Sir R. Abercromby, by Westmacott; Capt. Faulkener, by Rossi;

Capt. Burges, by Banks; Sir W. Hoste, by Campbell; Earl St. Vincent, by Baily; Lord Rodney, by Rossi; Lord Duncan, by Westmacott; Marques Cornwallis, by Rossi; Sir W. Jones, statue by Bacon; Bp. Heber, by Chantrey, cost £1300; Maj.-Gen. Gillespie, by Chantrey; Capt. Mosse and Riou, by Rossi; Capt. Westcott, by Banks; Gen. Ponsonby, by Baily; Maj.-Gen. Gore and Skerett, by Chantrey; Maj.-Gen. Hay, by Hopper; Gen. Sir T. Picton, by Gahagan; Maj.-Gen. Dundas, by Bacon; Capt. Cooke; Capt. Duff; Capt. Hardinge; Maj.-Gens. Mackenzie and Longworth; Maj.-Gen. Houghton; Sir S. Myers; Maj.-Gen. Bowes; Maj.-Gen. Le Marchant; Maj.-Gens. Crauford and Mackinnon; Sir Isaac Brock; Col. Codagan; Maj.-Gen. Ross; Sir W. Ponsonby; Maj.-Gens. Pakenham and Gibbs.—In the crypt or vaults are the remains of the old monuments of Dr. Donne, his figure in a shroud, carved by Stone; Lord Chancellor Hatton; Sir Nicholas Bacon, in armour, and others saved from the old Cathedral; and the names of Sir Christopher Wren, whose tomb is nearly under the site of the high altar of the ancient Cathedral; Sir Joshua Reynolds, Barry, Opie, and West, celebrated painters; Mylne, architect to the Cathedral, and builder of Blackfriars bridge; Rennie, engineer; learned and eccentric Abraham Badcock; and the yet more eccentric upholder of animal magnetism, John Benoist de Mainaudoc; Doctor Boyce, eminent musician; Nelson and Collingwood, under the centre of the cupola.—St. Paul's, from the Reformation to the Commonwealth, was a general thoroughfare for every traffic, and the resort of all sorts of beggars and loose and disorderly people.—In the Cloister called Pardon Churchyard was painted the "Dance of Death," executed by Jenkyn Carpenter, Town Clerk, 1430.—In the Trophy Room is the rejected model of Sir Christopher Wren for the Cathedral.—The great bell weighs 11,474 lbs. being the largest in England next to that at Oxford, which weighs 17,000 lbs.

Among the eminent men educated at *St. Paul's School*, were Sir Anthony Denny, Sir W. Paget, Lord North, statesmen; Leland and Burton, antiquaries; W. Camden; MILTON; Scarborough, physician; Pepys, diurnalist; Calamy; Duke of Manchester, ob. 1721; JOHN DUKE OF MARLBOROUGH; many prelates; Earl of Orrery, philosopher; Roger Cotes; the pious Robert Nelson; the two Gales, antiquaries; Strype, editor of Stowe; Halley, astronomer; Sir Philip Francis; and Taylor the Platonist. The first Master was LILLY, the Grammarian.

Of *St. Peter le Poor* Bishop Hoadly was rector.

Of *St. Stephen*, Coleman Street, was incumbent the Rev. John Goodwin, a violent republican; author of a pamphlet, entitled "The Obstructors of Justice," in justification of the death of Charles I. He was ejected from his living, and his pamphlet burnt by the hangman. He afterwards kept a private conventicle in Coleman Street, and died in 1665.

In *St. Stephen*, Wallbrook, Dr. Wilson the rector, who died 1784, erected a marble statue to Mrs. Catharine Macaulay, in the character of History, and with a highly complimentary inscription, during her life, but it was removed by order of the Bishop of London.

In *St. Thomas Apostle* was Ringed Hall, a residence of the Earls of Cornwall before the time of Edward III.

In *St. Vedast Church*, Foster Lane, was buried the antiquary Leland.

In *Salisbury Court*, Fleet Street, lived Samuel Richardson, novelist.

In *Salters' Hall* is a curious dinner bill for 50 members of the Company in 1506, framed and glazed. The whole expense was £1. 13s. 2½d. A sum of 4d. is charged for 36 chickens.

In *Sambrook Court* resided Dr. Lettsom, the physician.

In *Scotland Yard*, Westminster, was formerly a palace, built for the reception of the Scottish kings when they visited England—Here resided Sir John Vanbrugh, poet and architect.

At *Smithfield*, in the middle of the pens, a large gas light stands on the spot where the martyrs were burnt.

Soho Square was called Monmouth Square, on account of its being the residence of the Duke of Monmouth, whose watch-word at the battle of Sedgmoor was " So ho!"

The *Company of Stationers* is of great antiquity, long before the invention of printing. They were also called Text-writers, and sold the A B C, Paternoster, Ave, Crede, Grace, and all sorts of books then in use. Hence the names of the Streets near the Hall.

The STRAND, from Charing Cross to Temple Bar, was at one time ornamented with numerous mansions of the great, the sites of which are marked by the streets and courts which still bear their names.—The House of the Duke of Buckingham was previously a house of the Archbishops of York, and known as York House It was granted to him by King James. The Parliament in 1649 bestowed it on their general, Lord Fairfax, whose daughter conveyed it by marriage again to the Villiers family. The site is known by the names of *George* Street, *Villiers* Street, *Duke* Street, *Of* Alley, and *Buckingham* Street, thus preserving the name and title of the owner, who disposed of the estate to be built upon.

In *Suffolk Street* is the residence of Mr. Cresy, the architect, a fac-simile of the house of Andrea Pallacho, at Vicenza.

In *Sweedon's Passage*, Cripplegate, was a house, pulled down in 1805, occupied by London's two great citizens, Sir Richard Whittington and Sir Thomas Gresham.

At *Temple Bar*, the banking house of Child and Co. is the

oldest in London. Adjoining it was the Devil Tavern, to which Goldsmith and his contemporaries used to resort.

In the *Temple Church*, within the circular area of the vestibule, are two groups of ancient sepulchral effigies, evidently congregated here from their original places in various parts of the edifice. These effigies, nine in number, are greatly mutilated and defaced; they have been sculptured out of blocks of freestone, two feet in thickness, and are lying on platforms of similar stone. The attitudes vary, but the figures are all recumbent, and represent knights in mail armour, with surcoats. Only one is bare-headed, and wears a monk's cowl. Their shields are of the heater or Norman form, but differ in size. Five of them are cross-legged, a position acknowledged to indicate actual crusaders, or knights who had taken the vow to engage in the Holy War against the infidels in Palestine. Only three or four of these persons can now be satisfactorily identified; and only one of them is considered to have been immediately connected with the order of Knights Templars. The first figure in the southernmost group is Geoffrey de Magnaville, made Earl of Essex by King Stephen, and mortally wounded in besieging the castle at Burwell in 1148; the second figure is William Le Marechal, the first and famous Earl of Pembroke, who died 1219; the third figure, a youthful looking knight, bare-headed, is referred to Robert Ros, a Templar, who died 1227; the fourth figure is supposed to have been intended for William Marshall, 2d Earl of Pembroke, who died in 1230. Not a single figure of the northernmost group can be decidedly appropriated, but the fifth, or that which is cross-legged, was probably meant for Gilbert Marshall, third Earl of Pembroke, who was killed by a fall from an unruly horse at a tournament, near Ware, in Hertfordshire, in 1241.

At *Tothill Fields*, Henry III. to punish the presumption

and reduce the wealth of the Londoners, who had bought his crown jewels, in 1248, granted to the Abbot of Westminster the privilege of holding an annual fair for fifteen days, during which all trade should cease within the city.

Calvert's Brewery, *Thames Street*, is on the site of the old mansion of Cold Harbour. The Earl of Huntingdon entertained Richard II. here. It was severally inhabited by Edmund Earl of Cambridge, 1398; Henry Holland, Duke of Exeter, 1472; Bishop Tunstall of Durham, temp. Henry VIII.; Earl of Shrewsbury, 1553.

TOWER: Once a fortress of great strength and consequent importance, now a town of houses, offices, and barracks. In it were confined numbers of royal, noble, and illustrious prisoners. Too many of them perished, either within its walls or precinct; some justly, but the far greater number without other crime than that of having unfortunately got into the hands of the powerful; and many are the records which have been preserved of their feelings and amusements during their solitary hours, spent in dreary cells and cold vaulted rooms, in the shape of carvings and writings on the walls of their apartments. It would occupy too much space to recapitulate the names of all whose lives and characters are historically interesting; but a list of the most distinguished and remarkable is absolutely necessary. Hubert de Burgh, Earl of Kent, Justiciary, most inhumanly treated, 1232; WILLIAM WALLACE, Scottish Hero, 1305, besides many northern chiefs, their Sovereign and his son; David Bruce, King of Scotland, 1346; the famous *Charles de Blois*, liberated 1356; John King of France, and his son Philip, 1357; Richard II.; James son of Robert III. King of Scotland, 1406; Lord Cobham, for Lollardism, 1413; the famous Owen Tudor, grandfather of Henry VII. 1438; Henry VI. mild and religious monarch, 1471; George Duke of Clarence, traditionally said to have been drowned

in a butt of malmsey, 1477 ; Sir Thomas More, Lord
Chancellor, 1535 ; Queen Anne Boleyn, 1535 ; Mrs. Anne
Askew, celebrated Martyr, 1546 ; the renowned Henry
Earl of Surrey and his father Thomas third Duke of
Norfolk, 1546-7 ; the Protector Somerset, 1549, beheaded
1552 ; Thomas Lord Seymour, beheaded 1548-9 ; Lady
Jane Grey, amiable and unfortunate, 1554, beheaded ;
Queen Elizabeth, while Princess ; Sir John Cheke, 1549,
an ornament to literature ; the Earl of Essex, the noble
but hasty, the beloved but unfortunate favourite of the
Queen ; Earl of Southampton, a name dear from his patron-
age of Shakspere ; the gallant, generous, witty, and learned
RALEGH, whose virtues and accomplishments would have
added brilliancy to any brilliant court, spent almost a life here ;
Lady Arabella Stuart ; Sir Thomas Overbury, the victim of
one of the vilest transactions that ever disgraced the name
of a civilized people ; Earl of Strafford and Archbishop
Laud, victims to popular frenzy ; the unfortunate Prince
James Duke of Monmouth ; and Simon Lord Lovat, and
others of the Pretender's friends.—In the church of St.
Peter ad Vincula, lie the remains of many very distinguished
personages ; among others, of the lovely Anne Boleyn ;
John Fisher, Bishop of Rochester ; the great Sir Thomas
More ; Queen Katharine Howard ; Queen Elizabeth's Earl of
Essex ; and the headless bodies of the Scotch Lords executed
in 1747.—The Armories (which were visited in 1840 by
98,000 persons) contain a great many ancient and foreign
arms and armour, which have been taken from or used
against the enemy, or have been presents to our princes.
The public are much indebted to the care and attention bestowed in the arrangement and explanation of these interesting curiosities, by Sir Samuel Rush Meyrick, in the year
1826. The Grand Storehouse was destroyed by fire in
1841 ; and many thousand stand of arms lost, besides some

of the old and curious military trophies. Among those saved is a large iron chamber gun, of the time of Henry VIII. which was part of the furniture of the Mary Rose, sunk off Spithead, in 1545, and had been just recovered from the wreck and placed in the armory. A beautiful brass gun formerly belonging to the Knights of Malta, with its elegant carved wooded carriage, with some others of much interest, were also saved. The Jewels are between forty and fifty in number, and of great value and beauty. Among them is the ancient imperial crown; the coronation regalia; the ampulla or golden eagle brought by St. Thomas à Becket from the Abbey of Sens, in France, where it was valued as the actual gift of an angel from heaven; the staff of St. Edward the Confessor, who reigned in 1041; the rock ruby worn by Edward the Black Prince; &c. They were safely secured during the fire which destroyed the Armory, and have been since placed in the new Jewel House.

Tower Royal, was formerly a residence of the Kings. It was afterwards the Queen's wardrobe.

Trinity Priory, Aldgate, was given by Henry VIII. to Mrs. Cornwallis and her heirs, because she presented him with some fine puddings. It was afterwards the residence of Sir Nicholas Throgmorton, in the time of Elizabeth, who was buried in Cree Church.

At the corner of *Tufton Street* and *Peter Street*, Westminster, resided the notorious Colonel Blood.

In *Turnwheel Lane*, Cannon-Street, was Herbert Inn, a mansion which belonged to Edward III. The Earl of Salisbury, brother to the great Earl of Warwick, lodged here in 1458, with 500 men.

In the vestibule of *University College*, London, is a marble statue of Locke, by R. Westmacott, which cost £1000.

On the site of *Uxbridge House, Burlington Gardens,*

was Queensberry House, built by Leoni, for the celebrated
Duke of Queensberry, in which the poet Gay for many years
enjoyed the patronage of the Duke and Duchess of Queensberry, who here rendezvoused the most brilliant people of
the time. Uxbridge House was designed by Vardy, assisted
by Joseph Benomi.

Warwick Lane, Newgate Street, takes its name from the
house of the King-making Earl of Warwick; where it was
said as many as six oxen were often eaten at breakfast.—At
the corner of Newgate Street, is a stone tablet representing
the famous Guy Earl of Warwick, with the date 1668.—At
the Bell Inn, Archbishop Leighton died. The old College
of Physicians (now a meat market) built by Sir Christopher
Wren.

In WESTMINSTER ABBEY fifty monarchs have been
crowned. Of the illustrious dead who have memorials here,
or have found a resting-place for their ashes, a long list
might be made. Some of the principal must be mentioned :
William Shakspere, monument by Scheemakers; "O rare
Ben Jonson;" Spenser ; Chaucer ; Butler; Milton ; Gray;
Prior ; Thomson ; Gay; Addison; Dryden ; Cowley; Dr.
Johnson; Goldsmith; Davenant; and Sheridan, all poets;
Mrs. Rowe; Garrick, actor; Casaubon, scholar; Gifford, editor
of the Quarterly Review ; Camden, antiquary ; Thomas
Parr, ob. aged 152 years; Sir Godfrey Kneller, painter ;
General Paoli; Major André, interred here from America,
1821 ; Banks, the sculptor ; Dr. Mead ; Sir Isaac Newton ;
Lord Stanhope, monument by Rysbrach ; Drs. Arnold,
Croft, and Burney, musicians ; Perceval, Pitt, Fox, Grat-
tan, Londonderry, and Canning, statesmen ; Lord Mansfield, judge ; Jonas Hanway; Lady Nightingale, Roubiliac's
chef d'œuvre. Besides these, there are some fine old monuments worthy of particular attention. By the altar are those
of Sebert, founder; Anne of Cleves; Aymer de Valence,

Earl of Pembroke, and his Countess; and Edmund Crouch-back, Earl of Lancaster. In Edward the Confessor's Chapel is an interesting sculptured frieze of the incidents in his life; the Saint's Shrine, executed by Pietro Cavalini, by order of Henry III.; the coronation chair, with the stone brought as a trophy from Scotland by Edward I. and said to have been Jacob's pillow; iron sword of Henry I. a part of his shield, and the helmet and shield of Henry V.— Henry the Seventh's Chapel, is a fine specimen of the ex-uberantly decorated Pointed style; the gates are of brass, most curiously wrought; Henry's tomb is a work of great magnifi-cence. Here are also monuments to the mother of Henry VII.; Queen Elizabeth; the three infant children of James I.; Mary Queen of Scots, &c. In the royal vault are the remains of Charles II.; William III.; Queens Mary and Anne; Prince George of Denmark; George II. and his Queen Caroline; Frederick Prince of Wales and his Prin-cess Augusta; William Duke of Cumberland; and several other children of George II. and of Frederick Prince of Wales.—In the *Jerusalem Chamber* died Henry IV. whose death was prophesied to occur in Jerusalem. — In the *Sanctuary* was born Edward V. where his mother had taken refuge. — In the *Chapter House* of the Abbey, the Commons of Great Britain first held their meetings in 1377. It is now used as a depository of Crown records. Among these is the celebrated Domesday Book, in two folio volumes, written on vellum, in the 11th century. The Records of the Star Chamber proceedings are also here preserved.—There is a very curious crypt underneath, where the pix, containing the standards of the Coinage, is kept.

The first Parliament held in *Westminster Hall* after the completion of the extensive repairs by Richard II. was for the deposing of that monarch.

Among the Masters of the *Westminster School* or *Col-*

lege, were, Camden, the antiquary ; Doctor Busby, of flog-
ging and classical notoriety, who held it upwards of fifty years;
Dr. Markham, afterwards Abp. of York; Dr. Carey, now Bp.
of St. Asaph ; and Dr. Vincent, afterwards Dean of Westminster. The great Lord Burghley ; the poets Jonson, Cowley, Dryden, Prior, Churchill, and Cowper; Gibbon, the
historian; great Earl Mansfield ; many bishops and eminent
divines ; the dramatists Colman the elder, and. Richard
Cumberland; Betterton the actor; WARREN HASTINGS,
whose name in gilded letters on the walls of the dormitory,
still attests his victory at the age of 14, on the examination
for the foundation ; &c. were scholars.

White Friars obtained many privileges and exemptions
from James I. Becoming a resort of thieves, swindlers,
debtors, &c. and the scene of much bloodshed and many
quarrels, it obtained the name of Alsatia, and lost all its peculiar privileges by Act of Parliament, temp. William III.

At *Whitehall* was a house which originally belonged to
Hubert de Burgh, Justiciary to Henry III. and then to the
Archbishops of York. On the death of Wolsey, Hen. VIII.
seized it, and it became a royal palace till the reign of
William III. when, in 1697, the greater part was burnt
down.

List of Works consulted.

1. A Survey of the Cities of London and Westminster. By John Stowe. Edited by John Strype, M.A.—fol. 1754, 6th edit.

2. A new View of London. By Edward Hatton.—2 vols. 8vo. 1708.

3. Repertorium Ecclesiasticum Parochiale Londinense ; an Ecclesiastical Parochial History of the Diocese of London. By Richard Newcourt, Notary Publick.—2 vols. fol. 1708.

4. The Antiquities of London and Westminster. By N. Bailey. —12mo. 1734.

5. A Survey of the Cities of London and Westminster. By Robert Seymour.—2 vols. fol. 1734.

6. London and Middlesex Illustrated. By John Warburton, Esq. Somerset Herald.—8vo. 1749.

7. London and its Environs described.—6 vols. 8vo. 1761.

8. A new and accurate History and Survey of London, &c. By Rev. John Entick, M.A.—4 vols. 1766.

9. History of London. By William Maitland, F.R.S. continued to 1772, by Rev. John Entick, M.A.—2 vols. fol. 1772.

10. A new History of London. By John Noorthouck.—4to. 1773.

11. Some Account of London. By Thomas Pennant.—4to. 1791.

12. The Microcosm of London : or, London in Miniature.— 3 vols. 4to.

13. The History and Survey of London. By B. Lambert.— 4 vols. 8vo. 1806.

14. London : being an accurate History and Description of the British Metropolis. By David Hughson, LL.D. (Dr. Pugh). —6 vols. 8vo. 1806.

15. Londinium Redivivum, or an ancient history and modern description of London. By James Peller Malcolm.—4 vols. 4to. 1802.

16. Anecdotes of the Manners and Customs of London during the 18th century. By J. P. Malcolm.—4to. 1808.

17. Anecdotes of the Manners and Customs of London from the Roman Invasion to the year 1700. By J. P. Malcolm.—4to. 1811.

18. The History of London and its Environs. By the late Rev. Henry Hunter, D.D.—2 vols. 4to. 1811.

19. Beauties of England and Wales, vol. x. 4 parts, 1814.

20. The History and Antiquities of London, Westminster, South-wark, and parts adjacent. By Thomas Allen.—4 vols. 8vo. 1827.

21. Public Edifices of London. By John Britton, F.S.A. and Augustus Pugin, architect.—2 vols. 8vo. 1828.

22. Londiniana; or, Reminiscences of the British Metropolis. By Edward Wedlake Brayley, F.S.A. &c.—4 vols. 12mo. 1829.

23. The Original Picture of London. Re-edited by J. Britton, F.S.A. &c.—18mo. 1829.

24. Allen's Panorama of London.—12mo. 1830.

25. The History of St. Paul's Cathedral. By Wm. Dugdale. New edition by Henry Ellis, Esq. F.R.S.—4to. 1818.

26. Westmonasterium : or, the History and Antiquities of the Abbey Church of St. Peter, Westminster. By Mr. John Dart. —2 vols. folio. 1723.

27. The Antiquities of St. Peter's, or the Abbey Church of Westminster. By Jodocus Crull, M.D., F.R.S.—2 vols. 8vo. 1742.

28. An Enquiry into the first Foundation of Westminster Abbey. By Richard Widmore, M.A.—4to. 1743.

29. The History of the Abbey Church of St. Peter's, Westmin-ster. [By William Coombe.]—Ackermann. 2 vols. 4to. 1812.

30. The History and Antiquities of the Abbey Church of St. Peter, Westminster. Illustrated by J. P. Neale ; and described by E. W. Brayley.—2 vols. 4to. 1823.

31. Some Account of the Collegiate Chapel of St. Stephen, Westminster. By John Topham, Esq. F.R.S.—folio, 1795.

32. Antiquities of the City of Westminster. By John Thomas Smith and John Sidney Hawkins, Esq. F.A.S.—4to.

33. Historical Notices of the Collegiate Church, or Royal Free Chapel and Sanctuary of St. Martin-le-Grand, &c. By Alfred John Kempe.—8vo. 1825.

34. History and Antiquities of St. Leonard, Shoreditch. By Henry Ellis.—4to. 1798.

35. Antique Remains from the Parish Church of St. Martin Outwich. By Robert Wilkinson.—4to. 1797.

36. A History of the parish of St. Lawrence Pountney, London. By the Rev. Harry Bristow Wilson, B.D., F.S.A. Rector of the united parishes of St. Mary Aldermary and St. Thomas the Apostle.—4to. 1831.

37. The History and Antiquities of the Tower of London, with biographical anecdotes, &c. By John Bayley, Esq. F.S.A.— 2 vols. 4to. 1821.

38. Historical and Antiquarian Notices of Crosby Hall. By E. J. Carlos, Esq.—12mo. 1832.

39. An Architectural and Historical Account of Crosby Place, London. By Edward L. Blackburn, architect.—8vo. 1834.

40. Antiquities of the Inns of Court and Chancery. By W. Herbert.—8vo. 1804.

41. The History of the Twelve Great City Companies of London. By William Herbert, Librarian to the Corporation of London. —2 vols. 8vo. 1834.

42. Some Account of the worshipful Company of Grocers, of the City of London. By John Benjamin Heath, Esq.—8vo. 1829.

PRINTED BY J. B. NICHOLS AND SON, 25, PARLIAMENT STREET.

www.ingramcontent.com/pod-product-compliance
Ingram Content Group UK Ltd.
Pitfield, Milton Keynes, MK11 3LW, UK
UKHW021312020126
9870UKWH00003B/90